D-DAY 1944

To Dad

From

Dan — January
2010

D-DAY
1944

VOICES FROM NORMANDY

ROBIN NEILLANDS
AND
RODERICK DE NORMANN

CASSELL

Cassell Military Paperbacks

Cassell, an imprint of Orion Books Ltd, Orion House,
5 Upper St Martin's Lane, London WC2H 9EA

Chapter head drawings and maps by Terry Brown

A catalogue record for this book is available from the British Library

ISBN 978-1-4072-1462-7

Printed in Great Britain by Mackays of Chatham plc, Chatham, Kent

The Orion Publishing Group's policy is to use papers that are natural,
renewable and recyclable products and made from wood grown in
sustainable forests. The logging and manufacturing processes are expected to
conform to the environmental regulations of the country of origin.

www.orionbooks.co.uk

The authors and contributors wish to dedicate this book to all those who fought along the coast of Normandy on D-Day 1944 and did not survive the day.

'Think not only upon their passing.
Remember the glory of their spirit.'

---

*US Military Cemetery
St Laurent, Normandy*

CONTENTS

ILLUSTRATIONS

Juno Beach, D-Day (private collection)

4th US Infantry Division, Utah Beach (Imperial War Museum)

Commanders Montgomery, Eisenhower and Tedder (Imperial War Museum)

S/Sgt Wallwork, Glider Pilot Regiment (Wallwork, private collection)

Men of the Glider Pilot Regiment (R. A. Howard, private collection)

S/Sgt R. A. Howard, Glider Pilot Regiment (R. A. Howard, private collection)

Pfc John Robert Slaughter, 29th Infantry Division (J. R. Slaughter, private collection)

Captain H. A. Shebeck, 82nd Airborne Division (H. A. Shebeck, private collection)

Guillaume Mercader, Chef de la Résistance, with General Koëning (G. Mercader, private collection)

Preparations: the bombing of railways (Imperial War Museum)

U S infantry train on Dartmoor, England (Imperial War Museum)

Transport aircraft and gliders in D-Day markings (Imperial War Museum)

Troopers of the 508th Parachute Infantry Regiment on a training jump in England, April 1944 (David Pike, private collection)

Aerial reconnaissance before D-Day over the beach obstacles near Arromanches (Imperial War Museum)

Bombardment warships sail for Normandy (Imperial War Museum)

Canadian infantry wait offshore (Imperial War Museum)

British tanks and infantry under fire, Sword Beach (Imperial War Museum)

Omaha Beach, 7 June 1944 (Imperial War Museum)

Troopers of 508th Parachute Infantry Regiment in Normandy (David Pike, private collection)

ACKNOWLEDGEMENTS

A great many people and organizations helped us with this book. Our thanks go to everyone involved, including those whose accounts we were unable to include through lack of space. They were all useful, either as a check on other information or as background to the story. We received nearly 1,000 contributions, stories, tapes, letters and photographs, from all over the world, to support our own interviews. Without such assistance, this book could never have been written.

Within that broad framework, some particular thanks are due to: the Imperial War Museum, London; the Musée de la Débarquement, Arromanches; the Army Museum, Ottawa, Canada; the D-Day Museum, Portsmouth; the Airborne Museum, Ste-Mère-Eglise, Normandy; the Tank Museum, Bovington, and Major & Mrs Holt's Battlefield Tours, UK.

We would also like to thank the American, Royal British and Canadian Legions for publishing our appeal for help, or supplying lists of possible informants. Thanks go also to the D-Day and Normandy Fellowship and the Normandy Veterans Association, and to many Regimental Associations – especially the Queen's Own Rifles of Canada, the 29th Division Association, the Royal Marines Association, the 1st Division Association USA and the Retired US Officers Association – and to Stephen Ambrose of the Eisenhower Center, New Orleans, Alan C. Aimone of the US Military Academy, West Point, and Arthur Chaitt, Society of the First Division. Thanks also to Keith Howell for contacts among the Normandy veterans, and Toby Oliver of Brittany Ferries for assistance with visits to France.

IN THE UNITED KINGDOM

Among a host of individuals – all of whom we thank – we would like to record a particular vote of gratitude to Colin Kitchen, RNVR for permission to quote from his copyright account; the late Brigadier Peter Young, DSO, MC of No. 3 Commando; Geoff Peters of the 2nd Warwicks; Colonel Robin McGarel-

Groves, RM; Captain Dan Flunder, MC, RM of 48 Commando; George Price of 12 Bn, the Parachute Regiment; Albert Herring; Frederick Hall, RASC; Brigadier Tom Collins, CBE; Ken Beard, RAF; Syd (Sticks) Lancaster, RM; Don Kelly of the Normandy Veterans Association; Warrant Officer 'Baron' Humphries, RAF; Jack Horsnell, RN; James Hinton, RN; Reg Bettis, RM; Norman Harris, 10th Beach Group, RN Commando; Lt Jim Booth, RN of COPP; Charles Lofthouse, 7 Squadron RAF; Geoff Riley, the Commando Association; Sidney Hoy, RN; Sidney Goldberg, RAF; Eric Downing, 22nd Dragoons; Tom Lovell of HMT *Glenroy*; Frank Haworth, RN; Noel Chaffey, RAF; Colonel Mike Morrison, the 8th King's Regiment; P. Finnegan, the 8th Bn, the King's Regiment; Lt John M. Moore, the 8th Bn, the King's Regiment; John Walford; Don Clarke, the Pathfinders Association; Roy Howard and James Wallwork, the Glider Pilot Regiment; Stuart Lasson; Kenneth McCaw, RNVR; Squadron Leader Douglas Millikin, RAF; Alan Schofield, 620 Squadron; Austin Prosser, RN; Peter Chambers, RN; Emlyn Jones, Signals Troop, 45 (RM) Commando; Ralph Rayner, Royal Engineers; Flt Sergeant David Swynne, Inns of Court Regiment; Bob Armit, RAF; Reginald T. Atkins, 1st Bn, Dorsetshire Regiment.

IN THE UNITED STATES

Commander Robert J. Erickson, USN; Harvy P. Newton, 508 Parachute Infantry Regiment; D. Zane Schlemmer of Hawaii, 508th PIR; John Robert Lewis, USN, of Yardley, Pennsylvania; A. A. Alvarez, 16th Infantry Regiment, 1st Infantry Division for his account of 'Omaha'; George M. Rosie, 101st Airborne Division Association; Anthony J. Di Stephano, 29th Infantry; Gene Owens, *Roanoke Times & World News*, Virginia; Milton Chadwick, 82nd Airborne; Leslie 'Bill' Kick of Westmoreland, New York, 82nd Airborne; David Pike for permission to reproduce extracts from *Airborne in Nottingham – the 508th PIR in England*; J. Robert Slaughter of Roanoke, Virginia, 116th Infantry Regiment, 29th Division for permission to reproduce extracts from his memoirs; Jack Schlegel of

Shandaken, New York, 508th PIR; Jack Jones, 4th Infantry Division; Jack Capell, 4th Infantry Division, for his support and his account of D-Day and after; Fred Tannery, 4th Infantry; Anthony M. Jele, 4th Infantry; Frank P. Schroen of Hamburg, PA; Louis Siebel; Colonel 'Red' Reeder, 12th Infantry Regiment, for permission to reproduce extracts from his book *Born at Reveille*; Mario Porcellini, 29th Infantry Division; Colonel James H. Watts, 1st Infantry Division; Colonel Gerald K. Griffin, 1st Infantry Division; Phil Sykes, USS *Frankford*; Daniel S. Campbell, 82nd Airborne Division Association, for publishing our appeal in *Paraglide*, the Division's magazine; Commander J. M. Suozzo, USN; Howard L. Huggett, 82nd Airborne; Captain Warren L. Hooker, 4th Infantry; Lawrence J. Bour of Williamsburg, PA, 16th Infantry Regiment, 1st Infantry Division; Bill Garvin, 12th Infantry Regiment; Walter F. Schaad, 4th Infantry Division; Robert L. Sales of Madison Heights, Virginia, who has built his own memorial to the men of Company 'B' who died on D-Day; Malcolm C. Williams Snr, 12th Infantry; Harold A. Shebeck, 325th Glider Regiment; Harper Coleman, 8th Infantry Regiment, Tucson, Arizona; Robert 'Bob' Salley, 326 Engineer Bn, 101st Airborne; Richard Willstatter, USN.

IN CANADA

Jack Jensen of Toronto, Ontario; Jane Fox of *The Legion*, the magazine of the Canadian Legion, Ottawa; Dorothy and William Ross, QORC; Lawrence A. Cornett, Port Credit, Ontario, QORC; P. C. Rea, QORC; Jack Martin of Scarborough, Ontario, QORC Association; S. W. (Wet Bird) Pawley, First Hussars Association; Alfie Hebbes of Rexdale, Ontario, Sherbrooke Fusilier Regiment (27th Canadian Armoured Regiment); Les Wagar of Red Deer, Alberta, QORC; Stanley Biggs, QORC; W. F. Lawson, 13th Canadian Field Regiment; Don Doner of Alliston, Ontario, QORC; Rolph W. Jackson, QORC.

IN FRANCE

Mlle M. Thomas of Caen; Henri Lamperière of Landelles et Compigny; M. and Mme Felix Reginensi of Condé-sur-Noireau, Normandy; André Heintz of Caen.

IN GERMANY

Ammegret Harmetz of Munich, for permission to reproduce the account of her late husband, Rainer Hartmetz; Oberst Helmut Ritgen, Panzer Lehr; Oberst Hans Von Luck, 21st Panzer; Herbert Muschallik, 352nd Infantry Division; Wolfgang Kittel, Deutsch Fallschirmjaeger.

Our thanks and appreciation are also due to Colonel E. G. Peters and Paul Reynolds for reading the manuscript, to Beverlie Flower for additional help with the correspondence, to Estelle Huxley for constant typing of the manuscript, and to Terry Brown for his work on the maps.

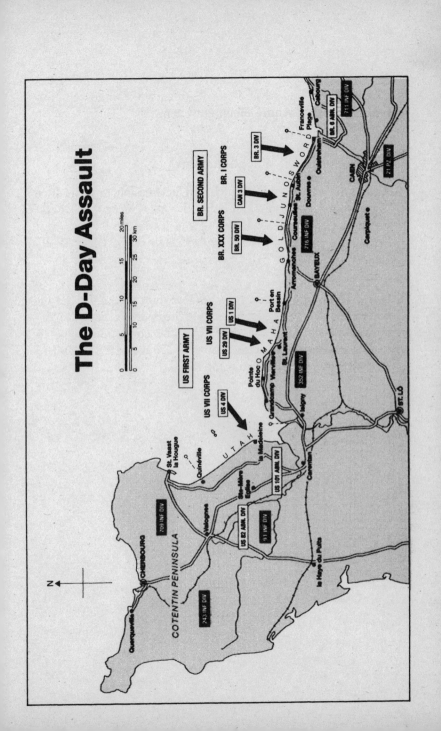

The D-Day Assault

N

COTENTIN PENINSULA

CHERBOURG

Querqueville

709 INF DIV

Valognes

243 INF DIV

la Haye du Puits

St. Vaast la Hougue

Quineville

U T A H

la Madeleine

Ste-Mère Eglise

US 101 ABN. DIV

US 82 ABN. DIV

91 INF DIV

Carentan

US VII CORPS

US 4 DIV

Pointe du Hoc

Grandcamp

O M A H A

Vierville

St. Laurent

Isigny

352 INF DIV

ST. LÔ

US FIRST ARMY

US VII CORPS

US 29 DIV

US 1 DIV

Port en Bessin

BR. SECOND ARMY

BR. XXX CORPS

BR. 50 DIV

G O L D

Arromanches

Courseulles

St. Aubin

BAYEUX

716 INF DIV

BR. I CORPS

CAN 3 DIV

J U N O

BR. 3 DIV

S W O R D

Douvres

Ouistreham

Franceville Plage

BR. 6 ABN. DIV

Cabourg

711 INF DIV

CAEN

Carpiquet

21 PZ. DIV

0 5 10 15 20 miles

0 5 10 15 20 25 30 km

Halifax bomber and glider tug

──────── CHAPTER ONE ────────

Dunkirk to D-Day 1940-1944

'Critics state that the strategy of World War
II was all wrong, that it would have been
better to have done this or that. Perhaps ...
but the fact remains, we did win the War.'
Omar N. Bradley
General of the Army

This is the story of one day, fifty miles of French coast and
about 200,000 men. This is the story of Operation 'Overlord'
and the most crucial day in the long and painful history of the
Second World War – the sixth of June 1944.

This is not an official history. It is a collection of stories,
drawn from the accounts of people who took part in Operation
'Overlord', of every nation, rank and arm of service. The effect
is to tell the story of D–Day in the words of the men who were
there.

This chapter will cover the years from the Dunkirk evacuation of 1940 to the time in 1943 when the Allied commanders
decided to launch Operation 'Overlord'. It will describe the
difficulties encountered by the invasion planners and how these
problems were overcome.

To tell such a story in simple terms is difficult and the very size and complexity of the D-Day operation is only one factor. All major operations of war are complicated and a seaborne invasion is the most complicated of all. What must be understood at the start of this story is the vital importance of 'Overlord'.

On the success of 'Overlord' rested the outcome of the Second World War, the swift liberation of Western Europe and the ending of a tyranny that had stalked the civilized world for five long years. Had the landings failed Hitler would have employed his 'V2' rockets against Britain with lethal effect; the atomic bomb might well have been deployed in Europe and the Red Army could have advanced to the Rhine or beyond, with incalculable consequences when the war was over. D-Day, 1944, prevented all that.

The story of Operation 'Overlord', the Allied invasion of Europe on 6 June 1944, really begins on the night of 4 June 1940, when a Royal Navy destroyer sailed from Dunkirk with the last of the British Expeditionary Force. Over 225,000 men, French and British, had been brought back across the Channel during Operation 'Dynamo', but there would be a painful four-year gap before a British army again set foot in France. After Dunkirk, the Axis Powers alone controlled the Continent of Europe.

By June 1940, the German Führer, Adolf Hitler, was sure that Britain was out of the war. If possible, he would now reach some accommodation with the British in the West, as he had done with Soviet Russia in the East before attacking Poland in 1939. If he could not make peace with the British, then his U-Boats would see that they starved, and his Luftwaffe would pound them into submission. Hitler had viewed the British, or at least some of their politicians, at Munich and had formed his own opinion of the British as a nation. 'They are worms,' he stated.

The British were relieved, even delighted, by the 'miracle' of Dunkirk, and Winston Churchill, Britain's lion-hearted Prime Minister, soon saw a need to put the Dunkirk evacuation in perspective. 'It was a defeat,' he pointed out in Parliament, 'and wars are not won by evacuations.' What was left of the British Army was home again but the military might of Britain had been blighted in the débâcle at Dunkirk and future prospects looked bleak indeed.

Although most of the soldiers got back to England, almost all their weapons and equipment had been left behind. The defence of Britain now depended on the Royal Navy and the Royal Air Force, but the British have an irritating habit of not being able to see the writing on the wall until their backs are pressed against it. After the capitulation of France at the end of June 1940, spirits in Britain became almost lighthearted. The King, George VI, summed up the national mood when he wrote in his diary, 'I'm glad we no longer need be polite to our allies.' Indeed, other than those few who had made their way to England, Britain had no allies; Britain and her embattled Empire now stood alone. The whole country became an arsenal, devoted to producing guns, tanks and aircraft. Every man and woman strained their sinews to produce munitions and the weapons of war, while every able-bodied young man or woman went into one or other of the fighting services.

The one bright spot for the British in mid-June 1940 was that a drawn-out trench struggle on the 1914-18 pattern had been avoided. This meant, however, that to free Europe from Hitler the British and their Allies must one day invade Europe, but this course of action was still a long way off in the summer of 1940. A more immediate prospect was of German forces invading Britain.

To do that, the Luftwaffe had first to eliminate the fighters of the Royal Air Force and gain air superiority over the Channel, as they had already done over Poland, France and the Low Countries. With its larger and more experienced fighter arm, equipped in the main with superior machines, the advantage here seemed to lie with Germany, but by late June 1940, it had not yet come to that.

First, Hitler tried peace offers and blandishments. When these failed he tried threats. Only when the British flatly refused to negotiate did he decide to invade: 'As England, in spite of her hopeless military position, has shown herself unwilling to come to any compromise, I have decided to begin preparations for, and if necessary to carry out, the invasion of England . . .

'The English Airforce must be eliminated to such an extent

that it will be incapable of putting up any substantial opposition to the invading troops.'

All military operations of any size have codenames. Hitler's planned invasion was codenamed Operation 'Sea-Lion' but Operation 'Sea-Lion' never took place. Throughout that long, hot summer of 1940, the skies over the English Channel and the south coast of England were ably defended by just 1,243 brave young men, the trained fighter pilots of the Royal Air Force, the famous 'Few', aided by pilots from the Commonwealth and Empire and American volunteer flyers of the two 'Eagle' squadrons. Together these men fought the mighty German Luftwaffe to a standstill.

The full story of the Battle of Britain, the defeat of the Luftwaffe and the abandonment of Operation 'Sea-Lion' belong elsewhere, but the lessons of 1940 still held good in 1944; the first requirement for a successful cross-Channel invasion was *control of the air*.

If Hitler could not invade England and finish the war, then it followed that one day the British and their Allies must go back to France. The first step on the road back was quickly taken; on the night of 22 June 1940, just two weeks after the Dunkirk evacuation, a small party of British Commandos made a reconnaissance raid on the French coast near Boulogne.

The raid achieved very little but it was the start of a long series of amphibious landings, large and small, along the German-occupied coast of Europe, that would develop amphibious operational techniques to a high state of expertise and gain for the Allies a mass of knowledge about the defences of the enemy coast. Here were two more of the invasion requirements; *skill in amphibious techniques* and *knowledge of the enemy defences*.

It was to achieve these objectives that the British Commandos were created, small units of men 'trained to act like packs of hounds', in the words of their creator, Winston Churchill. These Commandos came under the command of a new Headquarters, Combined Operations, and were only the first of several military innovations. Having seen the effect of parachute troops during the German 'Blitzkrieg' operations in France and Holland, Churchill also ordered the formation of parachute forces, initially a force of 5,000 men who could

swiftly seize strategic points on the battlefield and ho
until the main force came up.

The employment of raiding forces soon revealed the ne
another invasion requirement, a range of specialized landing
craft. In 1939, the British Navy, then the largest naval force in
the world, possessed exactly six landing craft. The best of these
had a top speed of five knots and drew four feet of water. The
US Navy had no landing craft at all. By the end of 1940,
however, work had begun on both sides of the Atlantic on an
expanding series of landing craft. These included the LCA
(Landing Craft Assault) which carried a platoon of infantry, and
the LCM (Landing Craft Mechanized) which could carry men,
a couple of tanks or some transport. Both were in service by
mid-1941, together with a most useful craft, the LCP(L),
imported into Britain from the USA which by 1940 was already
supplying Britain with a great quantity of war material.

Colin Kitchen, an RNVR officer, remembers them well:
'The letters LCP(L) stood for Landing Craft Personnel
(Large) – the adjective seeming rather odd as the boat was a
mere 37ft long; but there was an even smaller version, so there
had to be some means of distinguishing between them. LCPs
were made of seven-ply wood, with no armour protection. They
were driven by a petrol engine and could do about 22 knots.

'These craft were built by a US firm named Higgins of New
Orleans and the Americans called them "Higgins boats". The
story goes that they were originally designed to run liquor from
Cuba to the shores of Florida during Prohibition. With their
overhanging bows the boats were reasonably well suited to the
task of landing soldiers on beaches. They were the first craft to
be acquired by the Royal Navy for that specific job, pending the
introduction of purpose-designed landing craft.

'The LCP(L) flotillas' base was the aptly-named HMS
Tormentor on the Hamble river at Warsash, between Portsmouth and Southampton. I joined the flotilla in March 1942
and six such flotillas took part in the costly raid on Dieppe in
August 1942. My own flotilla carried the "floating reserve" of
French-Canadian troops on that occasion, and at 7 o'clock on a
brilliantly sunny morning we landed the soldiers on the central

promenade at Dieppe in the face of massive German fire; with no armour protection we lost heavily in men and boats.

'As a consequence of this experience Combined Operations HQ decided (very sensibly) that LCPs were unsuitable for landing assault troops. Most of the flotillas were converted into specialist smoke-laying craft, while some became even more specialized navigation or survey vessels used for clandestine operations off the enemy coast.'

Meanwhile, from early 1941, Britain's parachute battalions were being raised and trained. Among the early volunteers who later served on D-Day was George Price, who volunteered for parachute training in 1943. 'My old pal Bill Worley and I volunteered for the Paras in August 1943. In a very short time indeed we were sent to Hardwick Hall near Chesterfield for selective training, where in three weeks we developed muscles we didn't know we had. Everything we did had to be done at the double. If we were caught walking, no matter where to, we were for the high jump. The hardest part was the ten-mile route march – run a mile, walk a mile, in full battle order. At the end of it our socks were covered in blood. It was a really tough course and a good many of the lads were RTU'd (Returned to Unit), but Bill and I got through and were duly graded as A1+.

'From Hardwick we were sent to Ringway near Manchester, where we did our parachute training. The hangar we used looked more like a circus – we rolled, tumbled, and jumped from heights on to mats. Then came the dreaded balloon drops. I can still hear the shout: "Up 800 – 4 men dropping!" We did two daytime drops and one night drop from the balloon. After that came the real thing, from a hole in the floor of a Whitley bomber. It was pretty good fun really and we enjoyed it, especially the extra shilling a day (5p) after we got our parachute wings. (I still have mine, which are promised to my grandson.)

'In September 1943 we were posted to the 12th (Yorkshire) Parachute Battalion, which was originally the 9th Bn, the Green Howards, and consisted mainly of Northerners. This was a bit strange for Bill and I, he being a Londoner and me coming from Slough. We had quite a dialect problem for a while, but we soon got used to it, which was just as well because I eventually married a lass from the North.

'The training was very hard. We did many exercises, including being dropped in Wales and having to mock-fight our way back to Larkhill. I think in all I must have done about twenty jumps from various types of aircraft: Halifax, Albemarle, Stirling and the American Dakota – the C47. We once had a visit from General Montgomery while we were digging a slit trench, and he asked us what we were doing. I thought that was a bit daft, coming from him.'

George Price jumped into France on D-Day, and this story will pick him up again later. Meanwhile, the war had spread across the world. In December 1941, Japan attacked the American Fleet at Pearl Harbor and the United States entered the war, but many American soldiers had already been drafted into the Army. Fred Tannery, from Brooklyn, New York, was called up in November 1941. 'I was inducted into the Army at Fort Bragg and assigned to the Signal Corps. I remember Sunday, December 7, 1941, the day of Pearl Harbor, and knew that we were in for some extended service in the Army. I was eventually assigned to the 4th Infantry Division and we spent a lot of time training at different camps along the eastern seaboard of the USA, until January 1944. On January 12 we set sail in the USS *George Washington* for England. The trip took twelve days in a tremendous convoy full of all kinds of ships, and after a lot of zig-zagging we arrived at Liverpool, England, and were sent to join the rest of the Division at Tiverton in Devon. We stayed there training until we sailed for "Utah" beach.'

In 1943, while George Price was doing his parachute training at Ringway and Fred Tannery was serving with the 4th Infantry Division in the United States, the 82nd American Airborne Division arrived in the UK fresh from the battlefields of Italy. Among them was Sergeant George Maruschak of Chicago, Illinois, then serving in the 32nd Glider Field Artillery.

'I will start my tale in an area around Leicester, England, where we were stationed prior to moving to the staging area for the invasion of Normandy. We were stationed in a farm area around Leicester – our location was about 15 miles away at Husbands Bosworth. There were many, many of us in Leicester daily, with two main objectives – finding pubs that were open, and meeting young females! Enjoying the pleasures took a

setback when the Army located a battalion of black soldiers in a
park in Leicester. It appeared that the "American Indians" (I
don't know if the girls gave them that title or if the black soldiers
said that is what they were) bought the girls fur stoles and other
garments, and the girls preferred them to the paratroopers.
Anyway, there were fights and knifings. All troops were warned
and many passes to Leicester were abolished.

'I and two of my buddies were assigned to the Special
Services Dept to work on a musical revue, "Together We
Sing", to be presented to the troops and the people of Leicester.
I spent most of my time with a Sergeant in the British ATS
who, along with five other ATS girls and five civilian girls, was
also in our revue. General Eisenhower and high-ranking British
officers saw it and liked it so much that we were given permission to take it around RAF installations. We were also booked
into the Scala Theatre in London and Cavendish Theatre in
Nottingham. In London an air-raid alert was sounded and we
heard the noise of a V1 – a buzz-bomb – but our tour was never
completed. At the end of May 1944 we were ordered to report
back to our units. That could only mean that the time for our
next mission was not far away.'

Sergeant Maruschak's next performance would take place
near Ste-Mère-Eglise, a small town in Normandy.

Between 1940 and 1943, while these men and millions like them
were being recruited and trained, the war had spread. On 2 June
1941, violating the neutrality pact with the Soviet Union which
had enabled him to rape Western Europe with impunity, Hitler
invaded Russia and drove the Red armies before him in defeat.
Six months later, Hitler's ally, Japan, attacked the American
Pacific Fleet at Pearl Harbor and the United States entered the
war. A few days later, Britain declared war on Japan, and
America and Britain then forged an alliance with the Soviet
Union.

All these steps brought the cross-Channel invasion of Europe
perceptibly closer. Soviet Russia began to demand help, a
'Second Front' in Western Europe. Specifically, they
demanded a landing in the West, but this was, for the moment,
impractical, though aid was sent to the Soviet Union in im-

mense amounts. From mid-1941, first from Britain and later from the USA, munitions flowed to Russia in powerful convoys that fought freezing Arctic seas as well as German submarines and bombers to take Russia the weapons of war.

As soon as America entered the war, certain strategic decisions had to be taken between the Allies as to how the war should be fought. Two weeks after Pearl Harbor, on 20 December 1941, Britain's Prime Minister, Winston Churchill, and the American President, Franklin D. Roosevelt, met in Washington for what became known as the 'Arcadia' Conference. During this conference two decisions were arrived at which proved crucial to the future invasion of Europe.

The first step was the setting up of a unified Allied Command, the Combined Chiefs of Staff, to jointly direct the Anglo-American war effort and liaise with the Soviet Union. This was done in the light of the bitter experience of the Great War when the British and French armies fought under separate commands until near defeat in March 1918. In this war there was to be unity from the beginning and, although not without strain, this unity held firm to the end.

The second major decision taken at 'Arcadia' was the 'Germany First' policy. It was decided that the Allied effort be directed first and foremost to the defeat of Germany, and that American armies were to go into action against the Germans as soon as possible, probably in Western Europe. This met with the full approval of the Soviet Union, which did not in fact declare war on Japan until the Second World War was practically over.

This 'Arcadia' decision was based upon the well-established article of strategic doctrine which states that a nation faced with an array of enemies should defeat the strongest first. This done, the weaker elements may collapse and will certainly be more easily overcome. Although strategically sound, this decision caused controversy. Some American commanders had deep misgivings about how far the Allies could go in excluding the Japanese in the Pacific from these calculations and Admiral King, Commander-in-Chief of the United States Navy, only agreed to the 'Germany First' policy with the greatest reluctance.

The American Pacific Fleet had suffered a major and in-
famous attack at Pearl Harbor and the Japanese were now
swarming across the Pacific islands and the Philippines. Admiral King naturally wanted to hit back hard and fast, but revenge
apart, he did not see how the Japanese could ever be defeated if
they were given years to consolidate their conquests in the
Pacific. Assurances of total commitment in the Pacific from all
the British Empire and American forces immediately Germany
was defeated quite failed to reassure him. The Pacific would
also be primarily a naval theatre of operations, where Admiral
King's fleets would dominate Allied strategy, and he naturally
had no objection to that.

Admiral King's attitude to the European theatre was to have
one unfortunate effect on the cross-Channel invasion plans.
King controlled the allocation to theatres of the ships produced
in the bustling American shipyards and the Pacific was a mari-
time and amphibious theatre which needed a great deal of
shipping. As a result, the Allied cause in Europe and the
Mediterranean suffered from a chronic shortage of landing craft
and support vessels from 1942 until the end of the war. Britain's
shipyards were already working flat out, producing or repairing
warships and merchant vessels to fight the Battle of the Atlantic
and support operations in the Channel, the North Sea and the
Mediterranean. There was no spare capacity in Britain for
massive landing-craft production.

The next disagreement was over European strategy. American agreement to the 'Germany First' policy was given on the
understanding that the war was carried across the English
Channel and on to the Continent as quickly as possible. The
American intention was to build up an army in England in 1942,
and then strike directly across the Channel into France. Roosevelt and his advisers originally proposed to reach this stage by
the summer of 1942, just six months after entering the war. The
British were more than a little dubious about the wisdom of
such a venture and said so in unmistakable terms.

As American troops began to land in Britain in mid-1942, a
stream of high-ranking American politicians and military men
also began to arrive, urging the British into action. The
Russians were also demanding an immediate 'Second Front'

and General Marshall, the American Army Chief of Staff, conscious of the need to support Russia, proposed that the Allies might cross the Channel in the autumn of 1942 and establish a small bridgehead, perhaps in the Cotentin, the Cherbourg Peninsula. This they would maintain via the port of Cherbourg throughout the winter, emerge from this fortress in the spring of 1943 and advance into Germany. This operation bore the codename 'Sledgehammer'. Exactly what the Germans would be doing about this enclave during the winter of 1942–3 was hardly discussed, and the plan was soon seen to be unworkable.

Practical considerations alone made 'Sledgehammer' a non-starter. The Americans had entered the war with a very small army and instantly took on worldwide commitments. Thanks to the introduction of the draft of civilians for compulsory military service, the size of the American forces had been increasing steadily from 1940, but these forces had to be trained, equipped and transported overseas. All this could not be done overnight. Then the Battle of the Atlantic, the war against the U-Boat, was still being bitterly fought in 1942–3. The U-Boats were savaging the convoys and severely restricting the build-up of Allied strength in Britain. During the winter of 1942–3, German U-Boats operating in the North Atlantic sank over 800,000 tons of Allied shipping in one month alone.

Finally, the Luftwaffe were more than holding their own in the skies of France while the Allied air offensive against Germany had still to develop. When all these factors were taken into account, the invasion of France came some way down the list of immediate priorities.

Then, in August 1942, the impossibility of 'Sledgehammer' was bloodily underlined when the 2nd Canadian Division and three British Commandos, Nos 3, 4 and the Royal Marine 'A' Commando, together with a detachment of American Rangers, attempted a *coup-de-main* against the French port of Dieppe.

The Dieppe Raid has been described as a 'reconnaissance in force' and Lord Louis Mountbatten, then Chief of Combined Operations, stated later that the Battle of D-Day was won on the beaches of Dieppe, since the lessons learned there were crucial. This may well be true. The fact remains that the Dieppe Raid was a costly fiasco. Nearly half the men taking part were either killed or captured.

The Dieppe Raid taught the Allies several lessons. One was that they could not hope to capture an intact working port. To understand the lessons of Dieppe and the need for the prefabricated 'Mulberry' harbours of 1944 requires some knowledge of logistics, the branch of the military art concerned with supply.

The logistical problem is considerable for any army. Armies cannot function for long without large supplies of petrol, food, ammunition, medical supplies and men. For an invading army landing from the sea, the basic problem of delivering the right things in the right amounts to the right unit at the right time is compounded by the physical problem of getting them ashore, in all weathers and against a variety of opposition. This problem is greatly eased if the invading army enjoys the services of a functioning port. The enemy is equally aware of this fact and sees to it that all likely ports, as at Dieppe, are well defended and, if in danger of capture, extensively destroyed.

For the invasion to have a chance of success the Allies would need a port in good working order, through which their army could be supplied, the shipments safe from interruption by the weather. The big question to be answered was: was it possible to capture such a port by assault before the enemy has time to make it unusable? The Dieppe Raid made it bloodily clear that it wasn't.

Having accepted that to seize a port was impossible, it was clear that the invading army must take a port with them. Eventually they took two, the floating, prefabricated ports known as 'Mulberry' harbours, each as big as the Channel ferry port of Dover, one for the Americans at 'Omaha' beach and one for the British and Canadians at Arromanches. Parts of the latter port still remain offshore fifty years later.

The slaughter of Canadian infantry on the beaches of Dieppe also pointed out the need for the employment of tanks in the initial assault waves, while the inability of the standard tank to cope with beach obstacles and break out from the landing area led directly to the development of specialized armour. This would eventually include mine-clearing tanks, bridge-building tanks, armoured bulldozers and tanks mounting heavy mortars to destroy concrete obstacles, but the main item of specialized armour was the DD (Duplex Drive) swimming tank, which all the Allied armies were to employ on D-Day. Launched from ships anchored beyond the range of coastal artillery, these tanks could sail in with the infantry landing craft and hit the beach at the same time.

Patrick Hennessey, MBE, trained on the first DD tanks: 'One lesson learned from the disastrous raid on Dieppe in 1942 was that infantry landing from the sea without the support of tanks were doomed. Our task was to get tanks on to the beach before or as the infantry arrived, and the problem was to do that without alerting the enemy. The solution was to launch the tanks into the sea and swim them ashore, but a tank does not float readily in water so a new type was invented.

'The DD tank was a normal Sherman tank weighing some 32 tons. A metal skirt was welded round the hull to which was attached a canvas screen. This could be erected around the tank, supported by pillars of compressed air and kept rigid by metal struts. When in the water the tank floated, but there was only about 3ft of freeboard above the surface. Two small propellers were fitted at the stern of the tank, driven by the tank's engine, and these gave us power and steering. Once on the beach, the screen was collapsed, and there stood a tank, ready to fight.'

Lance-Corporal Henry Jolly recalls his DD tank training: 'We started training for D-Day in the summer of 1943 on some Valentine tanks which had been converted for swimming purposes. I was just nineteen at the time.

'We had to learn the use of the Davis escape equipment, which was used in submarines. The training took place in a water tank 12–15ft deep, with the driving and turret compartments of a Valentine tank placed in the bottom. We then had to get into the Valentine tank and thousands of gallons of water poured down on us, and we were not allowed to use the Davis equipment until the water reached our chins. Breathing through the Davis equipment, we then had to stay in the Valentine until the outside tank was full. Only then, on an order from an instructor, could we escape from the Valentine. After

this, and normal tank training, we started swimming and landing tanks from the sea on to the Isle of Wight.'

Meanwhile, in 1943, the tide of war was slowly turning
against the Axis. Two months after Dieppe, in October 1942,
the British Eighth Army in Africa, under General Montgomery, defeated Field Marshal Erwin Rommel's Afrika Korps at
El Alamein. In November 1942, American troops went into
action against the Germans for the first time when they landed
in Morocco under the command of Major-General Dwight
D. Eisenhower.

The North African campaign dragged on until the late spring of
1943, thereby effectively ruling out a cross-Channel invasion in
that year. There was no time left to plan the attack, reorganize
the troops and switch the landing craft to the Channel before
the summer ended. To keep up the pressure on the Axis, Sicily
and Italy were invaded in 1943, and the Italian government
capitulated. The Germans, however, fought on in Italy and
were still fighting there when the war ended in 1945.

Most significantly for the cross-Channel invasion in 1943,
the U-Boat menace was finally controlled, if not defeated, in the
Atlantic. With the decline of the U-Boats the naval, military
and logistical strength necessary for the invasion of France
could begin to gather in Britain, and by the end of 1943 there
were nearly one-and-a-half million American servicemen in
Britain. They joined hundreds of thousands of fighting men
from all the free nations now assembling for the invasion. There
were Canadian soldiers, Australian, New Zealand and South
African airmen, and contingents from all over the Empire, plus
thousands more from the occupied countries of Europe, the
Free French, Dutch, Belgians, Norwegians and Danes. The
invasion of Europe would be an international venture.

Among those arriving was Leslie W. Kick of the US 82nd
Airborne Division, a unit which had already seen action in
Sicily and Italy. 'Bill' Kick had been a paratrooper for just a year
when he arrived in Britain. 'In September 1942 I took the
four-week parachute course at Fort Benning, followed by a
two-week parachute communications course. In late October or
early November I was assigned to HQ Bty, 82nd Airborne

Division artillery at Fort Bragg as a radio operator. We landed on the docks at Casablanca, Morocco on May 10, 1943. In July 1943, being one of thirteen from HQ Bty, I was on a plane heading for the invasion of Sicily. When we flew over the US Navy ships laying offshore, we received heavy AA fire and both engines of our C-47 Dakota were knocked out. The pilot got over land and gave us the green light. We all got out without a scratch, but the pilot and co-pilot were killed in the crash.

'The division proceeded westerly along the south coast of Sicily to Trapani. We flew back to Africa in August, then back to Sicily in September. Then we took a trip from Palermo to Salerno by landing craft in late September. We entered Naples on October 1, 1943.

'In late November we took a three-week boat ride to Belfast, Ulster, where we stayed at Camp Ballyscullion, near Ballymena. About February 1944 we moved to Market Harborough, Leicestershire, in the English Midlands. Training from then until late May 1944 included a few weeks artillery firing in Wales.'

Another of those arriving in Britain from the USA at this time was J. Robert Slaughter of 1st Bn 116th Infantry, 29th Infantry Division, another unit destined for 'Overlord'. 'I joined the Virginia National Guard as a teenager in December 1940. On February 3, 1941 the Guard was inducted into Federal service and I was sent to Fort George G. Meade for one year's training. The attack on Pearl Harbor on December 7, 1941 changed our lives for ever. The song, "I'll Be Back In A Year, Little Darling" changed to "in for the duration!" We went overseas unescorted aboard the luxury liner, *Queen Mary* on Sunday, September 27, 1942.

'On Friday, October 2, a beautiful and calm day, 500 miles from our destination, Greenock in Scotland, the British Navy sent a light cruiser, HMS *Curacao* and a six-destroyer anti-submarine screen for our protection. *Curacao* zigged instead of zagging and we cut her in two, killing 320 British sailors. We limped into port the next day with a king-sized hole in the *Queen Mary*'s bow.'

Fifty years later, in a time when world travel is within most people's grasp, it is hard to imagine the impact the Americans had on the British people, or the curiosity the Americans felt about this war-weary little island. When the Americans arrived, the British people had been fighting Hitler for three long years and the strains were beginning to tell. Most of the men were in uniform, many of them abroad, and most of the women were in the services or working in the factories. Food rationing was in force and although most of the people were healthy enough, they were looking tired and thin. The centre of many of the cities had been reduced to rubble by German bombing, and the British people were in sore need of a little light relief. Into this scene erupted more than a million ebullient young Americans who seemed to have plenty of everything. Before long their trucks and troops filled the streets, and their music dominated the airwaves.

There were, inevitably, tensions. British reserve was frequently seen as sullenness, a resentment of America's wealth and power, while American enthusiasm was often taken as brashness and stupidity. British soldiers sourly remarked that the Yanks were 'over-paid, over-fed, over-sexed and over here'. The Americans replied that the British troops were 'underpaid, under-sized, under-sexed and under Eisenhower'. Relations between the Allied troops never became very friendly, though many American soldiers went to serve or train in British establishments. Robert Slaughter, for example, became a member of the 29th Ranger Battalion, which was trained by British Commandos at Achnacarry in Scotland.

Between the Americans and the British civilians – especially British girls – relations were much easier. Many Americans married British girls, and friendships were forged which endure to this day.

Fred Tannery, of 4th Infantry Division, remembers one of his English friends: 'In the five months before we went to France, I became very friendly with an English fellow, Gordon, who ran the Tiverton Theatre, the local movie house. He was the projectionist as well and I used to help him run the projector and take tickets in the lobby. We still keep in touch and I saw him on my visit to England long after the war. I met some very wonderful people in England, who I will remember as long as I live.'

Milton Chadwick arrived with a glider unit of 82nd Airborne: 'I loved England. Maybe the common language helped. I remember the flowers in the park at Market Harborough. I always used to swing the children in the park there and I was amazed that they remembered me when I came back from Normandy after six weeks' absence. The people treated us as their very own, and gave us a big welcome at the rail-road station upon our return from Normandy. I spent several pleasant Sunday afternoons with the Coleman family, who lived in Highfield Street in Market Harborough. I thought England was great, and if I could not have returned to the US after the war, I would have chosen England as my place to live.'

Jack Schlegel, now Chief of Police at Shandaken, New York, was then a twenty-year-old trooper in the 3rd Battalion of the 508th Parachute Infantry Regiment: 'After a few weeks in Portrush, Ireland, we came to our English base in Nottingham. English life and customs were strange to me, but I soon experienced the friendly warmth of the Nottingham people. Most of our time in Nottingham was taken up by training, but there were the lighter moments of pubs, romance, and rival fights between units. One incident always comes to mind; the killing of the King's deer in Wollaton Park. One day, a group of us decided deer steaks would be great, and since many of us were deer hunters in the USA, we felt the King would not miss a few. That night, several deer were shot, but the local constables got word of this, and several days after, a message from Col. Gavin's Headquarters put the 508th under base arrest with a warning that hunting deer was off limits in Nottingham. The deer steaks tasted great though!'

Alan Mitchell of Nottingham was a teenager when the American troops arrived: 'We used to hold dances in the youth club on a Saturday night, and as most of the local men were in the army, about four of us played in the band. It was really great playing such tunes as "You'll Never Know" and "My Devotion". The audience were mainly American paratroopers and the place was packed solid. Although I never heard them myself, the 508th had their own twelve-piece band, and they, too, used to play at the hall on numerous occasions. The stage was bedecked with different coloured parachutes.

'All in all, the GIs I met were a nice bunch, especially the Mexican boys. I used to walk home down Western Boulevard regularly with them as they walked back to Wollaton Park.'

Mary Hutton of Malmesbury in Wiltshire remembers another incident: 'My grandmother was a rather severe old lady and didn't approve of any girl going out with an American. Then one day, when she was going to the shops, a convoy went past full of American troops. One of them leaned out, gave a great wolf-whistle and called out, "Wish I was forty years older, Ma'am." The Americans could do no wrong in her eyes after that.'

The amazing thing is not that there were tensions but that, after the initial shock, the two peoples got on so well. Co-operation was necessary, for the day of decision was drawing closer.

The Allied leaders, Roosevelt, Churchill, Stalin, their Chiefs of Staffs and planners, were now meeting regularly, to plan overall strategy for the war, and in particular to plan the invasion of France. The decision to invade was finally taken by the Combined Chiefs of Staff in Washington in May 1943, with a provisional D-Day – the day of the actual assault – fixed for 1 May 1944.

In early 1943, the forthcoming invasion acquired a code-name. They called it Operation 'Overlord', while the naval part was given another codename, Operation 'Neptune'. From the beginning there had been agreement that the Supreme Commander of 'Overlord' would be an American, for after the initial landing in France the bulk of the ground forces would be American, and the appointment of an American as 'Supreme Commander, Allied Expeditionary Force' was therefore inevitable.

The Anglo-American and Canadian troops were lucky in the man chosen to lead them to France. General Dwight D. Eisenhower had commanded the American forces in North Africa. He was, by any standards, a good soldier and a fine man, but was unequalled as a leader of disparate Allied armies. He could handle prickly Army Commanders tactfully, or slap them down hard if he had to, but without causing lasting rancour. He was universally liked and respected; his smile alone was reputedly worth an Army Corps to the Allied cause.

Commanding a vast force drawn from many nations, Eisenhower was quite without nationalistic prejudice but, within limits, he could tolerate it in others, and his staff, following this example, worked together in an atmosphere remarkably free from friction. For internal disagreements among his officers, Eisenhower's rule was simple: 'If you disagree strongly with someone,' he said, 'you can call him a bastard if you have to. You may not, however, call him a Limey or a Yankee bastard.'

Eisenhower was not a fighting soldier. Before Operation 'Torch' (the American landings in North Africa at the end of 1942), Eisenhower had not even held an operational command. He was by profession a staff officer of considerable skill and experience and a protégé of General Marshall, the American Army Chief of Staff. This link with Marshall gave Eisenhower considerable political influence and a knowledge of how to get his views across to people in a position to help. Added to his universal popularity, this made him the perfect man for the job, while his staff experience proved invaluable for what was, in the end, a tremendous logistical task.

Eisenhower's appointment as Supreme Commander, Allied Expeditionary Force, was confirmed on Christmas Day 1943; from that moment Operation 'Overlord' was under way.

The Senior Command structure for 'Overlord' was as on p. 20.

As the diagram shows, the Army Field Commander for the invasion and build-up period was to be the British General, Sir Bernard L. Montgomery, the famous 'Monty', victor of El Alamein. His command would only endure for the invasion period or until sufficient American forces were ashore for Eisenhower to take up the Field Command.

Montgomery has had his critics, and not only in America, but you will not hear many critical voices among those who served under his command. 'With Monty, at least you knew what was going on ... and that is not always the case in military matters,' is one typical comment.

General Montgomery, or 'Monty' as he was universally called, was Britain's most charismatic commander and a

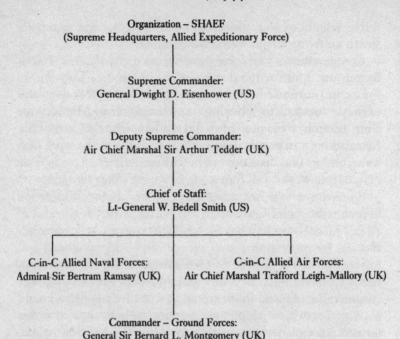

Organization – SHAEF
(Supreme Headquarters, Allied Expeditionary Force)

Supreme Commander:
General Dwight D. Eisenhower (US)

Deputy Supreme Commander:
Air Chief Marshal Sir Arthur Tedder (UK)

Chief of Staff:
Lt-General W. Bedell Smith (US)

C-in-C Allied Naval Forces: C-in-C Allied Air Forces:
Admiral Sir Bertram Ramsay (UK)   Air Chief Marshal Trafford Leigh-Mallory (UK)

Commander – Ground Forces:
General Sir Bernard L. Montgomery (UK)

professional fighting soldier. Commissioned into the Royal Warwickshire Regiment, he had been wounded on the Western Front during the Great War, and commanded a division in France in 1940. These experiences had left Monty with two firm convictions. First, that his men's lives were precious; no steps were too long or difficult if they saved lives. Second, that war was a chaotic business on which he must impose order by careful soldiering and meticulous tactics.

Monty's personality was often abrasive and he was undoubtedly arrogant. His attitudes brought him into conflict with his American colleagues who saw him as a cautious, even timid commander, while for his part Monty made little secret of his dislike of their bald-headed approach to battle. Monty's natural instinct to protect lives was compounded by the fact that by 1944 Britain's military resources, particularly in manpower, were almost at an end. He had to protect lives because his men were irreplaceable. Indeed, shortly after the D-Day landings it was necessary to break up one British division to supply reinforcements to other units; no other reinforcements were available. Whatever the difficulties caused by his attitude, Montgomery was the acknowledged master of the planned, set-piece battle and, like Eisenhower, he was acknowledged as the best man for the job that had to be done on D-Day.

Eisenhower and Montgomery had their first look at the plans already prepared for 'Overlord' at Marrakech in Morocco on New Year's Eve 1943–4. They did not like what they saw. This plan had been in preparation since 1942 and was the work of a team under the direction of a British officer, Lt-General F. E. Morgan and his American assistant, Brigadier-General Barker. Morgan's appointment was entitled 'Chief of Staff to the Supreme Allied Commander (Designate)' or COSSAC for short, and his proposals were therefore known as the COSSAC plan.

The war itself had laid down many of the requirements necessary for a successful invasion; air supremacy, surprise, adequate forces, specialized troops and armour, logistical support, the provision of ports. As more requirements became evident, so they were incorporated into the COSSAC plan. Now came the crucial problem of where the Allied armies should land ... and where the enemy's armies must be persuaded to *think* they would land. To these vital matters the planners now turned their minds.

Clearly, the invasion area must be within reach of Allied air cover. It must have weather-protected landing beaches which would also permit rapid deployment of the Allied armies inland after the invasion. The invasion area must be capable of being sealed off by bombing enemy communications, bridges, roads, and rail links, to delay the build-up of enemy counter-offensives, and have some reasonable port facility nearby that could quickly be captured, cleared of mines and obstructions, and brought into use. The planners spent hours and days poring over maps, seeking such a location on the French coast.

For the first requirement the Channel coast around Calais would be best. It was a bare twenty minutes' flying time away from the airfields in Kent and a beachhead there would give easy access towards Germany across northern France. It was so suitable that the enemy agreed with the Allies on this point and the defences along the coast around Calais were particularly strong. The Allied planners looked elsewhere. To the north of Calais the landing area was even more suitable, but a break-out would lead across the flood plain of Flanders on to the fatal ground of the 1914–18 War, and this fact alone tended to eliminate that area. The COSSAC planners then turned their eyes south, across the Seine and, beyond that, to the Calvados coast of Normandy.

The coast of Normandy, and in particular the area between the Cotentin Peninsula and the Bay of the Seine, lay only 80 miles away from the south coast of England. This was just within fighter range in 1943, and fighter range was steadily increasing – Allied fighters ranged 75 miles into Normandy on D-Day. The beaches between the River Orne north of Caen and the River Vire at the foot of the Cotentin Peninsula were wide and gentle, and the Cotentin – or Cherbourg – Peninsula, apart from offering the port of Cherbourg, would give some protection from the full fetch of any Atlantic gales coming in from the west. Moreover, the area could be cut off by the tactical bombing of some thirty bridges leading in across the Seine, thus isolating the area from German reinforcements. Finally, on this sector the coastal fortifications were nowhere near as strong as they were along the Channel coast. COSSAC, therefore, chose Normandy for the 'Overlord' invasion, on a 30-mile strip running west from the mouth of the Orne, 6 miles north of Caen to the River Vire.

Eisenhower and Montgomery had many reservations about the COSSAC plan and they wanted changes. With 1 May 1944 already set as the invasion date, they had only a few months to do much about it, but they did agree that the choice of a landing place was broadly correct. Thus the die was cast. Some time soon, in the coming year of 1944, the full weight of Allied arms would fall on the coast of Normandy.

—————CHAPTER TWO—————

The Defences of Normandy

'Rommel told me, "If the Allies will land
and we can't throw them back into the sea
within 24 hours, it's the beginning of the
end."'
Major Hans Von Luck
125 Panzer Grenadier Regiment
21st Panzer Division

Normandy, ancient dukedom of the English Plantagenet Kings,
is the largest province in modern France. As in all French
provinces, Normandy is sub-divided into a number of *départe-
ments*, of which two, Calvados and La Manche, were to be
directly concerned with the invasion, which fell on their northern and eastern coasts.

The Calvados coast runs west from the mouth of the River
Orne, north of the city of Caen, to the mouth of the River Vire,
north of Isigny. Before the war this was a holiday and tourist
area, noted for fine, safe, sandy beaches, for yachting and for
the abundant and excellent local seafood. The coast west of
Ouistreham, running through the little resort towns of Lion-
sur-Mer, Luc-sur-Mer, Langrune and St Aubin, is referred to
locally as '*Le Côte Nacré*', the Pearl Coast. Apart from some

modern tourist developments, like caravan parks, it is still very
much as it was fifty years ago, in the summer of 1944.

To the west, across the Vire, lies the *département* of La
Manche, which runs west through the market town of Carentan
and north up the Cotentin Peninsula, through the beautiful
little town of Ste-Mère-Eglise, to Cherbourg on the tip of the
peninsula. Cherbourg is the major port in this section of the
coast and the nearest port to southern England, some eighty
miles to the north. The beaches of Calvados and La Manche are
very wide, flat and sandy, gently shelving and backed with
drained salt marshes or low sand dunes. They do contain
patches of mud and there are offshore sandbars, but they are in
general very suitable for amphibious operations.

These beaches are broken only once on the Calvados coast,
between the River Vire and Arromanches, where steep cliffs,
100ft high, drop directly into the sea along twenty miles of
coast. These cliffs are broken only twice, by the small harbour
and town of Port-en-Bessin, and by four miles of beach below
the villages of Vierville and St Laurent. This beach – codenamed 'Omaha' – was to be the scene of bloody fighting on 6
June 1944.

The country behind the beaches is very varied. Around Caen
there are large open areas of arable fields interspersed with apple
orchards and low wooded hills, land flat enough to contain the
airfield at Carpiquet. South of the Cotentin Peninsula and
Port-en-Bessin lie the close, irregular fields of the Normandy
bocage. 'Bocage' is a Norman word meaning grove or copse; the
Normandy *bocage* consists of innumerable small, irregular
fields, divided by high, thick hedges set atop earth banks. This
was perfect defensive country if the enemy had the time and
forces to occupy it. Overall, the country is not unlike Hampshire or the flatter areas of Vermont and Maine in the eastern
United States. It is farming country, threaded with streams and
rivers, home to an industrious rural population.

Large towns are few. The capital of the region is the university city of Caen, six miles up the Orne from Ouistreham.
Caen and the city of St Lô, further to the west, would be the
scene of bitter fighting later in the Normandy campaign. In the
centre of Calvados, some ten miles inland from the coast, lies

the ancient cathedral city of Bayeux, famous down the ages for that remarkable relic of another invasion, the Bayeux Tapestry, which depicts the landing of Duke William the Conqueror in England nine centuries ago in 1066. There are no other towns near the coast, with the exception of the sizeable fishing port of Ouistreham at the mouth of the Orne, with a population in 1944 of about 5,000. Then there is Courseulles at the mouth of the River Seulles, and over to the west, Carentan, a market town of the southern Cotentin also with a population of around 5,000. Another place to note is the village of Ste-Mère-Eglise in the centre of the Cotentin, which had a population of some 1,500 in 1944 and was noted for the breeding of horses.

When the COSSAC planners' eyes first turned upon it in 1943, Normandy was a backwater in the European war, quiet, peaceful and relatively undisturbed. It had been that way since German forces overran France in 1940. Normandy was usually occupied by second-rank formations of the German Wehrmacht, units without motor transport or with obsolescent equipment, or by divisions resting after campaigns on the Russian Front. In late 1943 all that began to change.

The options open to generals are often limited. The Germans were able to predict when and where the invasion would probably take place simply by calculating what they would do in Eisenhower's place. By mid-1943 there was no doubt on either side of the Channel that an invasion was coming, and the Allied choice clearly lay between the Pas de Calais, which was favoured by General Von Rundstedt, the German Commander in the West, and most of the German High Command (the OKW), and Normandy, favoured for intuitive reasons by Adolf Hitler, the German Chancellor. Both parties felt that wherever the main invasion came in, there would be a major diversion in the other, to disperse the defenders and help the main assault. The main difficulty would be to decide which was the invasion and which the diversion.

Hans Von Luck, then a major in the 21st Panzer Division, had served with General Rommel in the desert and was with him again in Normandy. 'Before, and on D-Day, I was commanding a Panzer Grenadier Regiment of the 21st Panzer

Division, east of the River Orne. Our division was in Army Group "B" reserve and under strict orders not to move unless released by the Army Group on direct orders from Hitler's Headquarters.

'We didn't expect the invasion in Normandy because the distance was very long, there were a lot of cliffs, difficult to overcome, but we were training every night to get as familiar with the ground as possible. Rommel visited us several times, and he insisted that we had to take position and dig in, that the invasion might come in Normandy. General Marcks, who was the Corps Commander at that time, knew the British very well and he said, "I know the British. They will go to church on Sunday, they will land here in Normandy on Monday." So this was foreseen, only Eisenhower postponed the invasion for one day.'

The Germans had been building up their coastal defences, the so-called Atlantic Wall, since the invasion of Britain was abandoned in 1941. When completed, the Atlantic Wall was to run from Norway to the Spanish frontier, a thick belt of minefields, obstacles, strongpoints and artillery, the latter set in reinforced concrete blockhouses which could repel any invasion force. The snag was that even by the spring of 1944, the Atlantic Wall was not complete.

British Commandos and Allied agents crossed it with impunity night after night, and resources to complete it in terms of concrete, men or munitions were simply not available. The Pas de Calais was certainly strong enough and the Allied deception plans, which included stationing the American Third Army in Kent, fed the Germans the idea that this would be the area of the invasion, and that any attack in Normandy would only be a feint. However, Normandy needed much more attention before it could be considered secure. Hitler had some six months to prepare for the invasion, and clearly there was much work to be done. He did, however, have just the man to do it: Rommel.

Field Marshal Erwin Rommel, infantry colonel, Panzer leader, sometime commander of the doughty Afrika Korps, the most charismatic general of the Second World War, was glad to be summoned to the Führer's Headquarters in December 1943. The previous twelve months had not been happy ones for him.

Since his return from Africa in the spring of 1943 he had spent some time in hospital, recovering from jaundice and exhaustion following his efforts in the desert. He had kicked his heels for a while at Hitler's Headquarters, and in November 1943 was commanding an Army Group based in Bavaria and northern Italy.

This was not an active fighting command, and Rommel's time in office there was plagued with trouble from the SS, the soldiers drawn from the ranks of the Nazi Party. SS Divisions, while under Wehrmacht control for operations, were not under control in matters of discipline and the savage behaviour of SS troops toward the Italian civilian population proved a continuous source of trouble for Field Marshal Rommel. His complaints about their behaviour were referred to political leaders such as Himmler, and then ignored. Though unpopular, SS units were nevertheless excellent fighting divisions, and through their political influence usually had the pick of manpower and equipment. Well trained, well equipped and often fanatical, SS troops, in particular the 12th SS Panzer Division, were to play a significant part in the early Normandy battles of 1944.

Rommel was glad to leave Italy and looked forward to the new appointment outlined by the Führer. His first task was to inspect all the defences of the Atlantic Wall, from Denmark to the Spanish frontier, and report on their ability to repel the coming invasion.

Rommel began his task with a series of whirlwind inspection tours along the entire length of the Atlantic Wall; he was horrified by what he found. In all but a few areas the Wall simply did not exist. The major ports and possible Allied landing areas, such as the coast of the Pas de Calais, were certainly well protected with heavy guns in concrete emplacements and adequate garrisons secure in intricate defence systems, but elsewhere there were long stretches of coast where the defences were no more than a few mines and some strands of barbed wire. The problem now was what to do about it in the short time available before the Allies came ashore.

By 1943 the shortage of war material for the German forces was becoming acute, but the main blame for the lack of defences along the coast lay with the Oberkommando Wehrmacht (OKW), the German High Command. The OKW had made the fundamental mistake of believing their own propaganda.

Following the bloody repulse of the Canadians at the Dieppe Raid of 1942, Goebbels, Hitler's Minister of Propaganda, had made great play with the impregnability of the Atlantic Wall, citing Dieppe as evidence of what would happen to any invader who dared put a foot in Fortress Europe, the Germans' '*Festung Europa*'. The German people and Army were bombarded with propaganda which seemed to bear out Hitler's claims that the Allies could never set foot in Europe until Hitler's long-promised V-weapons, the V1 and V2 rockets, were able to shatter Britain and end the war ... and these rockets and their launching sites were ready for deployment by the summer of 1944.

Since 1940 France had been listed low in the priority scale for men and equipment, and had become a rest area for divisions mauled on the Russian Front. The permanent garrison consisted largely of low-grade divisions, often containing Poles or Romanians, or elderly and unfit Germans, even renegade Russians. Some indication of the diversity in these divisions is indicated by the fact that in some of their battalions, eight different types of paybook were necessary, for Russians, Cossacks, Armenians, Georgians, Turkmen, Tartars, and so on.

The development of thick defences, especially of beach obstacles and strongpoints, was hampered by a shortage of steel, concrete and manpower, for the main German labour force, the Todt Organization, was kept busy repairing bomb damage to factories in the Ruhr. Rommel reported his dire findings to OKW and to Field Marshal Von Rundstedt, commanding Army Group West, but little was or could be done to rectify matters.

Rommel therefore decided to take a direct line in the affair. He went to Hitler and applied for command of Army Group B, which consisted of the German armies stationed between the Netherlands and the Loire. The invasion would certainly come somewhere in this area and Rommel would therefore be the Commander of the German anti-invasion forces. As Commander of Army Group B, Rommel was responsible directly to

Von Rundstedt, the Chief of Oberkommando West, command-ing all the troops in Western Europe. There might have been friction between the two men, since Rommel had gone over Von Rundstedt's head to obtain his command. Von Rundstedt was the doyen of the Offizier Korps, while Rommel was regarded in some Wehrmacht circles as an upstart who had gained his rapid promotion by the favour of Hitler. Fortunately, Von Rundstedt had little interest left in fighting the war and was happy to give Rommel his head.

In June 1944, Von Rundstedt had, at least on paper, 60 divisions, 11 of them Panzer divisions, to meet the Allied invasion, but these were deployed all down the western coast of Europe and their men and equipment varied widely; 24 of these divisions were deployed in Holland or Belgium, 11 were in the South of France and 6 south of the Loire. Some units had little or no transport, while the others relied heavily on horses, even for artillery haulage, a method which had long since been abandoned by the Allied armies.

Von Rundstedt's authority in the West was continually undermined by interference from Hitler and he was quite content to let Rommel have a free hand if he wanted one. Rommel's disputes with Von Rundstedt's headquarters, Army Group West, were over supplies and tactics, and his main opponent here was not Von Rundstedt but the Commander of Panzer Forces in the West, General Geyr Von Schweppenburg. Their main disagreements centred on where the invasion would come and on what tactics should be employed to repel it.

Rommel's appreciation of Allied intentions fell somewhere between that of Hitler and the OKW. He felt that Normandy was more likely than the Pas de Calais, but decided that an assault around the mouth of the Somme was the most probable of all. It was therefore in this area and in Normandy that he concentrated his efforts, setting out to develop the coastal defences in depth, driving his men hard, using energy, in-genuity and his genius for improvisation to overcome a chronic shortage of material.

Rommel's intention was to halt the Allied invasion on the beaches. Here his views differed from those of Field Marshal Von Rundstedt, most of the General Staff, and certainly of

Geyr Von Schweppenburg. Von Rundstedt felt that with over
1,500 miles of coast to defend and the Allied command of the sea
and domination of the air, the invasion simply could not be
prevented. Therefore he did not propose to try and prevent the
Allies getting ashore. Rather, he proposed to concentrate on
defending major ports and on building up a strategic reserve
which, once the main invasion had been located, would move
against it with overwhelming force and push the landing forces
back into the sea.

This was a classic defensive strategy. Rommel appreciated
the thinking behind it, while totally disagreeing with the concept. He felt that the Allied command of the air would be
decisive and prevent the movement forward of any German
strategic reserve. Such forces as were able to move would be
shattered by Allied air strikes long before they got near the
landing areas. He therefore intended to work well forward and
defeat the invasion on the beaches, and on the first day – the
'longest day', as he called it. Within his own command he made
preparations to do just that, but his preparations were constantly hampered by disagreements on this basic policy, particularly with Geyr Von Schweppenburg, who controlled the
best equipped divisions in the West, the Panzer divisions of the
Waffen SS. Rommel and his superiors were still arguing over
the fundamental points of his policy when the Allied troops
came ashore. There were only 18 German divisions in Normandy and Brittany, between the Seine and the Loire, and the
disputes between Rommel and Von Rundstedt over the best
invasion tactics led to a compromise in their deployment.

In the actual invasion area were two German armies, the
Seventh to the south of the Seine and the Fifteenth to the north.
The Seventh Army was to bear the brunt of the invasion, which
fell on the three infantry divisions, the 709th, 91st and 243rd in
the Cotentin, and two infantry divisions stationed along the
Calvados coast, the 716th and 352nd. Of these, only the 352nd
was a first-class, well-trained and properly equipped assault
infantry division, although the 91st was up to strength and had
been trained in anti-invasion tactics.

The only Panzer division near the coast was an ex-Afrika
Korps formation, 21st Panzer, deployed between Caen and

Falaise, and the only tactical reserve was the first-class 6th Parachute Regiment deployed around Carentan. Other formations available in support included the troops of 84th Corps deployed along the coast from the Orne to the Seine, and two more Panzer divisions, 12th SS Panzer, deployed around Bernay and Evreux, and Panzer Lehr, which was positioned further south, on the wide plains of the Beauce, near Chartres. The headquarters of the 1st SS Panzer Corps was at Rouen, while Rommel took up his headquarters at the château of LaRoche Guyon, further up the Seine, near the base of the 116 Panzer Division.

Apart from the 21st Panzer Division, the 352nd and 91st Infantry Divisions, and the 6th Parachute Regiment, the troops along the Calvados and Cotentin coast were second-rank formations. Many of the soldiers had chronic complaints, stomach ailments or poor feet, or were Russian or Polish renegades, serving here to avoid forced labour. They lacked heavy weapons and motor transport, and got about on bicycles. Even at this stage in the war, most German infantry divisions in whatever state of readiness still used horse transport. Even so, these German formations were dug-in and prepared to make a fight of it when the day came. They had very little choice and could reflect that the normal attack:defence ratio, where one defending soldier was held to be worth three attackers was increased when the attackers had to land and attack from the sea.

Sergeant Rainer Hartmetz had arrived in Normandy from the Russian Front and was an experienced infantry NCO. 'When I came to Normandy I was stationed some kilometres east of Caen on the main road to Pont l'Evêque. It was different from those awful days in Russia, I remember the time the Russians assaulted us three times in one day, the last time with about 120 tanks. The company was stationed in Frénouville, a small village on the Caen–Lisieux road, with about 200 inhabitants. Each morning the company disappeared into the fields or forests for combat training by squads, platoons and companies. We practised with all our weapons, and the training became a kind of sport. We didn't know much about the other German troops in France. Our battalion came from Russia, and that was another world. We knew we would have to fight another adversary – the British. We didn't think of the Americans; they were not known to us. We had the feeling that fighting with the British would be a more human fight. We knew the British would be tough fighters but there would be humane rules.

'We never got the idea to surrender to the British, but there was a certain temptation to give up sooner than necessary, and that had been the problem of a lot of discussions between us and our officers. We fought this temptation with our feelings of honour and responsibility. Honour as a soldier, responsibility for Germany, but what was Germany? My parents, my teachers, my girlfriends, my younger friends in the Hitler Youth, the Nazi leader on the block, those fat guys in brown uniforms with big patriotic words in the mouth?

'What about Hitler? That simple soldier of World War I, four times wounded. He must have suffered like we did, but he couldn't have wanted what happened. We knew that there had been some things wrong and bad but he seemed, to us, sacrosanct. We fought for Germany against the Russians, and now we had to fight against the British, who helped them.

'After this war there would be a second one, to get rid of the Nazis. It was a very simple and primitive way of thinking, but it came out of our emotions, education, experiences and propaganda. Germany, our country, seemed to be strange to us, even our parents. We got furlough and felt alone at home. Being together with our parents, there was nothing to tell, and the things we wanted to talk of they didn't understand.'

Another of the German defenders was Herbert Muschallik, a soldier in the 352nd Infantry Division. 'I was not an NCO but an ordinary soldier. I was born in Buethen in Silesia in 1926, so I was just seventeen when I was sent to Normandy. We were shipped west in cattle trucks and I got there in September 1943, after just six weeks' infantry training at a place called Oppeln. I can't remember my company or regiment, but I was on an anti-tank gun crew, a Pak 38, and we trained with that a lot. We were stationed in a village near Bayeux, but we didn't go out much, and if we did, we had to be back by ten o'clock. We trained and trained and waited for the invasion, but when it came it was a surprise ... but I was only a soldier. Maybe the officers knew more about it.'

Oberst Helmut Ritgen was then serving with Panzer Lehr, a crack German armoured division. The word 'Lehr' means 'training', but Panzer Lehr was no training division. It was the demonstration division for the German Panzer Corps, equipped with the latest tanks and staffed by first-class men, including a high percentage of experienced officers and NCOs. Panzer Lehr was deployed to the south of Caen and was one of the units which Rommel was eager to bring up towards the beaches.

Helmut Ritgen has left an account of the pre-D-Day period. 'All German field manuals on operations contained the phrase "Frictions and mistakes are commonplace phenomena". In 1944 such frictions thwarted the last possible effective counter-attack against the Allied landings in Normandy. This was to have been a violent and co-ordinated counter-attack by I SS Panzer Corps with three Panzer divisions within 48 hours of the landings. The beaches along the Calvados coast, on what were to be Gold, Juno and Sword, the British and Canadian beaches, were defended by 716th Infantry Division, a static division which was almost without any means of transport, even horses, and was made up of elderly soldiers who had no combat experience. It was insufficiently armed, mostly with captured French equipment.

'In the front line, on the dunes of "Juno", where the Canadians would land, two weak rifle battalions clung to a chain of pill-boxes and strongpoints near the shore, partly armed with 50mm, 75mm or 88mm guns. Beach obstacles and minefields, some still under construction, had failed to delay the invaders landing even at ebb tide. The German coastal and divisional artillery, lacking any means of fire control, was only capable of firing single-battery, not multi-battery missions.'

Apart from a shortage of manpower the Germans needed to develop their coastal defences to a depth capable of bringing the invasion to a grinding halt under artillery and machine-gun fire. Rommel's defences therefore began well below high-water mark, in the area between the tides. Beams and tree trunks were driven deep into the sand, the tops projecting seawards and crowned with sharp steel cutters to rip open the hulls of landing craft. Other poles were draped with fused mines. Concrete tank obstacles, obsolete ashore, were dragged into the sea to hamper craft beaching, and naval mines were secured in the shallow coastal waters with lines attached to their horns. The obstacle which was to prove most difficult to overcome was called 'Element C'. This obstacle came in various forms but consisted of a heavy steel fence supported by wooden posts and mined. There were also steel girders welded together like enormous starfish, and wooden ramps, mines, barbed wire, and another barrier known as 'Belgian Gates' which consisted of concrete dragon's teeth and metal barriers, armed with fused shells.

Singly or in combination these obstacles offered a number of possible terrors. They might succeed in sinking landing craft outright, or in blowing the occupants sky high. They might impale the craft and expose them, stuck fast, to shell-fire from the shore. They might force the landing craft to disembark the troops too far out at low tide, well beyond the obstacles, where they could be machine-gunned as they waded or ran ashore. They might let craft in, but probably in the confusion the craft would not get out again to bring up reinforcements. At the very least, these underwater obstacles would disrupt the landings. The beaches themselves were sown with an assortment of anti-tank and personnel mines, screened with wire and covered by guns, anti-tank emplacements, flame throwers and machine-gun posts and artillery set in reinforced concrete bunkers.

Rommel made great use of mines. In the four months before June 1944, four million mines were laid along the Channel coast. Had time permitted, Rommel intended to lay between 50 and 100 million mines before his preparations could be considered complete. As with everything else, there was a shortage of mines, which Rommel partially overcame by employing old French shells attached to obstacles or buried on the beach, fused to explode on contact.

Unless they are covered by machine guns, minefields and barbed-wire entanglements can be rapidly cleared, so behind and above the beaches Rommel constructed pill-boxes and concrete emplacements for heavy machine guns, 81mm mortars and field artillery, notably the formidable 88mm anti-tank gun. These guns, and all the emplacements close to the shore, were usually sited to fire along the beach rather than out to sea. Their seaward wall was protected by reinforced concrete many feet thick, covered and camouflaged with earth and sandbags against naval gunfire, the slits positioned to enfilade troops and tanks crossing the beach and so deny the invaders any exit from the landing beach, which was converted into a killing ground.

Behind the beaches came more minefields and wire, and the trench lines of the defending infantry. Rommel instructed the coastal divisions to entrench *everybody*, soldiers, cooks, clerks and drivers, all in deep dugouts linked by connecting passages to permit movement from one post to another under cover from enemy fire. All open fields inland considered likely spots for airborne landings, either by parachute or glider, were thickly studded with posts designed to smash the gliders as they came down. These became known as 'Rommel's Asparagus'. The posts were linked with barbed wire and many fields were mined with anti-personnel and anti-tank devices.

It was also possible to flood a number of tidal areas along the Normandy coasts and along the numerous rivers, notably around Ste-Mère-Eglise and Carentan, along the Vire and the Merderet, as well as in the flood plains east of Ranville along the River Dives, by destroying banks or breaking sluices, and in the east below the heights of Ranville, along the Orne and Dives. Both these areas were flooded, either by damming the rivers until the banks overflowed, or by breaking the banks themselves, allowing the water to flow out into the fields to a depth of between two and four feet. In the ditches, the water would be much deeper. The British, American and Canadian paratroopers would find these floods a considerable obstacle. Many men were to drown in them, trapped in their parachute harness, weighed down with their equipment and ammunition.

The flood waters quickly became covered with weed, and the floods were therefore invisible to Allied reconnaissance aircraft which by the spring of 1944 were making regular photographic flights over the invasion area. Many of these flights came in at wave-top height, to build up a 'soldier's eye' view of the invasion beaches for the assault craft coxswains and the invading troops.

Squadron Leader Jim Palmer flew many such sorties over the Normandy beaches. 'I was then an Army captain, an Air Liaison

Officer (ALO), assigned to No. 239 Recce Squadron RAF. I was posted to No. 35 (Recce) Wing RAF, which comprised No. 4 Squadron equipped with the PR (Photo-Reconnaissance) Spitfire for high-level vertical photography; and with Nos 2 and 268 Squadrons equipped with American P-51 (Mustang) aircraft for low-level oblique and vertical photography and also visual recce backed up with photographs. I was assigned to No. 239 Squadron as ALO.

'We were employed in the main with taking low-level oblique photographs of the French coastline, covering not only the Normandy beaches which would eventually be used but also a much greater length of coastline in order to confuse the enemy as to our actual intentions. We paid quite a lot of attention to the Pas de Calais area where the Germans expected us to land. This supported the deception supposedly made by FUSAG, the 4th United States Army Group set up in South-East England and which actually consisted of only a handful of officers and men – mainly wireless operators who successfully hoaxed the German "Y" Service – their interception service.

'A great deal of the coastal cover was undertaken at low tide to show the obstacles erected in the sand below high-water mark as a deterrent to our landing craft. Most of these obstacles were steel sections welded into a tripod (in some cases old railway lines were used). Explosive mines were attached to these. Others were of reinforced concrete "Dragon's Teeth". The photographs were taken by a camera with very little depression, mounted behind the pilot's head. This meant that the pilots had to fly extremely low and were vulnerable to anti-aircraft activity. The main reason for flying so low was to obtain photographic cover of the beach obstacles, and to get a panoramic view of the landing beaches. These pictures were eventually used by the landing craft coxswains to guide their craft ashore as the church steeples and distinctive elevation of the beaches shown on these photographs were a far better guide than any map or chart.'

Other aircraft were engaged in aerial interdiction, sealing off Normandy from the rest of France. Ken Beard was then an RAF air gunner: 'I cannot recall air crews associating raids with any particular strategy for winning the war. In other words, we would go into briefing, be given a target and get on with the job. It must be realized that we lowly air gunners would attend the general briefing only, whereas navigators particularly would have their own additional briefing when, no doubt, they would be given more information regarding the target and its significance. Perhaps I ought to say that even at general briefings we would be given something of a background to the target, i.e., "electrical equipment for German fighters is manufactured here", or "lorries are made here".

'Air crews were very single-minded about their function in the war, and I have no recollection of anyone being particularly interested in the general aspects of what was happening elsewhere. For example, although obviously aware of newspapers screaming that it was time for the Second Front, that Russia was demanding it, and so on, I never recall air crew losing any sleep about the purpose of raids. We would have been stupid, on the other hand, not to have realized that as we did more and more raids on targets "nearer home" the Second Front was in the offing. As evidence of this I can itemize the raids in which my crew took part during the month of May 1944.

'1 May: Malines (Belgium) Railway Centre locomotive sheds. 7 May: Mantes-la-Jolie (on the Seine); stores depots and locomotive sheds. 10 May: Lens, Pas de Calais; railway yards. 22 May: mine-laying off enemy coast. 24 May: Aachen, two railway yards (442 aircraft involved – 25 lost – 14,800 people bombed out of their homes). Aachen was an important link in the railway system between Germany and France.'

The photo-reconnaissance aircrews noted, among other things, the construction of several battery positions, probably containing heavy guns, near the village of Merville, east of Ouistreham, and on the cliffs of the Pointe du Hoc on the west coast by the mouth of the Vire. These were thought to contain massive 155mm guns, with a range of twenty miles, enough to embarrass any anchored invasion fleet discharging troops off the Normandy coast. These positions, and a thousand more, were noted on the planners' maps and pondered over. This was a game of cat and mouse, of finding an obstacle and taking steps to eliminate it, each side attempting to gain a march on the other.

In this game, the Allied planners were greatly helped by the
activities of the French Resistance. All along the coast of
France, the men and women of the Maquis were taking note of
the German defences as they developed and passing the information on to London. This activity was not without risk. On 6
June, even as the Allies came ashore, the Gestapo were shooting
French patriots in the prison at Caen.

Mlle Thomas was a member of the Resistance. 'On 6 June
1944 we were at Caen, except for my sister Madeleine, who was
still in the prison at Lisieux, from which she was eventually
liberated by the bombing. Our father had been arrested and
sentenced by a German Court Martial on the night of 9 November 1943, having been picked up by the Gestapo in early
October. We were part of the "Century" network, and gathered
intelligence on enemy fortifications, movement of troops, and
so on, right up to the moment of the invasion.'

Monsieur Reginensi was another Resistance fighter. 'I was
not in the Normandy region at the time of the landings. I was
with a unit of Maquisards in the centre of France, where we had
tried to attack and immobilize the movement of German troops
north towards the beachhead.'

In June 1944 the French Resistance could muster some
100,000 men and women, many of them well armed and trained.
The German Army were already making sweeps against the
Resistance, and the attacks mounted by Monsieur Reginensi
and his comrades often led to savage reprisals, most notably
when the 2nd SS Division surrounded the village of Oradour-
sur-Glane in the centre of France and killed all the inhabitants,
more than 600 men, women and children.

For defending the Normandy beaches, Rommel's main requirement was men. All these new positions demanded men,
especially trained fighting infantry and artillery men, men who
could hold their positions in spite of what came at them, as well
as reserves to back them up and counter-attack when the first
rush of the invasion subsided. Most of all, Rommel needed
Panzer divisions close to the coast. More men were available in
plenty, but Rommel could not move them to the Calvados.

North of the Seventh Army, lay the Fifteenth Army, which
had 250,000 men in 20 infantry divisions and 4 Panzer divisions.

Allied deception plans, plus the stubborn belief of the German High Command that Calais would be the real invasion area, would keep the Fifteenth Army out of the D-Day area until it was too late to intervene, and Rommel had to make do with what he had.

Normandy was now the scene of frantic activity. Throughout the spring of 1944 Rommel and his men worked and waited, while their defences grew and grew, becoming ever more secure. The morale of the men also improved as Rommel's constant badgering and inspection tours produced new equipment. Even as the Allied invaders were lucky to have Eisenhower, so were the German defenders of the Atlantic Wall lucky to have Field Marshal Rommel. Rommel was not quite the good chap of 'Desert Fox' legend and subsequent histories. He served Hitler loyally and well until he became convinced that Hitler was losing the war. His views were not noticeably liberal, nor was his information always accurate.

On 26 April, five weeks before the invasion, he wrote to his wife: 'In England morale is bad. There is one strike after another and the cries of "Down with Churchill and the Jews" are getting louder. These are bad omens for the coming offensive.'

Rommel had one other disadvantage; he was not lucky. He had the unfortunate knack of being away from his headquarters when the crucial battles began. When the Alamein offensive began in 1942, Rommel was in Rome. When the Allies landed in Normandy, Rommel was in Germany. On the other hand, he was an inspiring general, who led his men from the front.

Rommel was never an easy man to work with, but he knew his job. The troops knew where they were with him and what he wanted. In case there was any doubt, Rommel spelt out his requirements in simple detail: 'I give orders only when necessary. I expect them to be obeyed at once, and to the letter. No order shall be ignored, changed, or delayed by lack of zeal or red tape.'

Rommel's declared intention was to defeat the Allies on the beaches. His men were to stay in their positions and carry out his intentions, whatever the problems and difficulties, and these were men of the German Army, products of the war machine which had conquered most of Europe. 'I've fought a lot of people,' said Brigadier Peter Young, DSO, MC and Bar, then a lt-colonel, who was to lead No. 3 Commando ashore on 'Sword' beach on D-Day, 'but if you haven't fought the Germans, then you don't know what fighting is.'

Although the defences of Normandy were nowhere near complete when the attack finally came, they were vastly improved from 1943 and manned by resolute troops. To overcome them would be a mighty task indeed.

--------CHAPTER THREE--------
COSSAC to 'Overlord'

'There it is ... it won't work. I know it
won't work, but you'll bloody well have to
make it work.'
General Alanbrooke
Chief of the Imperial General Staff

The basis for Operation 'Overlord' was the COSSAC plan.
During 1942, an Allied committee, the Combined Commanders' Committee, had drawn up a series of ever more gloomy
forecasts for the forthcoming invasion of Europe. After the
Casablanca Conference at the end of 1942, where Churchill and
Roosevelt finally agreed to meet Marshal Stalin's demands for
an invasion, the British Lt-General Frederick Morgan and his
American assistant, Brigadier-General Barker, heading the
COSSAC team, were handed the Combined Commanders'
proposals. The Combined Commanders' Conference had concluded that a cross-Channel invasion, in sufficient strength to
guarantee success, could only be made if there was enough
shipping to lift ten divisions. There was only enough shipping
available to lift five. 'Well, there it is,' said the British Chief of
the Imperial General Staff (CIGS), General Alanbrooke,

handing the Combined Commanders' proposals to General Morgan. 'It won't work. I know it won't work, but you will bloody well have to make it work.' Trying to make it work kept COSSAC busy until the end of 1943.

Apart from considering the options and selecting the area for the assault, COSSAC analysed most of the problems the invaders would have to face and had gone some way towards providing the answers long before Eisenhower and Montgomery took up their appointments. COSSAC decided on a landing between the Orne and the Vire, but when Morgan and Barker got down to detail they found that combat-loaded vessels, where the men and their equipment are loaded ready to go into battle as they come off, could only lift three infantry divisions, not five, and that the aircraft available could only lift two airborne brigades, far short of the number needed. COSSAC worked and reworked the plans, using the men, aircraft and shipping available, but when Eisenhower and Montgomery saw the final COSSAC plan in the New Year of 1944, they promptly rejected it.

Brigadier Tom Collins CBE had been appointed Director of Movements for Combined Operations in October 1943: 'I had a splendid American staff and I had to work with Admiral Ramsay on the details for mounting the invasion. When Montgomery arrived back from Africa at the end of 1943, he studied the COSSAC plan and asked the Joint Chiefs if they wanted the invasion to succeed. Not surprisingly they said they did. He then said that either the assault or the follow-up forces must be doubled. The original date for the invasion was 5 May 1944, but this request meant the date had to go back ... and he had the prestige and the backing to make his demands stick.' Montgomery relayed his doubts to Eisenhower, asking, 'Will you hurl yourself into the contest and get us what we want?'

The main disagreement that Eisenhower and Montgomery had with the COSSAC plan concerned the proposed weight of the assault. Three seaborne divisions and two airborne brigades were not sufficient to get ashore and stay ashore. As General Omar Bradley wisely remarked, 'You can almost always force an invasion but you can't always make it stick.' The size of the assault area, thirty miles of coast between the Orne and the Vire, meant that the landing would not be strong enough or wide enough to permit the build-up of Allied forces before the Germans could counter-attack.

This was no reflection on the ability or work of General Morgan. His COSSAC planners were fully aware of the limitations of their plan, but the size of the assault was necessarily restricted by a lack of suitable shipping. Shipping, transportation and supply played such a major part in 'Overlord' that it was treated as a separate operation and received a separate codename, Operation 'Neptune', which will be fully discussed in the next chapter. Eisenhower and Montgomery saw that 'Neptune' was simply not sufficient to ensure the success of 'Overlord', but unlike Morgan they had the authority to insist on changes. The invasion was Eisenhower's responsibility and he had the authority to get what he needed. The first things he needed were more men, more ships and more time.

After taking up his appointment at SHAEF, Eisenhower went directly to Washington to confer with Roosevelt and Marshall. He sent Montgomery ahead to London, instructing him to examine the COSSAC plan in detail and make proposals for the necessary changes. Montgomery decided that if 'Overlord' was to succeed, then whatever the difficulties, the whole invasion must be enlarged, both in strength and area.

The point at issue went far beyond the problems of getting men to the coasts of France and putting them ashore. It was necessary to examine the strategic objective of 'Overlord', the defeat of Germany, and the destruction of the Nazi regime, and then work back to the force necessary to achieve that end. The strategic objective of 'Overlord' was the liberation of France and the defeat of Germany. Montgomery's whole plan for the 'Overlord' operation had that strategy in mind from the first.

A tactical defeat on the beaches would stop 'Overlord' in its tracks, but even if the invasion force got ashore and stayed ashore, Montgomery considered that to achieve the strategic objectives of the plan, the landings must be on a much larger scale. He therefore proposed to enlarge the assault force to five seaborne divisions, backed with three airborne divisions supported by two Commando brigades (then called Special Service Brigades), and detachments of their American equivalent, the

United States Rangers, plus as much armour, artillery, air and naval support as he could find.

He accepted the landing area along the Calvados coast but, to broaden the area of attack and as a step towards the capture of the vital port of Cherbourg, he suggested a parachute and coastal landing in the Cotentin. This, plus parachute landings east of the Orne at Ranville, would broaden the invasion front to about fifty miles. There would, of course, be gaps in this front, as dictated by the terrain, but the beaches could be quickly linked into one bridgehead by British Commando units and American Rangers making flank marches.

Eisenhower and the Combined Chiefs of Staff swiftly accepted these amendments. Montgomery then proceeded to prepare detailed plans for the actual landings, in his role as Commander-in-Chief, Ground Forces, for the invasion phase. In this he had the support of General Omar Bradley, commanding the American First Army.

Montgomery's plan called for the three airborne divisions, the British 6th, and the US 82nd and 101st, to drop after midnight on D-Day and seal off the flanks of the invasion area and seize certain vital features in the invasion area before the seaborne forces came ashore the following morning. The British 6th Airborne Division would seize two vital bridges over the Caen Canal and the River Orne at Bénouville and capture the high ground east of the Orne at Ranville, as well as the formidable Merville Battery which overlooked the invasion coast. The two American airborne divisions, the 82nd and the 101st, were to establish bridgeheads in the Cotentin Peninsula around Ste-Mère-Eglise and Carentan as a step towards seizing the Peninsula and capturing Cherbourg. They would also secure the causeways off the eastern beaches for the American 4th Infantry Division landing on the Cotentin coast around dawn. The 4th Infantry Division would land on a beach codenamed 'Utah'.

There would be four more assault areas along the Calvados coast. Two American divisions, the 1st and 29th Infantry Divisions, would land two Regimental Combat Teams on that gap in the cliffs near Isigny-sur-Mer on a beach codenamed 'Omaha'.

One of the men who would go ashore on 'Omaha' was Robert L. Sales from Madison Heights in Virginia, who was serving in 'B' Company of the 116th Infantry Regiment, the 29th Infantry Division. 'I loved England and I have always wanted to get back there, though what with one thing and another it will have to be in 1994 for the 50th anniversary. I was a Staff Sergeant in "B" Company on D-Day, though I was just twenty-one years old, and I expected to go to France with the 29th Ranger Battalion. That was formed from picked ranks of the division when we were at Tidworth. We went to school at Achnacarry in Scotland, which was the training school for the British Commandos and the toughest battle school in the world. The discipline was unbelievable and we were on British rations up there ... if you didn't think you'd ever starve to death, you should try that! We started speed marches at seven miles and went on up and up, and if you fell out, you washed out. But I was young and fit and when I passed out I got a week's leave in London, where you just had to have a good time.

'The Ranger Battalion was broken up just before D-Day and the men sent back to their units. I really wanted to fight with that battalion, and when it broke up it near broke my heart. Anyway, I went back to "B" Company as personal bodyguard and radio man to Captain Ettore Zappacosta, and went ashore with him on "Omaha" beach.'

Further east, the British 50th Division would land at Arromanches on a beach codenamed 'Gold' and capture Bayeux. The Canadian 3rd Infantry Division would come ashore astride Courseulles, St Aubin and Bernières, on a beach area codenamed 'Juno'. Finally, the British 3rd Infantry Division would land on 'Sword' beach, link up with 6th Airborne and advance on Caen.

All these landings would be supported by air attacks, naval bombardment, artillery and armour, especially the swimming DD tanks. On the British and Canadian beaches, the specialized armour of the British 79th Armoured Division would play a vital part, but the great weight of the assault would rest on the shoulders of the infantry.

For the pre-invasion softening-up phase, Eisenhower had two

Air Forces under his direct control, the American Ninth Army Air Force and the British Second Tactical Air Force. These were largely equipped with medium bombers like the American Mitchell and Boston, fighters like the Spitfire, Lightning and Typhoon, and fighter-bombers like the British Mosquito. These Tactical Air Forces were to provide pre-invasion bombing and interdiction of railway and road links, plus providing air cover and tactical support to naval and ground forces during the landing phase. Eisenhower also demanded and obtained, at least for the invasion period, operational control of the two strategic bomber forces operating out of Britain at the time, the American Eighth Army Air Force and RAF Bomber Command. The latter was obtained in the teeth of opposition from Air Marshal Sir Arthur Harris of the RAF. These air forces were equipped with long-range heavy bombers, the American B-17 and B-24, the British Lancaster and Stirling, and were busy at the time destroying German factories as part of the 'Pointblank' Directive, the long-term plan for paralysing German industry and thus ending the war.

In the spring of 1944, the heavy bombers switched their attacks to the marshalling yards and rail links between France and Germany, with a view to reducing the build-up of German forces and material in France before D-Day. In this task the air forces were highly successful. By mid-May 1944, rail traffic between France and Germany had fallen by 50 per cent; inside France it was down to 20 per cent of the January level. The tactical fighter and fighter-bomber forces then joined in, strafing train and troop convoys, shooting up stations and rail junctions. In the three months between March and June, over 1,500 French locomotives were destroyed, some 50 per cent of those available. Other rolling stock suffered in proportion.

Another air force task was to assist in sealing off the Normandy bridgehead by destroying the bridges across the Seine. Bridges are difficult targets and all were heavily defended, but the aircraft pressed home their attacks until by 1 June only 3 of the 26 bridges over the Seine were usable, and even these were damaged and under attack. This action was a vital part in the pre-invasion preparation, for the Germans would need these bridges either to pump reinforcements into Normandy, or for a speedy withdrawal to the east if the Normandy position became untenable.

Air force efforts in France were supplemented by the operations of the French Resistance, the Maquis. By June 1944, the French Maquis had a trained and equipped force of 100,000 men and women, ready to attack and disrupt German troop movements throughout France, reinforced by special parachuted teams of British and American soldiers, notably by men from the 2nd SAS Regiment. All this had a cumulative and debilitating effect on the German war machine. Damage that might have taken two days to repair in January was taking two weeks by June.

Henri Lamperière, a member of the French Resistance, was a gendarme in the village of Bretteville-sur-Laize on the outskirts of Caen. 'I joined the Gendarmerie to avoid forced conscription for work in Germany, but I was soon involved in resistance activity. I started by handing over to my friend, Foucu of the OCM (Organisation Civile et Militaire), the arms which the gendarmes had collected in 1940 and stored in a barn outside the city. I was also able to pass on information concerning the movements of German troops and German installations. My uniform enabled me to circulate freely by day and night and carry on my espionage work.

'I was able, for example, to penetrate the V1 rocket site at Quilly on the pretext of searching for a terrorist, but there was always danger from the Gestapo and their French auxiliaries, who were particularly dangerous, and did not spare the Gendarmerie. The complete brigade at St-Georges-du-Vièvre in the Eure, for example, was arrested and deported to the death camps for having given information and help to the Maquis Surcouf of Robert Leblanc at Pont Audemer. None of them returned.

'In April 1944, the OCM in our sector came under the orders of the Special Operations Executive and received two parachuted agents, Capitaine Jean Renaud-Dandicolle from Bordeaux, the leader, and his radio operator, Maurice Larcher, who came from Mauritius. On 3 June we received a parachutage of arms and explosives at Ste Claire and the drop zone was protected by the gendarmes of Pont-d'Ouilly. To give you some idea of the spirit of the Gendarmerie I can give you two stories.

'One morning, two Germans from the *feldgendarmerie* at Falaise arrived at our station. They were seeking an evader who had been denounced to the Germans by a neighbour (that happened frequently, alas). I slipped out to a nearby café, phoned a friend and told him to pass the news on to the evader. When I got back to the station the adjutant, André, asked me simply, "Have you done the necessary?"

'On another day, André called me to his office and said, "I know you work for the Resistance, but it's none of my affair as long as you don't implicate me." André himself had difficulties with the Prefecture for having demanded the closure of a café which was popular with the Germans. He. alas, was killed in the bombardment of Bretteville on 10 June, together with his wife and two children.'

Heavy bombing and Resistance sabotage were augmented by low-level attacks from the RAF. 'Baron' Humphries was a British Mosquito fighter-bomber pilot flying sorties into France. 'I was sent to Lasham in Hampshire to join 613 Squadron, 2 Group, in the 2nd TAF, where I was overjoyed to find them converting to Mossies (Mosquito VIs), so I kept my old observer, Flt Sgt Joe Carroll.

'The squadron began operations in late December 1943, and my first effort was on 26 January 1944. We were then on "No Ball" ops, daylight low-level attacks on V1 rocket launching sites in the Pas de Calais. Joe and I did eight of these, collecting a bullet which starred the windscreen and on another trip a very tattered tailplane.

'By March we had to change to night flying. From then on 2 Group was given the job of low-level night intruder work, ready for D-Day, to bang away at anything we could find on the ground. On 11 April 1944, by which time I was a Warrant Officer, while six of our planes hit the Gestapo HQ in The Hague, the rest of us started three weeks of camping at Swanton Morley doing exercises with the Army. Then back to Lasham to continue intruding, mostly over France.

'About three days before 5 June we were given details of the invasion plan and a pep talk by Air Marshal Cunningham. After that we were confined to camp. 2 Group's task for the night of 4/5th June (later changed to 5/6th because of bad weather) and onwards was to search for and attack enemy ground movement in a patrol area inland from the beaches; 613 Squadron had the area roughly bounded by the towns St Lô, Argentan, Caen and Vire, with each aircraft in turn doing a spell of half to three-quarters of an hour over the land. At briefing I saw that my name was last on the list, due to return just before daylight on 6 June, as the Army boys went ashore.'

Thanks to all this activity, the Wehrmacht's ability to react to the invasion was severely crippled before the first invader set foot in France, yet to maintain security and spread doubt about the real invasion site, at least as many bombs were dropped around Calais as on the approaches to Normandy.

The main preoccupation of the planning staff of SHAEF during the winter and early spring of 1944 was to increase the weight of the assault and get the men safely ashore. This was the responsibility of the naval phase, codenamed 'Neptune'. The 'Neptune' staff were soon in dire difficulties finding enough shipping for the extra divisions required by Montgomery's plan, and at the end of January 1944 it was decided that the invasion must be put back one month, to a date on or about 1 June. Careful consideration of tides and moon showed that the only days suitable for the invasion – with half-tide around dawn – were 5, 6 and 7 June. Thus 5 June was chosen as D-Day. Apart from giving the Anglo-American forces more time to build landing craft and train crews, this extra month would enable the invasion to coincide with the Russian summer offensive and prevent the Germans moving forces west. It also gave everyone a little more breathing space, for planning and training had now commenced on detailed aspects of the plan.

The hard lessons learned on the Dieppe Raid were now proving useful, in particular the necessity of giving the infantry armoured support in the actual moment of assault, and the need for various kinds of specialized armoured vehicles to get the tanks and other vehicles off the beaches, clear the obstacles and let the landing craft come in as the tide rose.

Montgomery's plan here was highly original. The traditional

pattern for an assault was a bombardment followed by an
infantry advance supported by tanks. Montgomery stood this
concept on its head. He decided to land his tanks first, followed
by the specialized armour, variously designed to deal with
different types of beach opposition and obstacles, and so clear
the way for the infantry in the assault landing craft. Then
regular heavy infantry would land from LCAs or LCIs to mop
up the beach defences. Finally, up to an hour later, the Commandos would come ashore, to deal with any strongpoints and
begin the necessary flank deployment and link up the bridgeheads. This is almost exactly the opposite of the then accepted
order, and shows a high degree of original thinking, with an
ability to face facts, however unpalatable, and find solutions,
however radical.

The seaborne landings were timed for half-tide on the flood,
a compromise between giving the infantry too much open beach
to cover and having all the obstacles exposed for the attention of
the assault engineers. The DD tanks and armoured bulldozers
would land in front of the beach obstacles and must clear them
away before the tide could cover them.

Montgomery maintained that the tanks and specialized
armour would have to clear a way through the beach defences
for the infantry. Otherwise the infantry would be held up
offshore in their craft or cut down in swathes by machine-gun
fire from concrete emplacements as at Dieppe. He also saw that
the tanks themselves would be neutralized by the defences
unless some means could be found quickly to breach the various
obstacles that Rommel had prepared to stop the assault on the
beaches. Montgomery knew all about these obstacles, for parties of men were now swimming ashore on to the Normandy
beaches every night to examine the defences.

One of the men swimming ashore was Jim Booth, then a
sub-lieutenant in the RNVR. 'I joined the Royal Navy in 1939
and served on convoy escorts in the North Atlantic for a while.
Then I thought I would try something different, so I volunteered for Chariots – human torpedoes – but I didn't get in, so I
tried for COPP and got accepted.

'COPP – Combined Operations Pilotage Parties – was
created after the Dieppe Raid. Dieppe was a disaster, partly

because the tanks couldn't find the beach exits or get off the shingle, and the troops were unloaded in deep water – no beach survey beforehand, you see. Anyway, our job was pre-invasion recce and we did a lot of them, in Sicily and Italy. We went in big submarines which surfaced offshore and then we paddled in canoes to the beaches. There were always two men, a naval surveyor who did his stuff below the tide-line, and a Royal Engineers officer who did the beach above the low-water mark.

'We would put in a peg on the water-line and swim about, taking offshore depths at 25-yard intervals. I suppose the Army chap did the same on the beach. Then we'd paddle back and rendez-vous with the submarine and plot it all on a chart. I enjoyed it – jolly good fun.

'Now, when we came to do the Normandy beaches we had a problem. Big submarines were too big to go inshore, so we had to use midget submarines – X20 and X23 were allocated to COPP, and we had two COPP teams; COPP 1 and COPP 9. We couldn't get our canoes into the midget subs and they were very slow, so a big sub would tow us into the mouth of the Bay of the Seine night after night, and then the midget sub took us to within 200 yards or so of the beach and we would swim in from there. My CO, Lt Jeff Lyne, surveyed a lot of the beach obstacles, and we did the gradients, while the REs took sand and beach samples, finding mud or quicksand and so on. All this was done well before D-Day. You didn't have to be a very good swimmer, incidentally, but I was twenty-three at the time and very fit. It was a good job and we didn't have many casualties – they wanted us back with the information, I expect, and took care to recover us.'

With this information, plans and equipment could be prepared to overcome and destroy the obstacles. Montgomery had one powerful answer to Rommel's obstacles in the wide range of specialized armoured vehicles contained in a unique British formation, the 79th Armoured Division. This unit had been raised in 1943 by Major-General Sir Percy Hobart, a pioneer of armoured warfare and a genius at training armoured forces. In the 1930s Hobart's ideas for the use of armour had been so revolutionary that the War Office rewarded him with desk jobs and an early retirement.

By 1940, after being sacked from command of the famous 7th Armoured Division in Egypt, General Hobart was serving his country in the only post open to him, as a corporal in the Home Guard. Hobart was rescued from this oblivion by Winston Churchill, who called on his ingenuity in the development of armoured devices for use in the forthcoming invasion. Hobart's machines, popularly known as 'The Funnies', were to play a vital part helping the British and Canadians ashore on the fire-swept beaches of Normandy. The 79th Division never fought as a unit, but was deployed in small groups to tackle obstacles located by beach reconnaissance.

The main item in Hobart's armoury was the Duplex Drive or DD swimming tank, which has already been described. The Germans suspected the existence of such a vehicle but until it appeared on the D-Day beaches they had no definite proof of its existence.

The big advantage of the DD tank, apart from surprise, was that it enabled tanks to land with the infantry and support them in places and at times where it was impossible or suicidal for the large tank-carrying vessels (LSTs or LCTs) to beach. The DD could be launched in deep water well offshore beyond the range of enemy artillery and plough ashore with the infantry landing craft (LCAs). Almost invisible till the tracks hit the sand, the DD was designed to give the defenders a very nasty turn when it lumbered out of the waves and opened fire. Around 900 DD tanks, mostly converted Shermans, were used by the British, Canadians and Americans on D-Day.

As well as the DDs, the 79th Division contained a wide variety of obstacle-clearing tanks. They had 'Crab' tanks bearing a huge flail that could beat a path through minefields for other tanks and infantry to follow. There were 'Bobbin' tanks which could unroll a carpet to make a path across mud or quicksand, and 'Petard' tanks, with a heavy gun, which could blast a hole in pill-boxes or through concrete sea walls. They had fearful 'Crocodiles', flame-throwing tanks, to scorch out machine-gun nests, and bridge-carrying tanks to mount walls or cross gaps, and 'Fascine' tanks, carrying a great bundle of logs to fill a shell or bomb crater, and many more. The British built these devices into their assault plans, combat-loading them into the ships in the order they would be needed ashore. They also had AVREs, armoured bulldozers, which could push or haul obstacles aside to let the landing craft in or the tanks deploy on the beaches. The AVREs gave the sappers of the Royal Engineers vital protection at their most vulnerable time.

The specialized armoured vehicles were combat-loaded to go ashore and tackle the difficulties revealed by beach reconnaissance. For example, the first obstacle might be a patch of tank-bogging mud, so the first tank out would be a 'Bobbin', to lay a path across it. Then came the minefield, so a 'Flail' followed to beat a path through the minefield to the sea wall, clearing the way for a bridge-building tank, which then helped to scale it, or a 'Petard' or 'Flame' tank to blast a gap or deal with the pill-box on top. Meanwhile, a 'Fascine' laid its logs to reduce the drop on the far side or filled in the anti-tank ditch. Behind them would come the other armour, the DDs supporting the assault infantry streaming through the breach, bursting through the Atlantic Wall with the minimum of casualties or delay.

Hobart's 'Funnies' were demonstrated and offered to the American assault forces, but General Bradley turned them down. This was partly because they were, in the main, based on the British Churchill tank, which might cause spares and maintenance problems, and partly because the two American beaches were more open and not backed with the small towns that lay along the British and Canadian front. He also considered the 'Funnies' a rather unnecessary frill. Bradley favoured a frontal assault by his infantry and combat engineers, and Montgomery could not order him to do otherwise. Bradley took the DD tanks, which were Shermans, and some armoured bulldozers, but he declined the rest. One thing Bradley did want which the British could not supply were 'Firefly' tanks, Sherman tanks mounting the British 17-pounder anti-tank gun. Only 'Fireflies' could match the powerful German 'Tiger' and 'Panther' tanks armed with the 88mm gun, but there were simply not enough of the 17-pounder guns to go round and equip all the tanks available. The British only had enough 'Fireflies' to supply one for every tank troop, but they proved very useful when the German Panzer divisions began to probe the invasion perimeter.

The outline of the invasion tasks now began to emerge from the original COSSAC plan. In military parlance an attack goes in phases, calculated from a precise time on the day and hour of attack. The day of attack is called 'D-Day' to separate it from other relevant days, which are set forward or back from D-Day as necessary. For example: before D-Day, D−1 (D minus 1), D−2, D−3, and so on, or following D-Day, D+1, D+2. In the same way, the hour of attack is H-Hour, and preparations taking place beforehand are timed for H−1, H−2, or afterwards to H+1, and so on.

The date and timing of D-Day was now set for 5 June 1944, but the timing of H-Hour varied from beach to beach because of the tide, which floods up the Channel from the Atlantic to the west. The assault would be undertaken by the First US Army and the Second British Army and the First US Army would deploy the VII Corps and the V Corps against 'Utah' and 'Omaha' beaches, landing at 0630 hrs while the Second British Army would deploy XXX Corps and I Corps against 'Gold', 'Juno' and 'Sword' about 0730 hrs. The seaborne landings would be preceded by airborne assault to secure the flanks astride the Orne and in the Cotentin.

Just after midnight (2359 hrs) on the night of 4/5th June, the three airborne divisions would land by parachute or glider, the British 6th Airborne Division astride the Orne, the American 82nd and 101st in the Cotentin. The invasion beaches, from 'Utah' to 'Sword', were subdivided into unit assault areas by a combination of the phonetic alphabet and naval port and starboard colours. 'Easy Red' and 'Easy Green' are still remembered from 'Omaha'; 'Mike Green' appears in the Canadian accounts; 'Queen White' saw much action on 'Sword'.

The seaborne landings would commence in the west when the US 4th Infantry Division, commanded by Major-General Raymond O. Barton, would land at 'Utah' on the east coast of the Cotentin. The 4th Infantry were to link up with 82nd Airborne around Ste-Mère-Eglise, while the 101st Airborne took Carentan. At the same time, twenty miles away on the

Calvados coast, two Regimental Combat Teams, drawn from the 16th and 116th Infantry Regiments of the American 1st and 29th Infantry Divisions respectively, would go ashore on 'Omaha'.

At 'Omaha', 1st Infantry Division of the US V Corps were to swing east to link up with the British at Port-en-Bessin, while the 29th Division were to swing west and take Isigny by the evening of D-Day, aiming for a link-up with the 101st Airborne in Carentan. Between 'Utah' and 'Omaha', on the promontory of Pointe du Hoc, it was thought that a battery of heavy guns commanded the ship assembly areas for both beaches. This battery was to be heavily bombed and shelled, then assaulted by three companies of the 2nd US Rangers commanded by Lieutenant-Colonel James E. Rudder.

The fishing port of Port-en-Bessin was set as the dividing line between the Anglo-American armies and was to be captured by No. 47 (Royal Marine) Commando; 47 Commando would land on the west flank of the British Second Army at Arromanches and make a ten-mile advance through enemy territory to attack Port-en-Bessin from the rear late on D-Day. Port-en-Bessin was important as it was a designated point for the petrol terminal of PLUTO, the Pipe Line Under The Ocean.

The British Second Army, commanded by General Sir Miles Dempsy, would land two corps on three beaches on a thirty-mile front between Arromanches and Ouistreham with an H-Hour of 0730 hrs on D-Day. On the western beach, codenamed 'Gold', the 50th (Northumbrian) Division of XXX Corps would land between Le Hamel and La Rivière, drive west to meet the Americans and inland to take Bayeux.

Next, on 'Juno', the Canadian 3rd Division, also of XXX Corps but later to form part of the Canadian Army, would land between Graye-sur-Mer and St Aubin, and proceed inland towards Caen. Also at St Aubin, No. 48 (Royal Marine) Commando would come ashore, behind the Canadians, turn east and clear defences along the coast, including the strongpoint at Langrune, and link up with No. 41 (Royal Marine) Commando, which would land on the west flank of the British 3rd Infantry Division at Lion-sur-Mer. The 3rd Infantry Division formed part of British I Corps which had 6th Airborne Division and 1 and 4 Special Service (Commando) Brigades under command for 'Overlord'.

The British 3rd Infantry Division's beach ran from Lion to the outskirts of Ouistreham, and was codenamed 'Sword'. The town of Ouistreham would be captured by No. 4 Commando from the 1st Special Service (Commando) Brigade. The remainder of 1st Commando Brigade would advance across country to link up with 6th Airborne in their positions astride the Orne and the Caen Canal at Bénouville where the bridges would have been taken by a glider force commanded by Major John Howard of the Oxfordshire and Buckinghamshire Light Infantry. The British paratroopers and the Commandos would then hold the left flank of the invasion area on the heights of Ranville. Thus, the D-Day bridgeheads would run from the high ground around Ranville east of the Orne, to the flood-waters of the Vire around Isigny, then north to Carentan and the American drop zones, and finally to Ste-Mère-Eglise. This line should be complete on D+1, and embrace a front of 50 miles and a depth of up to 10 miles – if all went well.

In this, as in all plans, there were a large number of impon-derables. First, there was the weather. An analysis of meteoro-logical records for past years seemed to suggest that the May–June period, after the early spring gales, offered the best chance of fulfilling the necessary requirements for a successful landing. These were for at least four calm days, with the sea no rougher than a slight chop, good visibility of not less than 3 miles, a cloud base of more than 3,000 feet and, for the para-troopers, a surface wind of not more than 15 miles per hour. While the May–June period offered a chance of this, the odds were still calculated at 12 : 1 against. A further requirement for the paratroops was a late rising moon, so that the parachute aircraft had cover of darkness for the flight and moonlight during the drop. Finally, the optimum conditions for the sea-ward assault called for half-tide conditions around dawn, so that the beach obstacles could be avoided or destroyed, and the infantry would not be over-exposed as they crossed wide beaches.

At low tide, while most beach obstacles would be visible, the troops and tanks would have to advance up to 500 yards, over a quarter of a mile, across a flat beach under fire, before they got to cover in the dunes. On the other hand, at full tide the beach obstacles would be covered and difficult to locate and would certainly cause havoc among the assault craft. Beside this, the narrow strips of beach left above the high-water mark would be insufficient to let all the troops, tanks and vehicles deploy. Therefore half-tide was chosen as the optimum state, but speed was vital, for the beach must be captured and cleared of obstacles before the tide rose and covered them.

Because of the fifty-mile spread of the invasion beaches, it also followed that, to land at half-tide, the British forces in the east would have to land one hour later than the Americans in the west, as the incoming tide flooded up the Channel from the Atlantic. The next great imponderable was the reaction of the enemy. Allied Intelligence, with the advantage of the ENIGMA transcripts of German coded signals, was reasonably well informed about German troop movements, strengths and dispositions in Normandy, but the information on which their estimates were based was difficult to collect, delayed in transmission, and subject to change. Intelligence could never be fully up-to-date, and everyone was painfully aware that the unexpected appearance of even one Panzer division in the wrong place could have a serious effect on the landing.

Brigadier Tom Collins, CBE, recalls Operation 'Overlord': 'The follow-up force in an operation of this type is usually the deciding factor of whether the beachhead can be held or not. Montgomery based his plan of maintaining the beachhead on the amount of armour that could be loaded by D+3. He came to my HQ in Fort Southwick above Portsmouth and went closely into our loading tables for those first days. Every assault brigade had a tank regiment. All guns in the assault and follow-up waves were 25-pounders mounted in Sherman chassis, and there were also two armoured divisions plus the 79th and the DDs.

'A further complication was waterproofing vehicles for the assault and follow-up. Any vehicle landing over open beaches had to have its engine protected against the possibility of having to wade through three feet of water. This had to be done in three stages because the final stage (watertight) meant that the vehicle could only travel five miles before seizing up.

'In loading the follow-up forces, on which the long-term success of the operation depended, it was essential to keep the embarkation points filled with troops and vehicles so that returning ships and craft were never kept waiting. The organization consisted of concentration areas in the centre of England, from which units moved to marshalling areas, 15–20 miles from the coast. In these marshalling areas, units from the concentration areas were marshalled into the exact craft or ship loads in which they would be transported to the far shore. Once in a craft or ship they never moved out of it until arrival in Normandy.

'Once the loading commenced each area was filled from the one behind as it emptied, and a continuous process began in which the whole Allied Expeditionary Force, nearly 200,000 men, the tanks and guns, transport and equipment, ammunition and stores, began to move towards the South Coast. This gigantic movement began six days before D-Day and gave rise to one final complication, bigger than any previously tackled – the possibility of postponement which must require a halt and possibly even a reversal of the whole process.'

Apart from gradually concentrating forces in the South of England, opposite Normandy, the D-Day planners had to persuade the Germans that the invasion would come on some other part of the French coast. Knowing that the two best invasion areas, Normandy and the Pas de Calais, would be as obvious to the Germans as they were to the Allies, great pains were taken to hint discreetly, and apparently accidentally, at a large diversion in Normandy, followed a day or so later by the major assault in the Pas de Calais. This deception plan was known as Operation 'Fortitude'.

Obvious preparations for a landing were made in South-East England. Dummy landing craft were moved on the Thames and Medway, and dummy gliders appeared on the airfields of Essex and Kent. Montgomery's coded signals were sent by telephone to Kent and transmitted by wireless from there, creating a large volume of radio traffic for the Germans to monitor. General Patton's Third Army, one of the follow-up forces, assembled in Kent, and their massive tanks and field parks were clearly seen by German reconnaissance aircraft making quick darts across the Channel. This was a shrewd move, for Patton was recognized as a front-line field commander and he was, in fact, senior in rank to General Omar Bradley.

Meanwhile, in neutral capitals all over the world, German agents were receiving hints that the Pas de Calais would be the invasion area and any information to the contrary was part of a cunning Allied plot. Even the essential air attacks were made to contribute to this deception. For every ton of bombs dropped on Normandy, four tons went down in the Pas de Calais, where there were, in any case, many more targets. It all contributed to the massive all-out effort to confuse and disperse the German opposition.

Along with deception went security. From February 1944 the British Isles were sealed. No civilian traffic was permitted with neutral countries like Eire or Portugal, which swarmed with German agents. In April 1944 the coast of England was closed from the Wash to Land's End, for up to ten miles inland. Civilians were evicted from their homes in vital areas and military staging camps were set up to contain the invasion armies. Roads became clogged with military convoys, trains laden with tanks and guns and men rumbled by day and night, all heading in one direction – south. British civilians were then subjected to further restrictions in the use of the Post Office facilities and telephones in order to free the communications networks for military use. All overseas mail, even diplomatic bags, was either stopped completely or subjected to censorship.

Throughout the spring of 1944 the Allied armies were training, rehearsing their assault plans, exercising in landing craft, taking part in exercise after exercise, trying to get the plans just right, waterproofing vehicles and preparing their weapons, honing their skills.

'We also decided to beef up our fire-power,' said Peter Young, then CO of 3 Commando, a unit destined for 'Sword' beach. 'So we double-indented for Brens, magazines and ammunition. We got the extra guns in a few days. Things happened quickly in 1944, with no bloody red tape to worry about.'

Colonel 'Red' Reeder of the 12th Infantry Regiment in the

American 4th Infantry Division also had problems getting more fire-power. 'I soon became acquainted with a worry of the regiment. The 12th Infantry lacked 4 .30-calibre machine guns and 8 Browning automatic rifles. Major Kenneth Lay, the regiment's supply officer, told me, "I try every day to get them but all we receive are promises. To give our men training we swap guns around, but this wastes time."

'I asked the General and he told me it was my problem, and when I got back to the barracks I met Major Lay and a lieutenant.

'"Sir," Lay said, "this lieutenant has a boyhood friend in a supply depot twenty-five miles from here. He called his pal, who's a master sergeant, and if we'll go up there tonight with a truck, he'll slip us those guns. Otherwise we may not get them until about June 1."

'"What the hell kind of army is this?" I asked. "*Slip* us the weapons? Get me Lieutenant Mills."

'William Mills, from North Carolina, was about 6 feet 2 inches tall, spoke with a drawl, and was one of the best officers in our regiment. In the regiments of 1944 a Colonel was allowed three liaison officers, who could be given almost any kind of duty. Lieutenant Mills was one of these.

'"Mills," I said, "you'll have to go with this lieutenant and get the weapons. I don't want to send Lay. I'm saving him for a real emergency. And don't get caught or we'll all be hanged."

'"I can't go," Mills said. "Tonight's the night of the Division Commander's map-reading exam."

'"Mills," I said, "I am going to examine you now in map reading. What's the declination of the compass in Nome, Alaska?"

'He looked puzzled. "Sir, I don't know."

'"Well, what is the exact distance in inches from San Francisco to Brisbane, Australia?"

'Mills gave me his wonderful smile. "I don't know, sir," he drawled.

'"Can you tell me the exact location of Hitler's headquarters?"

'"No, sir."

'"Well," I said, "you missed three questions. I know you

know all the rest. I am awarding you a grade of 97 per cent. Now go get those guns!"'

At sea there was already plenty of action. K. G. Hancock was in the Channel, serving in the Hunt-class destroyer, HMS *Garth*. 'E-boats were the problem in the Channel. There was always a destroyer on patrol, escorting the small convoys of tramp steamers which sailed each night from London or Rosyth. There were never enough destroyers to go round, so we were usually at sea closed up at action stations throughout the night, breaking down to two watches at 0730 hrs. This would go on day after day until we became short of oil or ammunition, when we would return to Sheerness for a night before sailing again. We had a German Jew aboard working the radio, and he would try and pick up the German radio transmissions and hear what they were talking about. One night we beat off a real determined attack on a convoy. They sank two ships but we got one E-boat as she was blazing away and the skipper rammed her, cutting her in two. We picked up five Germans and two dogs.'

John Brown, a Royal Marine on an anti-aircraft landing craft, LCF(L) 19, recalls the final training phase in the Solent. 'LCF(L) 19 was the first of the Mark 4s fitted with eight Oerlikons and four Bofors anti-aircraft guns, and later the single Oerlikons were changed to twins. Two shipmates went ashore one night and were set upon by some American sailors. One was stabbed. The next night all the LCF (Landing Craft Flak) and LCG (Landing Craft Gun) crews went ashore to seek retribution. The result was satisfactory apart from the fact that we were then dispersed for a time. LCF 19 found herself on the "trots", the moorings at Bucklers Hard out on the Beaulieu River. Ever tried reaching a pub from the trots at Bucklers Hard?

'We spent much time on manoeuvres, gunnery practice and escort duties for smaller landing craft, but wherever we went along the south or south-west coast, it was noticeable that the Big Day was not too far away. We had one very bad scare off Bognor Regis when a severe storm blew up during the night. We sailed into the tide, took in a lot of water, but kept afloat. In spite of the earlier fracas with the Americans, we all tried to get

on the big LSTs. They had limitless coffee, doughnuts, chocolate and ciggies. Every day we observed more and more landing
craft wherever we went, with lots of troop movements ashore,
so we went to Beaulieu and stored up.'

While the invasion forces were mustering ashore, the Channel was the scene of almost nightly engagements between the
Royal Navy ships and German coastal forces. Stuart Lasson was
an able seaman on board HMS *Rutherford*, an American-built
frigate. 'In the months before 6 June, the Channel was split into
patrol areas, all numbered numerically – omitting No. 13. The
aim of our work was to clear the Channel of marauding German
E-Boats, very fast and dangerous small craft which would strike
at Channel convoys and coastal shipping. I was a submarine
detector, operating the HFDF set, and we were able to discover
and sink a number of E-Boats, taking the prisoners back to
Harwich. We often set sail at night on patrol, and the information of exactly where we were and what we were doing was
only known to the officers. I feel that this duty was a difficult,
monotonous task, and we were very much in the dark, but on
the whole we carried out our tasks successfully and must have
played a vital part in the invasion.'

The German Navy was still active in the Channel as the
nights grew longer, and sometimes the E-Boats got through.
Throughout April and May 1944, at ports all over the country,
the ships and landing craft were being loaded with vehicles and
heavy equipment, and participating in large-scale landing exercises. Not all these were successful or free from enemy action.
In 1944, on Exercise 'Tiger' off Slapton Sands, a force of
landing craft carrying American troops was intercepted by
German E-Boats, which sank several assault craft with great
loss of life.

Kenneth McCaw was then a midshipman and First Lieutenant of LCT 974. 'This was a Mark IV Landing Craft which
could take 13 three-ton lorries, or 8 Churchill tanks or other
assorted loads. We were sent to the River Dart where the load
turned out to be a USA tank support group of lorries, Jeeps and
trailers, plus a one-star general. It transpired that our flotilla of
12 LCTs was to take part in Exercise "Tiger". After that we
worked entirely with the Americans, subsequently landing on

"Utah" and "Omaha" beaches, making about twenty Channel crossings in all.

'During "Tiger" we set sail for Torbay and landed our troops successfully on Slapton Sands. Our route was inshore of the passing American LSTs, which were much faster than us. We could just about see the outlines of these big ships as they passed us to seaward, perhaps a mile away. I was on watch in the early hours when I saw flames break out on the two torpedoed LSTs. There was a red blaze across the water, reflected by the water.

'We were in convoy at the time and I think unescorted, and we just carried on. Had there been any communication (we had radio silence but kept in touch with Morse Light) it would have been simple for one of the lightly loaded LCTs to be despatched to pick up survivors. I never knew what had really happened until later, when we received our D-Day briefing. We had a full sack of instructions which we had to pore over (and burn those not required), and this disclosed the news of the E-Boat attack and that many men had put on their life-jackets upside down in the water and drowned.'

On 1 June 1944 the troops went into special holding camps near their embarkation points. There they received their final briefing, drew French money and were subject to complete security control. No messages, letters or phone calls could be made. The troops were only allowed out for route marches, closely flanked by military police. In the camps they were able to inspect models and aerial photographs of the Atlantic Wall, study maps, and see how and where they were to attack it, with every man and every tank playing a special part. Eisenhower, Montgomery, and many other dignitaries, including King George VI, visited many of the assault units, right down to battalion level, calling the men round their Jeeps to give them some orders or encouragement for the forthcoming attack.

Howard Huggett, then a 2nd lieutenant, 2nd Platoon Company 'C' 326th Airborne Engineer Battalion, 101st Airborne Division, remembers this time. 'Ten officers were billeted on the upper floor of Basildon House in the village of Pangbourne, near Reading. On 28 May 1944 my platoon left Reading by rail for the marshalling area at Merryfield Airport in southern England to prepare for the invasion of Europe. The 2nd platoon was attached to the 501st Parachute Infantry Regiment to provide engineer support. Upon entering the marshalling area at Merryfield we were sealed in and not allowed to leave the area.

'The platoon was billeted in squad-size tents with cots for sleeping and all the comforts of home including latrines within walking distance. Once we were settled, Lt Jones and I briefed the platoon on our mission including where, when and how we were to participate in the invasion of Europe. Our mission was to prepare the bridge over the Douve river for demolition and destroy the bridge only on orders from the Regimental Commander. We calculated that approximately 600 lbs of C-2 explosives would destroy the stone, dirt and asphalt paved span of the bridge. During the next few days in the marshalling area we packed the parachute bundles with C-2 explosives, attached the equipment bundle parachutes, and continued to brief the platoon on their mission and combat duties.'

On 2 June the infantry went on board their assault ships and the naval bombardment forces, the battleships, cruisers and monitors, sailed south from their bases at Scapa Flow, Belfast and the Clyde. Everything was ready, but everything now depended on the weather and D-Day was still scheduled for Monday 5 June, the first date when both moon and tides would be favourable. The final command 'To carry out Operation "Overlord"' must come from SHAEF not less than 36 hours before H-Hour, so that every ship and aircraft had time to follow the plan. Then there was a pause, while it seemed that everyone in Britain held their breath. All that could be done had been done, and it only needed the word from General Eisenhower to set this juggernaut rolling into action. Then, on Saturday 3 June, only 48 hours before the assault, the weather broke.

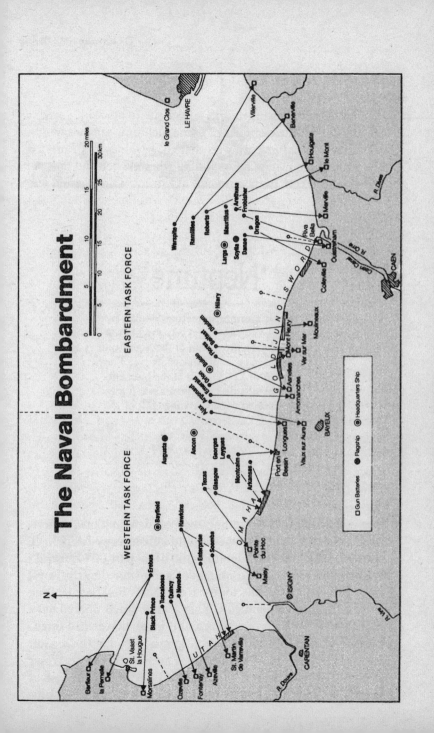

The Naval Bombardment

CHAPTER FOUR

'Neptune'

'Early this morning numerous landing craft
and light warships were observed in the
area between the mouth of the Seine and
the eastern coast of Normandy .... The
harbour of Le Havre is at the moment
being bombarded. German naval forces
have engaged enemy landing craft off the
coast.'

*German broadcast
0700 hrs, 6 June 1944*

Although warships and landing craft of many nations, American, Canadian, Dutch, Norwegian and Polish, as well as British, took part in Operation 'Neptune', the naval part of 'Overlord', the operation was mainly commanded and planned by the Royal Navy. This was fortunate, for the Royal Navy had been landing troops in France for centuries. They had long ago worked out a basic routine for such operations, and in particular had established the point at which their responsibility for the assault ended and that of the Army began. This is at the 'High Water Mark of Ordinary Spring Tides', or HWMOST. The task of Operation 'Neptune', therefore, was to convey the Allied Liberation Army from ports in Britain up to HWMOST on the Normandy beaches, to support them on the way in, and supply them thereafter.

To do this required an immense fleet of ships and landing craft and specialized vessels of all types. Of necessity most of these had to be British. To explain this, we must hark back to Admiral King, for the shortage of landing craft which had frustrated the COSSAC planners and was to perplex those of 'Overlord' was one of allocation, not of availability. Most of the larger landing craft then in service, especially the all-important LSTs, were American-built. The British shipyards were at the time fully engaged in repairing war-damaged vessels, building convoy escorts and merchant ships and, more particularly, in making the parts for the prefabricated 'Mulberry' harbours. There was little spare capacity for the construction of a varied fleet of landing craft, although of necessity many smaller craft, LCAs and LCGs, were constructed by temporary factories set alongside rivers as far inland as Reading, sixty miles from the sea.

There was a sufficiency of landing craft flowing from the American shipyards to meet all the Allied requirements, but as the allocation of craft to theatre depended on Admiral King, the European theatre tended to get very little. There is little need to debate this for the figures speak for themselves.

On 1 May 1944, the US Navy had in service some 10,000 landing craft of various types. Of these, only 1,400 were allocated to 'Overlord', the major Allied amphibious operation of the war, and Operation 'Anvil', the invasion of the South of France, planned as a concurrent and supporting operation. This shortage of landing craft had forced the 'Overlord' and COSSAC planners to make continual adjustments to their plan.

In the event, D-Day was put back a month to June, which allowed an extra month to produce craft and train crews, while 'Anvil' was delayed until enough craft could be spared from Normandy to take the armies ashore in the South of France.

The command structure for Operation 'Neptune' was as follows:

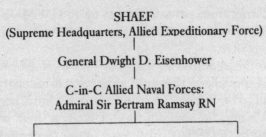

The Western Task Force would take the Americans ashore on 'Omaha' and 'Utah', while Admiral Vian's force would escort the Canadians and British to 'Gold', 'Juno' and 'Sword'. Under command of the two task forces were separate bombardment fleets, allocated to the various beaches, and therefore designated Force O (for Omaha), U, G, S and J, after their respective landing areas. Each beach area had a headquarters Control vessel from which the commanding general controlled the battle until he could set up his HQ ashore, and there was a wide variety of landing and support craft available, firing rockets (LCRs) or guns (LCGs), or anti-aircraft guns (LCFs).

These various forces mustered a total of 1,213 warships, from battleships and heavy gun bombardment monitors to midget submarines. In addition to this there were 4,126 landing ships and landing craft. There were, in addition, another 1,000 vessels involved in supply and in the 'Mulberry' project, plus merchantmen, tugs, command and close support vessels. The combined fleets mustered for D-Day totalled over 6,000 ships and vessels of various types.

About 70 per cent of these vessels were British or Canadian. The rest came from the US Navy or the Free French, Norwegian and Dutch Navies. The D-Day invasion produced the largest fleet that ever put to sea, a vast armada fleet that filled every port, estuary, roadstead and bay in the South of England in the weeks before D-Day. The shipping for the American beaches gathered in the west, in Weymouth and Torbay, the ships destined for the British and Canadian beaches in the east, along the south coast from Poole to Newhaven.

The 'Neptune' invasion plan issued by Admiral Ramsay for the guidance of his captains ran, with all its various appendices, to some 700 closely typed foolscap pages, a sight which so jolted the sailors that a directive had to be issued advising them that they need only read, learn and inwardly digest those parts directly concerned with their own activities. Even so, it proved a lot to learn, and still provides a fair indicator of the complexity of Operation 'Neptune'.

For clarity here, the naval forces for 'Neptune' may be divided into two parts, warships and landing craft. The warships, which had the task of bombarding the beaches and counter-battery fire against shore artillery, included 6 battleships: the British HMS *Ramillies*, HMS *Rodney*, and HMS *Warspite*, and the US battleships USS *Arkansas*, USS *Nevada* and USS *Texas*. The British also produced 2 bombardment monitors, HMS *Erebus* and *Roberts*. There were 16 British cruisers, including HMS *Belfast*, now a museum ship moored in the Thames near the Tower of London, and 3 US cruisers, USS *Augusta*, USS *Quincey* and USS *Tuscaloosa*.

There were 30 American destroyers, 57 British destroyers and various destroyers from the French, Dutch and Norwegian Navies, including HNMS *Svenner*. Apart from the 4,126 landing ships and craft, there were 736 ancillary vessels and 864 merchant ships. There were 189 minesweepers and 2 midget submarines of the Royal Navy, X20 and X23. Next to air power, naval gunfire support was to prove decisive in breaking up German counter-attacks on the beachheads.

The landing craft were of wide variety. Largest and most important were the LSTs, of which there were 236 in the assault, carrying the tanks and specialized armour as well as soft-skinned transport and armour. They were supported by 837 LCTs, the smaller Landing Craft Tank. The infantry went ashore in a variety of craft, ranging from attack transports, Landing Craft Personnel (LCPs), Landing Craft Assault (LCAs), Landing Ships Infantry [Large] (LSI[L]), and Landing Craft Infantry [Small] (LCI[S]). There were also the support landing craft, Landing Craft Rocket (LCRs), Landing Craft Guns (LCGs), and Landing Craft Flak (LCFs), the latter carrying quick-firing anti-aircraft guns. One of the more curious craft employed was the LB, or Landing Barge. Among these was an LBB (Landing Barge, Bakery), which cooked bread throughout D-Day for the troops ashore. Everything had to be considered, from shells for the 15-inch guns to bags of wooden pegs for hammering into bullet holes on the small landing craft.

Jack Horsnell was on LBF Landing Barge (Flak) No. 2 in the 26th Flotilla, heading for 'Gold' beach, the landing area of the 50th Northumbrian Division. 'These rather strange-looking craft were apparently intended as the original landing craft, but some sane person had noticed that in order to unload any cargo they would have to reverse before discharge, with an obvious loss of timing and life. Each craft comprised a naval crew and twelve soldiers of the Royal Artillery, who manned the two static Bofors guns.

'After the signal to sail we met up with many different types of craft assembling off Hayling Island and Portsmouth, appearing like corks out of a bottle from the inlets round about. Our skipper, Sub-Lt Tilley, told us that should anyone fall overboard, we would not be allowed to stop for rescue. Other craft had been allocated to look for survivors.

'The sea was very rough and we had the experience of wallowing in a deep trough and looking up at the propellers of a much larger vessel ahead, which will always stay in my memory. During the crossing we claimed a "hit", shooting down an enemy aircraft which was trying to fly the flag in that atrocious weather. Our last-minute orders were that we were to land on the beaches, the guns being used as air defence. What was to happen to us then was anybody's guess.

'Surprisingly, fate took a hand. We tried to follow our leader, who was a Lieutenant-Commander operating from a strengthened motor cruiser. He decided not to land but to turn in close to "Gold" beach at Arromanches and patrol up and down the coast. The reason that later reached us was that this officer was trying to get a fix by locating the "Mulberry" harbour of sunken ships, which were, of course, not brought out until D+1. One of my first recollections of Normandy was being on watch in the wireless cabin late on D-Day, and of our skipper looking very agitated because the Beachmaster wanted to come aboard. The Beachmaster was "Dod" Osborne of the fishing boat *Girl Pat* fame.

'Osborne launched into his story of the landing and of entering a house and killing all the occupants. As he was talking about the German Army we found his story rather hard to believe, but such was the man. His progress afterwards was rather chequered. The harbour of sunken ships protecting the "Mulberry", the "Gooseberries", was later used as billets for spare crews who had lost their craft and were available as working parties. The story goes that on seeking men for a working party, Osborne found no sign of life and proceeded to stir the occupants by firing a Tommy-gun down the hatches. This was not appreciated.

'It was also alleged that Osborne, needing a trip inland, hailed an American lorry, and on being refused a lift decided to press the point home with his revolver. This was the last straw and he was supposed to have been sent packing back to the UK. Anyway, here we were on D-Day, just patrolling the coast, looking out for doodlebugs (V1 rockets), and although we were battered by the subsequent storm that created havoc, we found life fairly easy. A few of the flotilla found themselves in trouble when patrolling up local rivers, getting between opposing forces, but as far as I remember there were no casualties. One of my shore memories later was of walking through Arromanches and being halted by a naval medical officer and torn off a strip as I had the bottom button of my jacket undone!'

Had it not been for the decision to postpone the invasion for a month, it is doubtful if Admiral Ramsay could have found enough shipping to convey the assault forces ashore. Eisenhower's requirements called for the navies to land 175,000 men, 1,500 tanks, 3,000 guns and 10,000 assorted trucks, Jeeps and other vehicles in the first 24 hours. To put this in perspective, it might help to realize that the American infantry for the 'Utah' and 'Omaha' assaults alone filled 200 large troop trains. To make room for all the men and their equipment it was necessary to cut the transport requirements of the assault divisions to the bone, but even so, the amount of necessary stores was daunting. On to the ships, apart from troops, weapons, ammunition and transport, went everything the armies might need, including a million gallons of drinking water.

The Royal Navy was also responsible for the design and

construction of the 'Mulberry' harbours. The 'Mulberries' were artificial harbours that could be floated across the Channel and sunk in position on the other side. Such ports were considered vital, and construction had been proceeding in prefabricated units, called 'Phoenix', all over the UK since the end of 1943. The plan called for two 'Mulberries' to be positioned, one off 'Omaha' for the Americans, and one off Arromanches for the British. Each would enclose an area about the size of Dover Harbour and accommodate ships of medium tonnage. The unloading piers were arranged so that they could float up and down with the tides, which in the Channel have a rise and fall of 19ft. The outer breakwaters, or 'Gooseberries', were composed of sunken merchantmen, and these would, in addition, provide shelter for the landing craft in the event of sudden gales. Once constructed, it was calculated that 7,000 tons of supplies could be unloaded daily through each port.

The 'Mulberries" components came to 400 separate units, totalling one-and-a-half million tons with the concrete caissons of the inner harbour, the 'Phoenix', displacing 6,000 tons apiece. To this could be added an outer ring of sunken blockships, or 'Gooseberries'.

Marine Syd 'Sticks' Lancaster went to Normandy on one of these 'Gooseberries', a Greek merchant ship. 'We had joined a Greek ship, the SS *Agios Spyridon*, and we sailed under the Greek flag. She carried her meat live, with at least a dozen sheep on board. I remember the sheep well, for when we first went aboard they roamed all around the upper deck, so we penned them into one area and cleaned up the rest of the deck. The crew consisted of the Greek Skipper, 1st Mate, Steward, Engineer, and about a dozen others. Among the Greek crew there was one other, a Canadian seaman. These people had all volunteered for the job, all except the Greek cook and he had a suitcase packed ready to leave the ship.

'The RN party consisted of Sub-Lt Saunders RNVR, "Dolly" Gray of Naval Signals, one Corporal and five Marines. Before leaving we were issued with emergency kit – knife, fork, spoon, tin plate, etc., plus two toilet rolls, and I remember saying, "My God . . . you've got some faith in us!"

'I remember the convoy going past Plymouth on Sunday 4

June, and saying to Lt Saunders, "The people on the Hoe who see us would have a fit if they knew where we were going." We received a signal to make for Arromanches – the signal being "Open Package A". The weather was pretty rough and very dark around midnight, and we were halfway across the Channel when Lt Saunders received another signal, "Open Package B", which was to "Abort and make for Poole Harbour". When we got to Poole it was crammed with ships, so we stayed outside.

'Our ships were to be used as "block ships" or "Gooseberries", to make a harbour for the landing craft, and should have been in place for the first wave to arrive, but owing to the postponement we sailed with the first wave.

'On the way across the Channel, the coal bunkers on the ship caught fire, so to put the fire out we signalled Commander Maude, the Beachmaster, for permission to take her in out of order. When we got in position, a boat came alongside to take off the crew and sink the ship, but as she was on fire and the charges were already in place, they were rather reticent. Lt Saunders said, "That's all right – my Marines will sink her." So the merchant crew was put ashore along with the sheep and hens (still alive) and we blew the charges and sank the ship. These ships did not sink out of sight, but left their upper deck above the water, forming a breakwater for the landing craft. As you can imagine, it was pretty chaotic on the beach that day and everyone forgot that we were still aboard.'

Albert Barnes was on a naval tug, towing one of the 'Mulberry' 'Phoenix' caissons. 'I was aboard HMRT *Storm King* on 6 June. We were one of the first blocks to arrive over there. The gale force winds and the high side of the block, plus the square bows and stern, made it one of the worst tows I had in seven-and-a-half years as a tuggie. We made many trips from Selsey Bill to Arromanches, towing blocks, landing stages and roadways, all in bad weather, until the harbour was complete.'

It took 160 tugs and 10,000 men to get the 'Mulberries' in position, and regrettably they lasted in full use for less than two weeks. On 19 June, a fierce three-day gale destroyed the American 'Mulberry' off 'Omaha' and severely damaged the British one at Arromanches. The American one was abandoned, and although the one at Arromanches continued to function, it was

discovered that ships could be safely beached at 'Utah' and their
cargo unloaded directly into trucks as the tide fell, the ships
floating off again, empty, on the next tide. Although of limited
use, the 'Mulberries' were vital while they lasted, and their
existence gave confidence to the staff at SHAEF who knew,
when planning the assault, that they would have no port available to supply the armies unless they took one with them.

Another necessary invention for D-Day was PLUTO, the
Pipe Line Under The Ocean. A force that would contain 15,000
vehicles on D-Day alone and thousands more with every day
that passed thereafter, would have a tremendous thirst for
petrol. This thirst could hardly be quenched by the use of
tankers operating through the 'Mulberries' or over open
beaches, and the planners' answer to this problem was
PLUTO.

As soon as Port-en-Bessin was captured by 47 (Royal Marine) Commando on 6 June, a fuel depot was to be established.
Here, where the US and British landing areas met, it could
supply both armies. An armoured pipeline, laid under the sea,
would receive fuel pumped from the tankers lying offshore, and
later on, the first cross-Channel pipeline was laid from the Isle
of Wight to come ashore at Querqueville near Cherbourg.
There were eventually four PLUTO pipelines, and their daily
deliveries of 2,500 tons of petrol kept the armies moving until
the Channel ports were cleared of obstacles and opened up
towards the end of July.

The troops were divided into three broad groups; the 'assault' formations would board their assault craft and sail with
the first fleet. The 'pre-loaded, follow-up formations' of first-
line reinforcements would be on board their vessels in British
ports, ready to follow ashore on D+1 or D+2 as the situation
developed. Later forces, earmarked for deployment on D+3 or
later, were in concentration areas close to the embarkation
ports, and they would be fed in as space permitted and the
situation required.

The Royal Navy had one other small but vital task during the
landings – to mark the beaches. Two midget submarines, X20
and X23, were to mark the beaches of 'Juno' and 'Sword',
surfacing as darkness fell and shining green lights seaward to

bring the landing craft in at the right place. At midnight on 2 June, X20 and X23 sailed for their stations off the coast of Normandy.

Jim Booth, the COPP Sub-Lieutenant and beach surveyor, was now embarked on a midget submarine. 'As I remember it, I was on X23, which is now resting outside the Submarine Museum at Gosport. There were buoys to lead the landing ships into the bay of the Seine and our task was to put out a radio beacon in a dinghy just offshore to mark the eastern end of the beach at "Sword" – that would be west of the Orne. We went across under tow by a big submarine on 3 June, all according to plan, and lay on the bottom all that night and the next day, ready to come up and put out the beacon on the night of 4/5th. When we came up we got the message that the invasion had gone back 24 hours, so down we went again.'

The infantry marched on board their ships on 3 June, and the western invasion convoys set sail from places like Falmouth in Cornwall, rolling before a stiff westerly gale as they turned towards the assembly area – known as 'Piccadilly Circus' – in mid-Channel, south of the Isle of Wight; but as the day wore on the gales steadily increased.

Don Kelly, then a regimental policeman, recalls the last days before the invasion. 'As a regimental policeman, it was one of my duties each morning to unbar the cells and kick in the boots, braces and trousers which were left outside the cell, but this day I found they were missing, and on entering the cell found it was empty, and after opening the third cell door I realized that all the prisoners had gone! I ran off immediately to find the Guard Commander in his bed. He was highly amused, and it transpired that all the prisoners had been taken away at 3.00 a.m. to join an advance party for the Second Front.

'A newsagent's errand lad rode along the quayside before departure and he was pelted with money for his newspapers by the troops on board, who had no further use for it. Finally he had collected so much money that he tied his errand bike on to a rope and we took it to France with us. We sailed down the Thames and passed a large munitions factory, with the workers on the roof displaying a huge banner inscribed: "The war workers wish you a safe journey and a speedy return." This produced a loud chorus of boos from the troops on board.'

At Eisenhower's Headquarters on 3 June the atmosphere was becoming fraught. Weather forecasting was not then as sophisticated as it is today; there were no satellites or computers to observe and predict weather patterns, but all the information available indicated that severe weather was sweeping in from the Atlantic and would hit the Channel hard on or about 4 June, just when the invasion craft were putting to sea. All that could be done had been done, but no one could control the weather.

All attention was now fixed on Group Captain Stagg, RAF, Head of the SHAEF Meteorological Unit. General Eisenhower had been getting Stagg's weather forecasts for months, in order to gauge their accuracy, and had built up a considerable respect for his ability. Stagg's forecast for the early hours of 4 June was of continuing bad weather for the next three days, with gales to disrupt the landing-craft fleets and very low cloud, which would certainly ground the air forces and paratroop aircraft. The latter was the critical factor since only air force interdiction could prevent the massive German counter-attacks that were sure to follow the landings.

Time for a final decision was now getting very short. At dawn on 4 June, Eisenhower reluctantly postponed the invasion by 24 hours, and recalled the vessels then at sea. One group of ships, Force U2, bound for 'Utah', could not be contacted by radio and had to be chased and turned back by destroyers. For the soldiers, crammed into the wet, stuffy troop decks, already apprehensive and seasick, the delay seemed unendurable.

The pressure on General Eisenhower was tremendous. Other people could offer advice but the decision to launch the D-Day attack was his alone. Because of the moon and tide requirements the invasion could not be long delayed; it had to go in on 5, 6 or 7 June. The next suitable date was weeks away and any long delay meant unpicking the entire operation, with a great risk of a breach in security. 'The question is,' said Eisenhower to his staff, 'how long can we leave this situation hanging there?'

The storm grew worse throughout Sunday 4 June, with

heavy seas pounding the beaches on both sides of the Channel. At 2100 hrs that evening, Eisenhower and his staff met again, and Group Captain Stagg had one slight chance to offer; the possibility that after the present front had passed, in about 24 hours' time, there would be a short period of reasonable weather, with moderate cloud and lower winds, lasting until the evening of 6 June. It was a small chance and a great risk, but the alternatives were equally unpalatable. The ships were ready to sail and if this chance went by, there would be a delay of at least two weeks until the tides would again be favourable. By dawn on 5 June, when SHAEF met again for another forecast and a final discussion, the issue could no longer be postponed.

By this time Stagg had a slightly more optimistic forecast; the break in the bad weather was now confirmed, from the afternoon of 5 June, and it would probably last until the evening of Wednesday 7 June. A small chance it might be, but it was all Stagg could offer. 'OK,' said General Eisenhower. 'We'll go.'

Two hours later the convoys began to sail. By the evening of Monday 5 June the minesweepers were off the Normandy coast, close enough to distinguish houses on the shore. The gales had moderated but the wind was still coming in hard from the west, blowing at fifteen knots and kicking up waves six feet high, causing surf on the beaches. The cloud base was around 10,000ft, but some cloud was down to 1,000ft.

Marine Jim Wilde was on the battleship HMS *Rodney*, sailing for 'Sword'. 'At the time of the D-Day landings I was serving on HMS *Rodney*, which was the battleship for the "Sword" beachhead. We had 3 turrets of 3 by 16-inch guns, 6 turrets of twin 6-inch guns, and were bristling with AA 4-inch pom-pom, and others too numerous to mention. At dawn on 5 June 1944, I could already see the outline of France. The sea was a bit rough, too rough for landing craft full of seasick soldiers, and the whole fleet turned about; "Mission Off", so back to port. Later that night we put to sea again and as the day dawned the crossing was more like a mill pond, at least from HMS *Rodney*, a miracle compared with yesterday. The sky was full of aircraft, some towing gliders.

'On arriving off "Sword" beach, I looked at the small craft busily going about their tasks. All at once a huge plume of water appeared right in front of P-1 and the look-outs reported the same to starboard. We were a sitting duck for the 15-inch guns on the Le Havre battery. We had on board the C-in-C, also the Senior Army Officer co-ordinating naval fire power. In all, I think they were too valuable to sacrifice, so we moved out some three miles and started to shell Le Havre.'

Phil Sykes was a communications officer on board the USS *Frankford*, a Fletcher-class fleet destroyer and flagship for Des-Ron 18, a squadron of fourteen US destroyers heading for 'Omaha' beach. 'Our particular assignment was to escort a whole mess of troop-carrying vessels, and supply ships, landing craft ... anything that could float to the Normandy beachhead, take up positions to provide screening and gunfire support. The seas were not in our favour and if you know anything about destroyers, they roll even tied up to dock. Everybody was affected by the seas.

'Since our ship was the flag ship, we were point ship for the squadron and took up a position somewhere between 500 and 1,000 yards off the beachhead. We were to give gunfire support to the landing parties, and being dead in the water and broadside to the beach, we had an overview of all activities. We were supposed to have communications with a beachhead landing party who would call in gunfire on targets, but unfortunately most of those people got blown out of the water, or simply didn't make it. If you take 14 destroyers all with 5-inch guns firing at one co-ordinated target, along with the 40mm and 20mm, you can create quite a stir. There was a lot of confusion, as everything was happening so fast. You can't imagine the amount of shipping that was present, but we were held up for a time due to several enemy gun emplacements on the high ground behind the beachhead raising hell with our forces.'

Apart from shelling, the 'Neptune' forces had to contend with mines. Denis Froment was an able seaman on HMML 185: 'Q-Queenie Minesweeping Flotilla left Portsmouth Harbour in the afternoon of the 4th. It was blowing a Force 8 gale, so we anchored off the Isle of Wight and remained there until Monday morning, 5 June. We left late afternoon and started to sweep until about 8 o'clock that evening. According to the wheelhouse chart we were in direct line for Port-en-Bessin. The first glimpse of the French coast came at about 0400 hrs and at 0430 hrs all hell let loose.'

Commander John Robert Lewis Jnr was then an ensign in the United States Navy on the staff of Rear Admiral Don P. Moon, Commander of Force U, destined for 'Utah' beach. 'Admiral Moon was a very intense man who slept for only about four hours a night, and our ship, the USS *Bayfield*, had been one of the ships involved in Operation "Tiger" when several LSTs were sunk. On June 1, Admiral Moon and his staff boarded the *Bayfield*, and on June 3 we picked up Major-General J. Lawton Collins (Commander of the VII Corps) and his headquarters troops, and also Major-General Barton, Commander of the 4th Infantry Division, along with his deputy commander, Brigadier-General Teddy Roosevelt Jnr.

'We then assembled with other ships of Force U and began our trip across the English Channel. During the cruise across we all assembled on the deck of the *Bayfield* and sang the "Battle Hymn of the Republic" and "Onward Christian Soldiers". This was a very sobering time to sing the words, ". . . *as God died to make men holy, let us die to make men free* . . .". We arrived off "Utah" beach at approximately midnight on June 5. At that same time, bombardment by our naval ships commenced, and we also disembarked our underwater demolition teams and rubber boats. They were to go on to the beach and clear the underwater obstacles.

'A few days after the landing the flag ships were visited by General Marshall, General Eisenhower, General Arnold and Admiral King. It was a great thrill to see these officers, and I will never forget shaking the hand of General Teddy Roosevelt Jnr, not too long before he died in action. For three weeks the *Bayfield* sat anchored off the "Utah" beach and the staff stood four hours on, four hours off watches during this entire time. Then, in early July, we sailed for Naples, to plan for the landings in the South of France. Just a few days before these landings, Rear Admiral Don Moon committed suicide aboard the USS *Bayfield*. He wrapped a towel around his .45 calibre pistol and shot himself during the night. It was later announced that Admiral Moon had taken his own life due to combat fatigue.'

Deryk Thomas, then aged twenty-two, was a telegraphist on board HMS *Bangor*, one of the 9th Minesweeping Flotilla. 'Our flotilla could not sweep the last two miles to the beaches and this task was taken over by the BYMS (Brooklyn Yard Mine Sweepers). We drew in sweeps and we had a huge mine in our wire which was being dragged inboard until the winches were stopped and the First Lieutenant grabbed an axe and cut the wire, first securing a buoy to mark the spot. D-Day was already over as far as we were concerned.'

The minesweepers were ignored by the German radar and no shells fell about them as they deployed their paravanes and began to sweep. The troopships began to arrive at their assembly points just after midnight, ten miles or more offshore, quietly and without lights. There was no confusion and in spite of the heavy seas the grouping of vessels at their various assembly areas went according to plan.

Tom Lovell was a Royal Marine LCA coxswain on the assault ship HMT *Glenroy*. 'As a young man of twenty-two I well remember the scene before me. Here I was, privileged to be present with the greatest invasion force the world had ever seen, and indeed was ever likely to see again. We talked to each other and expressed our fears about what was to come, and whether we would be returning. We were all highly trained, but it seemed to me that thoughts of wives, kids and so on were uppermost in the minds of everyone I met.

'When we reached the open sea the scene was incredible, with hundreds of ships, boats and tugs all going the same way. I well remember PLUTO, the oil line reels and the huge concrete harbour piers and cranes which were all heading for Arromanches. There were also huge rafts containing motor vehicles and guns. These were all bobbing up and down in the gale which by now had reached around Force 6. As night fell the Air Force began adding their bit to the scene and this went on all night with more and more bombers going our way.

'We went to our craft on the davits and all the necessary checks were made. We then took on board our charges – each LCA held some thirty men of the Royal Hampshire Regiment, whose goal was Bayeux. Like us, they were worried about what lay ahead, but seemed more concerned about whether we would reach the beach. I assured them that we would and that I would see that they went right up out of the water; this seemed to settle them down. Later I was pleased that I was able to keep my promise.

'The Navy lowered us into the water and we then experienced the swell. On the way in we were going with the sea and it was quite pleasant and fast, for which I was grateful. Our touch-down point was near to the village of Le Hamel, and I was consulting the panoramic strip photos (taken by aircraft prior to D-Day). Then we came up against the beach obstacles – huge ramps made from old railway lines set in concrete, all with mines. We negotiated all these and I then saw the opening I was seeking. I put the craft full ahead and hard to port and we were through. I beached and all hell was let loose. Down went the ramp and all my Hampshires got out safely. I know this because I saw them go right up the beach.'

Able Seaman Sidney Hoy was a twenty-one-year-old signalman in an LCPL. 'Our LCP was a small landing craft about 8 metres long, rather like a small speedboat and made entirely of plywood. Our flotilla consisted of about 12 boats commanded by a lieutenant and we had a crew of 6. I was more than pleased when we anchored off the French coast at dawn. We had been towed from Weymouth during the night by an LST, the rough seas had pounded our craft and we were taking in water. As soon as the LST anchored we tied up alongside it and went aboard up the scramble nets. This was not easy because of the rough seas.

'The ship was manned by Americans and I remember queuing up cafeteria style with a metal tray and being given some splendid food. I have to say that I only had a rough idea of what we were supposed to do, and we could not claim to be highly trained for the job. We were to go in first with the amphibious tanks, closely followed by the troops in the LCAs. Our task was to pick up survivors. By 0530 hrs all the DD tanks had been floated from the ramp of the LST and were taking up formation. The order came to attack and we started to make our way towards the beach, about three miles away. We were not the only group of floating tanks; many others had been launched from other LSTs. By this time the enemy had woken up and we came under heavy fire. About a mile off the beach some of the DD tanks were getting into difficulties. The sea tore their canopies and they sank, while others had been swamped by waves. Some of the crews had gone down with their tanks but others managed to get out and were floating in the sea.

'We had been instructed not to rescue anyone until the main body of tanks had made it to the beach. We finally got very close to the shore, where some of the tanks got caught on the beach traps, others were hit by enemy fire or blown up by mines. Once the tanks had landed, we were able to set about the task of rescuing the crews floating in the sea. Soon the first waves of landing craft were converging on the beach, and from where we were it looked like the landing had been a failure. We carried on making ourselves generally useful offshore for some time till we were hit by enemy fire. I was wounded in the neck and thrown into the sea. I was in the water for some time, and there were many men in the same situation. Finally I was picked up by a rescue ship and the following day I was taken back to England.'

Marine Ernie Knibbs was with 536 LCA Flotilla on board SS *Empire Cutlass*: 'We carried two assault companies of the East Yorks Regiment, and I slept quite well for a few hours on the way over. We arrived at our lowering position about ten miles offshore, and as we assembled at our LCAs I saw the trail of a torpedo pass across our bow. Not long after that a Norwegian destroyer was hit midships, her bow and stern sticking out of the water to form the letter "V". She held that position for quite some time before she sank, almost as though she was putting two fingers up in defiance. I later learned that she was HNMS *Svenner*.

'We were lowered away, nine tons of LCA plus the crew and troops. We were lucky and caught the swell as it came up and so were able to slip hooks first time. Some were less fortunate and took quite a hammering, as one minute they were afloat and the next they were high and dry, still on the hooks. Both hooks must be slipped at the same time or disaster overtakes and you are upside down.

'We circled round until all craft were clear of the ship. It was a good run-in, with plenty of LCTs around us. There was a heavy swell and sick-bags appeared to be "dress of the day" for the troops. With about five miles to go the LCA astern of us was taking in water fast, and her stern-sheets man had the semi-rotary pump going as fast as his arms would let him. He must have done a grand job as I saw them hit the beach later.'

Apart from the loss of the destroyer HNMS *Svenner* to a torpedo there was no German naval opposition off the beaches. The German E-Boats stayed snug in the harbours of Cherbourg and Le Havre, convinced that no invasion fleet would have sailed in such weather. Even Field Marshal Rommel thought the invasion so unlikely that he went home to Germany to visit his wife on her birthday, which fell on 6 June, and to try and persuade Hitler to move more Panzer units to the beach areas.

J.L. 'Les' Wagar was a rifleman in 'C' Company, the Queen's Own Rifles of Canada, and remembers the run-in to the beach. 'Before dawn on 6 June the Channel was black and drizzly, the ship rolling in the back swells of yesterday's storm, but this was truly a luxury trip. The last time our Company had been in the Channel was on an exercise, crammed into an LCI, and nearly everyone was sick, including the Navy.

'This time it was no flat-bottomed LCI – this was a real ship, an LSI, equipped to feed, billet and transport an entire beach assault group, ringed with scrambling nets and with LCAs slung from the davits. We had been aboard her since 4 June, waiting. She would carry us comfortably across the Channel and drop the first of us into our LCAs under cover of darkness, about three miles off the coast.

'Reveille was early on the 6th; it was still night and the LSI was still ploughing ahead into the darkness. I don't remember eating – the Navy may have ladled out some porridge and coffee. All we had were our compo-rations anyway, but they were for later. I recall lining up for rum ration, but only because somebody talked me into it. Since I was so queasy in the stomach, at least I could be a good pal and get an extra shot for a drinkin' man. The drinkin' man was smarter than I was. He poured both mine and his into his canteen, which was already half-full; a little something he was saving up for a party when the time was right.

'Then official noises began coming over the intercoms, people started giving orders and the engines slowed. We got into our gear and lined up on deck beside our designated LCAs. The sky was just beginning to lighten as the LCAs were dropped into the swell, and we climbed down the nets to get on board. At that point I don't remember anyone saying anything. Each man's job had been set and memorized days before, and there was really nothing to say. We knew the width of beach we had to cross, the mines we had to avoid, the bunkers, the gun positions, the wall we had to get over or through, the streets and the buildings of the town we had to take, the minefields, the possible enemy strength, the perimeter we had to establish for the next wave to go forward.'

The only sound that disturbed the night was the steady drone of aircraft engines. The bombers of the US Ninth Air Force and RAF Bomber Command began their attacks on the German batteries and beach defences soon after dark, which came late, at about 10 p.m. on 5 June. These raids had been going on for months now and caused no particular alarm ashore, and the sailors and soldiers on the invasion craft hardly looked up as the bombers flew over.

Kenneth Beard was flying in one of these aircraft. 'I was rear gunner in a Halifax "G-George", registration LV825, which took off from Melbourne (York) aerodrome at 0235 hrs on the morning of 6 June, and landed at 0425 hrs. Our target had been Mont Fleury, and I was flying with Squadron-Leader R. Kennedy, "A" Flight Commander, as pilot.

'We had been given no inkling of the nature of the mission, but as an experienced crew we suspected something special by virtue of the fact that we had an extra briefing prior to take-off. Even at the second briefing we were not told that this was the day we had all been waiting for, and the only luxury the Intelligence officer permitted himself was to announce, with typical British irony, "If you have to jettison any bombs please don't do it in the Channel as there will probably be a few extra ships around!"

'Weather to the target was good and there was no evidence of

German fighters or flak, but what stands out in my memory is the sight of a vast armada of ships below us. Our aircraft intercom was swamped, for disregarding all intercom discipline we virtually shrieked our delight, but we had to confess to each other later on that we were aware of the odd tear trickling into the flying helmet, and this from a hardened, experienced air crew.

'This was a very special trip for us as a crew who had flown together for thirty operations, most of them against heavily defended targets, but this was our final flight of our tour, so as we taxied to dispersal we bandied plans for our forthcoming celebrations. We weren't at all surprised to find the Squadron Commander waiting for us at dispersal, as it was usual for him to greet a crew returning from a final operation. Imagine our dismay when, instead of the congratulations we had expected, we were told that Air Ministry had requested all squadrons to provide as many aircraft as possible to give assistance to the landing troops, and that he would appreciate our "volunteering" to do another flight.

'We understood that "volunteering" was something in the nature of a euphemism, and so 2230 hrs saw us taking off, with the rest of 10 Squadron, for a target further afield, namely St Lô.'

Squadron Leader Douglas Millikin was then a Lancaster bomber pilot in 50 Squadron of 5 Group. 'Any man who says he wasn't frightened during the war either has no imagination or is a bloody liar. We took off from Skellington at about 3.30 a.m. on 6 June. We came over Didcot and crossed the coast near Bournemouth to bomb a battery of 15-inch guns near Cherbourg. We were not told that this was D-Day, and the Met. men had made a balls of it, offering cloud over England and clear skies over the French coast. It was as clear as a bell over England and got thicker as we crossed the English coast.

'Our bombing speed was 150 knots and we broke through the cloud at 2,500ft and saw the target indicators going down dead ahead. The bomb aimer said, "Left, left," and then "Bombs gone." In that half minute we saw a Lancaster go down, and only waited for the flash of the photo before we got up into the cloud again. Over England we could see the lights of the glider aircraft going over – hundreds of them. On the next night, 6 June, we went to Argentan to crater the crossroads and fields around the town to stop the Panzers getting up to the beaches. I did 45 operations in all and 50 was *the* Squadron for me – a wonderful Squadron. My second son is now in the RAF and has two commendations for valuable service in the air; one for the Falklands and one for the Gulf.'

Corporal Bill Fox of the RAF was at sea with the men of his airfield construction unit, preparing to go ashore in Normandy and build landing strips. 'We sailed with the Canadians, many of whom had cut their hair like Mohican Indians and carried hunting knives in their boots, saying they wanted to avenge Dieppe. On the way to the dock we stopped in Fareham, where a lady came out of a house and offered me a bath, which I was very grateful for. We then boarded an LCT at Gosport, and I remember sailing past the Needles on the way to France. I did not sleep well and awoke to see ships everywhere, and then a coastline dimly ahead towards which the LST was steaming hard. Then the ramp went down and more orders came – "Follow the white tapes as anywhere else is mined." I found out later that this was "Juno" beach and we had landed near the village of Courseulles.'

Ron Colledge was a flight lieutenant navigator in a Stirling bomber of 218 Squadron. 'My pilot was Flight Lieutenant John McAllister, an Australian, and we carried out one of the spoof invasions designed to make the Germans think that the real invasion would take place off Calais. For this operation each aircraft carried three navigators. One to operate the Gee-box, one to operate the GH, and the third to carry out the dead reckoning. We took off around midnight to a point in the English Channel east of the Isle of Wight.

'At that point the Gee-navigator was responsible for flying an accurate course towards Cap Gris Nez, while the GH operators were in charge of dropping bundles of "window" (radar distorting foil) out of the windows and chutes. The effect of this was to simulate a convoy approaching the French coast at a speed of five knots. I can't remember how many different GH co-ordinates had to be set to get the required effect, but it seemed a hell of a lot at the time. I see from my log book that it took four-and-a-half hours, and I can still hear the radio announcing that the invasion had started as we sat down to our bacon and eggs in the mess at about 6.30 a.m. on 6 June.'

The news of the landings had also spread to the French Resistance, as André Heintz recalls: 'I was a member of the Underground and had been warned of the approach of D-Day by hearing the first message, "*L'heure du combat viendra*", on the crystal set in my cellar on 31 May. I heard the last order, "*Les dés sont sur le tapis*" – "The dice are on the table", the signal for general sabotage, at 8.45 p.m. on 5 June. I was in Caen on D-Day, and after the second message I passed the word on and spent the rest of the night watching the Headquarters of the German 716th Infantry Division, which was near where I lived in Caen. The first despatch rider only reached the HQ at 3.30 a.m. We had heard many planes going overhead from 11.20 p.m. onwards, and after 3.30 a.m. the rumbling of intense shelling from the sea. I think the Royal Navy were destroying the defences, the positions and shapes of which I had sent over to England during the previous months.

'My mother had been unable to sleep because of the noise and said, "It must be the landings, André." I told her, "We had better get some bottles filled with drinking water because we don't know how long drinking water will be available." In fact, ten days later we were still drinking some of the water and it was still the best of our supply. My mother cooked some potatoes, because she said the gas would soon be cut off, and three days later it was, and not put on again for six months.'

Just before midnight there came another sound, deeper, more constant, ominous, the steady roar of countless aircraft flying over the darkened fleets, like a great swarm of bees. Hundreds of aircraft were coming over now, flying very low across the sea, but these were transport aircraft and they carried not bombs but men.

At midnight on the night of 5/6 June, by parachute or glider, 20,000 Allied soldiers from three airborne divisions began to land in Normandy. Operation 'Overlord' had started and D-Day had begun.

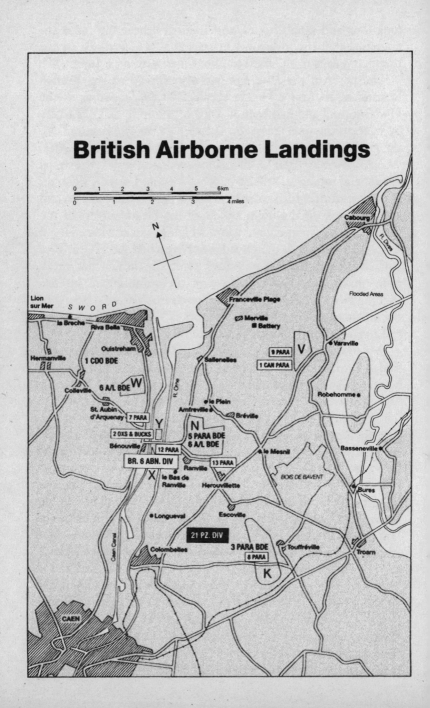

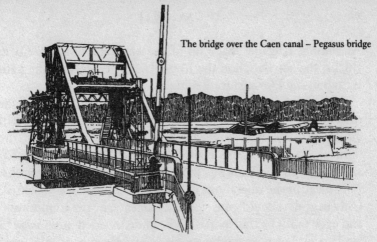

The bridge over the Caen canal – Pegasus bridge

---— CHAPTER FIVE ———

The Red Devils

'Gentlemen, do not be daunted if chaos
reigns: it undoubtedly will.'
Brigadier James Hill
3rd Parachute Brigade
6th Airborne Division

War is unpredictable. It is a sad fact but true, that in spite of the best efforts of all concerned, matters in war will frequently go awry from the moment the first shot is fired. Many commanding officers, like Brigadier Hill, were well aware of this fact, had advised their men accordingly and told them what to do; whatever happens, press on, do their best, take their objectives, kill the enemy. As a rule plans just don't work in any detail, and the airborne operations of D-Day went wrong from the start.

The British 6th Airborne Division was raised in England in the spring of 1943. A year later, in the spring of 1944, 6th Airborne was commanded by Major-General Sir Richard 'Windy' Gale and consisted of three brigades, the 3rd Parachute Brigade, containing the 8th, 9th and 1st (Canadian) Parachute Battalions; the 5th Parachute Brigade, containing the 7th, 12th and 13th Parachute Battalions, and a glider formation, the 6th

Airlanding Brigade, made up of the 2nd Battalion, the Ox &
Bucks, the 1st Battalion the Royal Ulster Rifles, and the 12th
Battalion the Devonshire Regiment.

An airlanding brigade consisted of three infantry battalions
turned over to an airborne role and landing by glider. Allied
glider formations at this time flew in three main types, the
'Horsa', a 24-seater, the 'Hamilcar', which could take 40 men,
and the 'Waco', which was more popular with the Americans.
For the airborne operations of the day the glider was essential.
Only in gliders could guns, jeeps, scout cars, heavy ammunition
and even tanks be transported. The glider needed no runway to
land on, and was, on landing anyway, strictly expendable; most
gliders crashed. They could stand up to very rough treatment
but needed skilled handling. The British gliders were piloted by
men of the Glider Pilot Regiment, a regiment of sergeants
trained in infantry fighting and ready, once their passengers
were landed, to join them in fighting the enemy.

The plan for 6th Airborne on D-Day called for the men to be
dropped on the eastern flank of the seaborne landings. The drop
zones (DZs) chosen were on the high ground around Ranville,
between the Rivers Orne and Dives. Here they were given three
main tasks: first, to secure the bridges over the River Orne and
the Caen Canal at Bénouville and secure the Ranville heights to
the east; second, to destroy the bridges over the flooded River
Dives, 8km beyond the drop zone, at Bures, Robehomme,
Troarn and Varaville, to seal off the bridgehead against
counter-attacks; third, and perhaps most daunting of all, to
destroy the 155mm guns of the Merville Battery at Franceville-
Plage. The guns of Merville enfiladed the beachhead to the west
and could easily sink the invasion shipping, destroying men and
stores offshore.

This part of the Normandy coast was defended by the
German 716th Infantry Division, commanded by Lt-General
Wilhelm Richter. The 716th was a second-rank formation, up
to strength but poorly equipped, especially regarding transport.
To the east lay another German infantry division, the 711th,
which was in a similar state of readiness. Far more formidable
was the 21st Panzer Division which lay south of Caen and could

be expected to move against the Allied flank as soon as the Allies were ashore.

The task for 6th Airborne, therefore, was a difficult and dangerous one. It exposed them to almost certain attack from an armoured division, the type of attack that lightly equipped paratroopers were least able to deal with, and if their heavy equipment and anti-tank guns should fail to arrive, or the seaborne link be delayed, they stood in considerable danger.

Most of the men of the 6th Airborne had not been in action before and were as untried as the division itself. They had, however, been intensively trained for their tasks and were confident in their ability to overcome any difficulty they might encounter. Their commander, General Gale, had spelt out their job in simple terms: 'What you get by stealth and guts,' he said, 'you must hold with skill and determination.'

The first task, the securing of the bridges over the Orne and the Caen Canal, was allocated to the 5th Parachute Brigade, landing to the north of Ranville and clearing landing grounds for the Advanced Headquarters and anti-tank guns that would arrive later by glider. For the actual capture of the bridges they had under command a glider force of 180 men from the 2nd Oxfordshire and Buckinghamshire Light Infantry and from 249 Field Company Royal Engineers, commanded by Major John Howard. This force would take the bridges at midnight on 5/6th June by *coup-de-main*.

Major Howard's plan was to crash-land his glider force beside the bridges and overwhelm the defenders before the shock of their arrival wore off. This plan appeared to suffer a setback some days before the invasion when anti-invasion posts sprouted in the fields around the bridges, but his glider pilots were not a bit disconcerted. They considered they could use the posts to run the glider wings against and slow their landing speed.

Sergeant James Wallwork and his co-pilot, John Ainsworth, were selected as the crew of the first glider to land. They and the other five crews started training for this operation in March 1944, flying out of Netheravon in Wiltshire, and Sergeant Wallwork recalls the training: 'No word as to why, in the usual glider pilot style, but on arrival we were addressed by Colonel

George Chatterton who pointed out a couple of triangles on the
airfield marked with broad white tape. Not very big but apparently, in his judgement, big enough. "You will be towed," said
the Colonel, "at one-minute intervals to 4,000 feet, which will
take about one hour. You will then release three miles away at a
point decided by your tug. Nos 1, 2 and 3 will land in this one,
making a right-hand circuit, and 4, 5 and 6 in t'other, from a
left-hand circuit. Now, hop off for lunch. All gliders are ready
and assembled on the towpath. Take-off 1300 hours."' All six
crews landed within the taped-off areas.

Another of the six glider pilots involved was Staff Sergeant
Roy Howard. 'For the next phase, a formation of trees close to
the east side of Netheravon Airfield had been selected. Each day
the 6 chosen glider crews, 3 from "B" Squadron and 3 from
"C" Squadron, were towed from Tarrant on the same height
and course and pull-off point to simulate the operation's requirements, of which we still knew nothing. Three gliders
would land in two very small fields. RAF ground crews were
there to get the "Horsas" back to Netheravon Airfield and
service them, but we could only do one of these "Deadstick"
landings each day.

'The operation required that the three gliders attacking the
river bridge had to shed height as quickly as possible, whereas
the three gliders attacking the canal bridge were to carry out a
longer and more orthodox approach. Our three gliders had only
about half the distance to fly, although from the same height of
6,000 ft, and in order to lose so much height in sufficient time,
we had to apply full flap as soon as we released. As soon as we
cast off, our Halifax tugs were to continue straight and drop
bombs on Caen.

'By this time we were training at night, at first with a few
lights on the ground, but as our landings became more precise
these were removed and we were told to do spot-on landings in
these small fields with no lights or aids of any kind. At first I
thought that it could not be done, but after one or two hairy
missions we found that it could.'

For the first of the practice landings the crews flew in empty
gliders, but Sergeant Wallwork recalls how this changed: 'Air
Vice Marshal Sir Leslie Hollinghurst, who exercised overall

Group Command, had expressly forbidden any live-load or passengers on the "Deadstick" practice flights. We graduated to half-load and then full-load. The latter comprising a Bailey bridge which filled the "Horsa" and finished with a steel cross-beam directly behind the two pilots at neck level. We all flew very, very carefully that night, haunted by visions of Madame Guillotine and said, "No thanks." In all we practised our "Deadstick" routine 42 times, so we should have been – and were – bloody good at it by June 1944.'

At the end of May 1944, the glider crews met their passengers – Major John Howard and his small group of infantry. Roy Howard again: 'On 28 May we met our load of Major Howard and his Ox & Bucks Light Infantry, and in my case Lieutenant Fox and his men. Then followed the most intensive briefing on the military side of the operation, greatly aided by an elaborate sand-table model. This showed every detail of the terrain with all the trees, and of course, the river and canal with its bridges, though we did not know where it actually was until about two days before D-Day.'

Lieutenant David Wood, one of the platoon commanders, also recalls the briefings. 'The company was increased to six platoons by the addition of two from "B" Company and moved into a sealed transit camp on 27 May 1944. There the officers were briefed on 28 May and the men on the 30th. We had a really marvellous model on which every house, slit trench and even tree in the landing zone was shown. We even knew the name of the English-speaking café proprietor near the canal bridge. We were not told where the bridges were but an issue of francs in our escape kit gave us a clue to the country concerned!'

Like most other airborne operations that night, Howard's task did not go entirely to plan. Of the 6 gliders, 4 landed on target, close to the canal and river bridges. One landed half a mile away, and 1 beside a totally different river eight miles away. There were still enough men at Bénouville to do the job and James Wallwork describes the attack: 'We took off at 2245 hrs through low cloud and into the clear at 6,000ft over the Channel, avoiding the Navy – that most trigger-happy service – who had done their best to shoot us down on our way to Sicily the year before.

'The troops, encouraged by Major Howard, sang and (thank heaven) none was airsick. We were right on time and dead on target, thanks to our tug crew, and we saw the French coast in plenty of time to get set. Five, four, three, two, one, Cheers! Cast off! Up with the nose to reduce speed while turning to Course I. That's when the singing stopped. We came in on the final leg at 90 miles per hour and touched down, crashing through several fences in the process and coming to a final stop half way up the river embankment.

'We made an awful noise but it seemed not to have bothered the German sentries who perhaps thought that part of a shot-down bomber had landed. Exactly one minute later No. 2 arrived, followed by No. 3, justifying all those "Deadstick" training flights.

'There was only one casualty on landing. The Bren gunner in No. 2 glider was thrown out and drowned in the pond in our field, about which everyone seemed to have avoided asking daft questions during briefing. Johnnie and I revived in a few minutes and with the aid of a medic I managed to crawl free of the debris, but it required two of us to drag Johnnie out. Nothing was broken except an ankle and a badly sprained pair of knees for Johnnie. The medic took him to the ditch which had been designated the Regimental Aid Post. That was the last I saw of him until back in the squadron several weeks later. I had taken a header through the Perspex nose and was bleeding from a head cut. Blood had congealed quickly in my right eye socket and I thought all night that I had only one eye left.'

Sergeant Roy Howard, heading for the Orne bridge, also had a successful crossing. 'We were at 1,200ft and there below us the canal and river lay like silver, instantly recognizable. Orchards and woods lay as darker patches on a dark and foreign soil. "It's all right now, Fred, I can see where we are," I said. I thought that it all looked so exactly like the sand-table model that I had the strange feeling I had been there before. I took off the flaps for a moment to slow our headlong descent and to ensure we had sufficient height. I put them back on as we shot towards the line of trees over which I had to pass, not by 50ft or we should overshoot and be crushed as we hit the embankment which I knew was at the end of our field.

'I had to just miss and scrape over the tree-tops as we deployed the parachute brake specially fitted to the rear of the glider in order to shorten our landing run to the minimum. Up with the nose and then the heavy rumble of the main wheels as we touched down a few minutes after midnight close to the river bridge. "You are in the right place, sir," I shouted to Lieutenant Fox, who seemed both happy and surprised at the same time. With a drumming and crash of army boots, he and his men disappeared into the night.

'It was only much later that we learned that No. 5 had undershot by some 400 yards, while No. 4, due to the tug navigator's error, was ten miles away, busy capturing a bridge on the wrong river. Realizing their error they were later to fight their way through the night to our bridge, an astonishing feat of skill and determination in itself.'

Major John Howard's small group scrambled out of their gliders and charged for the bridge. A white phosphorus grenade was thrown at the pill-box guarding the approaches, quickly followed by a grenade through a gun port. There was no time for the bridge guard to deploy fully, although the German NCO in charge did manage to get off a burst of machine-gun fire, killing Lt Brotheridge, the first British soldier to die on D-Day. The bridge was in Allied hands within minutes, the Royal Engineers then searching for and dismantling its demolition charges.

David Wood and his men flew in Glider No. 3. 'Quite suddenly, one of the pilots shouted, "Christ! There's the bridge," and we were descending for a rough and bumpy landing at about 90 m.p.h. with the skids throwing up sparks from flints in the ground. We thought they were rounds of tracer and that we were already under fire. The impact of landing broke the glider's back and I was pitched out through the side. I collected myself and my canvas bucket with its grenades still intact, which says something for the boys who designed the safety factor in those grenades. I reported to John Howard and pushed on across the road to clear the inner defences.

'The enemy had by this time come to life and Don Brotheridge was killed as he led his platoon on the far side of the Canal bridge. We were all a bit dazed but acted more or less automatically. There was a good deal too much firing and shouting, which is fairly typical of troops in action for the first time. I heard the success signals "Ham and Jam" on the radio before being sent for by my company commander. As I went towards him in the dark I was hit in the leg by a burst of fire, which also caught my platoon sergeant and my runner. I regret to say there were no heroics, although I had heard about folk who can run around on only one leg. I found I simply fell down and couldn't get up. My platoon medical orderly gave me a shot of morphia, applied a rifle splint and found my flask in my hip pocket. I always claim that I lasted 25 minutes in action, but I really cannot be sure how long it was.'

With both bridges in Allied hands, Major Howard and his small band dug in to await reinforcements. These were to come from Brigadier Nigel Poett's 5th Parachute Brigade. This brigade had been given the tasks of consolidating the capture of the two bridges and establishing a bridgehead both for further glider landings and against German counter-attacks. They were to be reinforced by Commando units from Lord Lovat's 1st Special Service (Commando) Brigade landing on 'Sword' beach, west of Ouistreham, six miles away, just after dawn.

Brigadier Poett hit the ground twenty minutes after midnight, but his brigade was well scattered. Strong westerly winds had carried 5th Parachute Brigade's pathfinders well away from their designated drop zone and over to the east. With no time to march back they set up their beacons where they were, with the result that the brigade main force, their aircraft harassed by anti-aircraft fire, landed well to the east and were unable to get back to the bridges before German infantry with armoured support began to probe Major Howard's defences. The battalion detailed to reinforce Howard's group, the 7th Parachute Battalion, could muster only 300 men to support the defenders at the bridges. This was just enough for the moment, and as the night wore on more 7th Battalion paratroopers arrived, trickling in alone or in small groups, obeying the old military dictum of 'when in doubt, head for the sound of the gunfire'.

One of those to drop with the 7th Battalion was Private Bill

'Ernie' Elvin, a member of 4 Platoon, 'B' Company. 'For me, D-Day started in the late afternoon of 5 June, when we boarded trucks at our concentration area on Salisbury Plain. As our convoy passed through the villages, groups of people waved us farewell. Some of the women were in tears; they had guessed that something big was about to begin. We arrived at Fairford in the early evening and were taken to our planes, which were four-engined Stirlings, twenty Paras to each plane. All our kit was unloaded and we then had parachutes issued.

'We looked like a lot of little Michelin men as we carried all our weapons and gear on our fronts. On our backs, of course, was a parachute. Being only 5ft 4in. I was as broad as I was long, carrying as much equipment as I weighed myself. With our faces blackened we settled down on the floor of the plane for the trip to France. If an officer had said to me, "You cannot go," I would have cried my eyes out, and so would many of my mates. We were all green, having never been in action before, but we all wanted to have a go.'

Another member of 'B' Company was Sergeant Bob Tanner: 'I joined the Parachute Regiment from the Royal Tank Regiment. Although an officer came round and explained what joining the Paras entailed, the hardships, training and relentless exercises, I did not catch on at the time. First and foremost was a desire to get away from ruddy Catterick Camp. My whole tank crew volunteered, and as far as I know, only two of us survived the war. I realized that I would be losing the protection of all that armour plating, but the horrors of seeing burned tanks and crews soon made me realize how lucky I was.

'Then came the day of reckoning – D-Day. The airfield, fitting chutes, checking equipment, last-minute instructions, the talk by our CO, Lt-Colonel Pine-Coffin, going to the toilets (they did a roaring trade). Some of us in "B" Company carried rubber dinghies for crossing the Caen Canal in the event of the bridge being blown. Last minutes to blacken faces and then emplane ... thinking about it all still gives me the willies! Engines started and finally we began to move. The plane seemed to be taking a long time before we lifted off. There was not much to see inside a darkened aircraft fuselage, and each man had his own thoughts. I remember deciding that I was going to come back. Although thoughts of death and injury cropped up, I made my mind up. I was coming back.'

The majority of the battalion was lifted to France in converted Stirling bombers. Joe Bedford was a sergeant rear-gunner in a Stirling of 620 Squadron. 'Our aircraft for the night was coded QS-T. We took off from Fairford in Gloucestershire at 2330 hrs on the 5th with a load of twenty-four paratroops for a dropping zone near Caen. As we crossed the south coast the cloud was seven-tenths with a bright moon above. A few miles out in the Channel there was a gap in the clouds and I could see hundreds of ships heading towards France.

'We crossed the French coast, descending to about 800ft, and were met with a hail of light flak which continued all the way to the DZ. I fired back at quite a few but I don't know whether I hit anything. I saw one aircraft shot down which exploded on hitting the ground, and in the few seconds of light caused by the explosion, I saw paratroops going down all around us. One stick was just above my aircraft and just to starboard. I still don't know how we missed them. We made our drop at about 0130 hrs on 6 June, climbed away and made our way home without further incident, although we had to make deviations to avoid other aircraft as the sky was a bit congested that night. We landed back at Fairford after a four-hour trip.'

Private Elvin recalls his first operational jump: 'Stirlings were large and heavy planes and it was just like riding in a double-decker bus, only not so comfortable. To get out of the plane we had to waddle to the rear and drop out of a large hole shaped like a coffin. There was plenty of back-chat and we all had something to say – excitement and nervous tension, I guess.

'When we got near the dropping zone it was a case of "Red light on; Hook up; Get ready to jump." The engines throttled back and it was Green light on "Go" and we were out and floating down over France. It was so silent, only the noises of the plane's engines going away from us. Where was the war? Where were the Germans? Then I looked down ... Where was the land?

'All I could see below me was water. I panicked and set off the air-levers on my Mae-West jacket under my parachute harness.

Suddenly there was I, being dragged over the water by my parachute, unable to release myself from the harness. Luckily one of my section was close by and he waded over and cut me free. I was then able to stand up waist-deep in water. We had landed in the flooded Dives valley.'

The flooding of the Dives valley had been noted by reconnaissance but the extent of it was not so easy to calculate once bushes and grasses had started to grow on the flooded plains. Many men, like Sergeant Tanner, found themselves totally alone when they landed. 'I didn't know where I was, apart from somewhere in Normandy. Although it was only minutes before I located our chaps, it seemed like eternity. I heard bugles going, then a noise, and I froze for a second or two. Was it ours or theirs? If theirs, I had to shoot them – would I be able to do it? I cocked my rifle in readiness and it seemed to me that the sound was deafening, till a good old Cockney voice bawled out, "What bleedin' unit are you in?" I can't explain the relief on hearing that voice. We eventually met up with others and finally made the Canal bridge, which by then was in our hands.'

Throughout that night small groups of paratroopers were roaming over the Ranville heights and the plain beyond, desperately looking for their own units, or setting off alone in search of their objectives. Having been released from his harness, Ernie Elvin found himself in just such a situation. 'There were six of us in the water, so we made our way to dry ground, which turned out to be a road. When we got there we had to make up our minds which way to go. We had no idea where we were or where the other members of our plane-load had dropped. It was pitch black and silent, like being in another world. We chose a direction and set off in file, not knowing where we were heading. We had not gone far when an order was given in German and two bursts of machine-gun fire and grenades were directed at us, then silence. I had dropped to the ground, my heart thumping, thinking that after all the hard training I had done I was now going to be killed without seeing a German. I had a grenade in my hand but did not throw it as the Germans had disappeared into thin air. I guess they were as startled as us and just as green.

'When we came to our senses there were only three of us left.

Where the other three had gone we did not know; their bodies were not there so they must have scattered in the confusion. The three of us who were left, all privates, decided to head in the opposite direction from the one we had been following, away from where the Germans were going. Had we continued with our original plan we would have ended up at Cabourg and been either killed or taken prisoner. In the event, we carried on and came to a farm just off the road. The buildings were partly concealed and there was a faint light showing in a downstairs room. The occupants had, no doubt, been awakened by the firing. We now had a chance to find out where we were, so I knocked on the door and the two others kept me covered with their weapons in case a German came to the door. Nobody answered but a face appeared at the window. It was a man with a moustache and glasses and he shook his fist and gestured at us to go away. We did not argue.'

Alan Schofield of Tasmania was a flight sergeant with 620 Squadron and also recalls the drop. 'We dropped our paratroops at 0058 hrs. I remember fierce flak, a huge explosion lighting up the night sky, revealing aircraft everywhere and parachutes descending above and around us like falling snow. I expected to find remnants of parachutes in the aircraft but only found shell holes caused by fragments. I know that our Flight Commander, a Canadian, Squadron Leader Pettit, was shot down that night. His aircraft was coned by searchlights and seen going down in flames.' This heavy flak, combined with the high winds, dispersed the aircraft and gave many of the paratroopers a scattered drop.

The 5th Brigade suffered nearly 100 casualties in the drop alone, and over 400 men were missing when they assembled next day, though most of the missing trailed in later. While 7 Para were mustering at the bridges, 13 Para began clearing the drop zone of obstacles ready for the arrival of the Airlanding Brigade. They also cleared the enemy out of Ranville, while 12 Para, though 50 per cent under strength, made for the brigade concentration area, the high ground south of Ranville, where they dug in to await the inevitable German counter-attack.

Lance-Corporal George Price was one of those who jumped with the 12th (Yorkshire) Parachute Battalion: 'I had joined the

12th Battalion in September 1943, having volunteered from the Royal Armoured Corps. I was twenty years old and looking for some adventure and a bit of excitement and the prospect of parachuting appealed to me. I was a member of the Anti-Tank Section of Headquarter Company attached to "C" Company for D-Day. My main weapon was the "Projector Infantry, Anti-Tank", or PIAT. This was a heavy spring-operated weapon, firing a hollow-charge round. It was very heavy, cumbersome, and, like others in the brigade, I landed in the wrong place.

'Here I was, lying on my back in a field in Normandy, taking part in the liberation of Europe, with only a couple of hand grenades in my belt. In the drop I had lost all my equipment. My rifle and ammunition, my PIAT and food, were somewhere in the orchard behind me – and I was lost. I scrambled out of my harness, got to my feet and took stock of my surroundings. Although it was dark the sky to the west was aglow with light from the fires in the coastal towns that were being bombed by the RAF.

'I could see the orchard a short distance away and thought of my kit bag. I could see figures all around me and they all seemed to be going in the same direction, so I joined them hoping that I would eventually reach my allotted position. Dawn was just breaking when we approached Ranville, having been dropped some four miles from the drop zone.'

Also jumping with 'C' Company, 12th Parachute Battalion that night was Ron Dixon of the Signal Platoon: 'Fortunately, I dropped on the right drop zone at Ranville, but I appeared to be the only person on it. I hadn't a clue where I was, only that I was in France and for me the war had just begun. Luckily, I linked up with our Company Commander, Major Stephens, and within minutes we arrived at the battalion rendezvous. We moved off some time later with only half the battalion, the remainder having dropped some distance away by mistake. We reached our objective, the Bas de Ranville village, around dawn, where an elderly French lady came from her farmhouse, which was on the land where we were digging in. Not being able to understand the French language very well, I could only guess that she was asking who we were and what we were doing. In the little French I knew, I told her that we were British and this was the invasion. She went back into her house and minutes later came out with a jug of milk and some bread. I had a block of chocolate in my camouflaged denison smock, which I gave to her.'

The original rendezvous for this battalion was a quarry on the Cabourg–Caen road. Those who got there found that very few of the battalion had arrived and, not being able to wait, the commanding officer ordered those who were there to start out for their first objective, the village of Le Bas de Ranville.

At 0330 hrs Divisional Headquarters came in by 'Horsa' glider, bringing the Divisional Commander, Major-General Gale, more ammunition and the all-important anti-tank guns. The German defenders were by now fully aware that a major parachute assault was taking place and began to send out fighting patrols and armoured cars.

Colonel Hans Von Luck of the 125th Panzer Grenadier Regiment recalls that night. 'Our position lay east of the River Orne and the Caen Canal. The bridges there were defended by a "second-rank" company, whose task was to make sure that Commandos or the French Resistance would not blow the bridge. Our division – 21st Panzer – was in reserve with a strict order not to move unless released by Army Group "B". However, I made a counter-attack on my own responsibility to support two companies of my regiment who were on a night exercise with dummy ammunition when airborne people dropped on their position.

'I am quite sure that had we been able to make a counter-attack at once, in the direction of the coast and Pegasus Bridge, it would have been successful.

'On D+2, part of my battle group met with Major John Howard – a very good friend of mine today – at Escoville, where he lost quite a large number of his company.'

Lieutenant David Wood recalls one of the first German probes: 'The enemy sent two armoured half-tracks down to the Canal bridge to find out what was happening; one was knocked out by a PIAT. There was a magnificent firework display as the ammo in it exploded and 7 Para thought we were still having a hell of a battle to capture the bridge. The commander of the local garrison, who had been out on the tiles for the night, returned across the river bridge in a staff car with an escort, which we shot up. Wounded and captured, he asked the MO to finish him off because his honour had been lost, but the MO would not oblige. Finally, the Germans sailed a gunboat down the Canal from Caen where it was swiftly despatched by a well aimed PIAT round.'

Some of the heavy equipment was now coming in and landing on the drop zones. Frank 'Snowy' May was a flight sergeant in 295 Squadron, flying an Albemarle tug towing a 'Horsa' glider. 'We were to tow a glider carrying a Jeep and field gun. Six aircraft took off half an hour before the main force to prepare the landing zone, but none of their gliders made it to the LZ. We took off at 0130 hrs on 6 June. As we approached the French coast I confirmed with the navigator that we were spot-on track. We verified our position by the mouth of the River Orne, and our LZ was on the east bank. There were no beacons to be seen, but thanks to the model of the LZ it was obvious we had arrived. I confirmed this with the glider pilot, and we all wished him luck as he cast off. As he neared the ground a beacon came on, so he must have been one of the first to land on that epic day.'

Another member of 295 Squadron was Flying Officer Ronald Sloan. 'My crew and I were not directly involved in the night-time operations of 6 June, and when we went into breakfast we knew the invasion had started, as a huge main glider force was waiting to be towed off later in the day. The main runway was crowded with stationary gliders, and at mid-day we were briefed to tow in these gliders to a landing ground in the Bréville and Ranville area.

'My glider was quickly airborne and in the "high tow" position before we were halfway down the runway, and we climbed away to take up a position about 100 yards behind and slightly to one side of the previous combination. Throughout the flight, which lasted about two hours, we were in constant conversation with our glider pilot through the telephone link in the tow rope, and we gathered their airborne infantry had a relatively smooth trip.

'We followed the glider stream across the French coast and

saw for the first time the smoke and flashes of a battlefield. The glider pilots had their own maps and knew exactly when they proposed to release. Suddenly across the intercom came the farewell Irish message, "Thanks for a smashing tow – we're off now." Before I could say "Good luck" I felt 8EA surge forward as the rope trailed free. We flew forward another minute for the purpose of getting rid of our tow rope, away from gliders which were spiralling down like huge moths seeking a spot to land. Our rear gunner gave a call, "I think he's landed OK, but it's chaos down there." Some gliders had piled into each other, some were on top of each other, and there was smoke everywhere. Clear of the dropping zone I pulled the release handle and the rope fell free.

'Back at base the airfield looked different. It was almost empty of "Horsa" gliders which had been part of the scenery ever since we had arrived.'

By the time this glider force arrived on the afternoon of D-Day, the battle around Ranville was taking shape, but the 3rd Parachute Brigade, commanded by Brigadier James Hill, had been having problems from the moment they landed. This brigade had three main tasks. First, and most vital, was the elimination of the Merville Battery, a task given to the 9th Battalion. Second, they had to secure the high ground at Le Plein, a task given to the 1st Canadian Parachute Battalion. Third, they had to destroy the four bridges over the River Dives at Troarn, Bures, Robehomme and Varaville. Having achieved all this the brigade was to concentrate close to Ranville in the area of the Bois de Bavant.

Among those to drop with the Brigade HQ was Gunner David King, a signaller with 53 Air Landing Light Regiment equipped with 75mm field guns. Like many others that night, David King had a very wet landing. 'I managed to jump but my kitbag was whipped away and I landed on my back in a couple of feet of water. I tried to keep my head above water and to release my parachute, and my Sten gun which was under my parachute harness, was swept away. I tried to feel for it for a while with no success and eventually managed to reach dry land. There I was, a twenty-year-old soldier, behind enemy lines, with eight magazines of Sten ammo in my pouches and no gun, no radio and no rations! After wandering about for what seemed like hours but was probably only minutes, I heard someone approaching. I was so relieved to hear him say the password for the drop, "Punch", I quickly replied, "Judy". This turned out to be an officer who carried a revolver and a Sten gun and he kindly gave me the Sten. Eventually we met other Paras, some heading for Le Mesnil – my target.

'We reached Le Mesnil without too much bother. There was no sign of my officer or fellow signaller and I was put as No. 2 on a Bren gun. My officer arrived that afternoon, followed by my fellow signaller, struggling in with the two heavy accumulators needed to operate our radio. He wasn't very pleased to discover that I had no radio to attach them to. However, a supply drop during the evening replaced the radio, and we were back in business.'

The Merville Battery still lies amid farmland south of the resort of Franceville-Plage. In June 1944 the concrete casements, six feet thick, enclosed four heavy 155mm artillery pieces, with a garrison of 200 men entrenched to defend the guns. These were protected by minefields, barbed wire, and fixed-line machine guns, and their living quarters underground had concrete head cover against bombing. The task of destroying the battery was given to Lt-Colonel Otway and 600 men of the 9th Parachute Battalion.

Otway had found an area near Newbury in Berkshire that resembled Merville and, having had the landscape bulldozed into the appropriate contours, exercised his battalion endlessly in the assault plan. The battery would be bombed by a Lancaster force just before the assault. Then, the minefields having been gapped by Royal Engineer sappers, the battery would be assaulted by the entire battalion. As they went in, another volunteer force, 50 men in 3 gliders, would crash-land right on top of the battery position. Finally, if all else failed, the battery would be engaged by the guns of the fleet. This was a fine, if complicated, plan and it went wrong from the start.

The battalion had a terrible drop, being scattered widely across the flooded valley of the Dives, where many men were drowned. Some men fell thirty miles from their proper drop zone, though Lt-Colonel Otway and his batman landed right by a German headquarters and were nearly captured while still in their parachutes. When Lt-Colonel Otway reached the battalion rendezvous he found he had only 150 men and none of the special equipment he needed except a few Bangalore torpedoes for clearing wire. Even so, the Colonel decided to attack immediately.

One of those to jump with Lt-Colonel Otway was Private S. F. Capon, in 12 Platoon of 'C' Company. 'Our drop was set for 0030 hrs, 6 June. It wasn't long before we heard the order: "We are approaching the coast of France", and suddenly our aircraft was sent into a turmoil with German anti-aircraft fire raining on us. We were hurled from port to starboard before despatch, when a voice shouted, "Stand by the doors – Get ready! Red light ... Green light ... GO!" I had always jumped to perfection but this time I wondered what the hell was happening and fell out like a sack of coal. As I jumped I could see the amber glow from the shells exploding around the aircraft. After a disastrous exit I floated down to the best landing I had ever made.

'About a hundred yards further on a group of about six men, including Lieutenant Mike Dowling of "B" Company, were lying in a patch of stinging nettles trying to find their bearings. We moved on along a narrow road when suddenly the noise of a lorry was heard. It was full of Germans so we laid low. When the lorry had disappeared we crossed the road to be greeted by a Pathfinder, and we joined the few men who had arrived at the rendezvous. The final number reached 150.'

On arriving at the assembly area near the battery, Otway found that some of his men had already arrived and had cleared a few tracks through the minefields, crawling out in the dark to dig up the mines with their bayonets. The attack went in as timed, and the 9th Battalion took the Merville Battery by storm, capturing thirty of the garrison and killing the rest.

Private Capon again: 'We arrived at the outskirts of the Merville battery where all was very quiet. We advanced to the assembly point and laid low, facing the four gun emplacements that we could now see. My Platoon was to capture the No. 1 gun. The thirty-two men under the command of Lieutenant Alan Jefferson, who had trained day and night back in England for this task force, were now reduced to Alan Jefferson, Eric Bedford, Harold Walker, Frank Delsignore, Les Cartwright, me, and perhaps one other. Seven men to do the job of thirty-two. This left Mike Dowling with a group to take No. 2 gun, and another group to take No. 3, and likewise No. 4. However, all was not lost. We had three gliders with fifty men of "A" Company, all parachutists, a *coup-de-main* force to land on the battery and cause havoc and maybe even take it.

'We laid low awaiting the gliders. The first one appeared, only to land well away from the target in an eleven o'clock position. The second glider hovered over the battery, and suddenly the German machine-gun tracer bullets raked the glider which veered behind us in a seven o'clock position, never to take part in the attack, though the survivors joined us later. The third glider never arrived at all.

'Our Colonel couldn't wait. Time was running out and the guns had to be silenced before the seaborne troops arrived. All eyes were facing the guns and awaiting the final words from Otway. He shouted, "Get in!" and Jefferson blew his little hunting horn, which he always did in training. Two blows on the horn and he fell wounded.

'I ran with my mates across the uneven ground, zig-zagging and firing as we ran. To my left I heard explosions and shouts of "Mines!" but I ran to my target. Within seconds I arrived with three others at the rear of the gun. Left standing with me were Eric Bedford, Harold Walker and Frank Delsignore – my mates, just four of us. Eric was now in charge and we threw grenades into the large emplacement. After the din and gunfire it seemed eerie, but after the exploding grenades, voices could be heard within the emplacement and the German prisoners pushed each other from the left-hand enclosure within the gun, across the corridor and out towards the opposite wing to us, with our guns pointing towards them. The last bespectacled German was shaking with fear.

'Colonel Otway arrived with some of the men he had kept in reserve and we proceeded out of the battery only to come under enemy fire from a machine-gun on the perimeter. After a few bursts, and on seeing the prisoners we had, the crew surrendered. Handing over the prisoners to Colonel Otway, we proceeded to pull out our wounded. The badly wounded were put on sledges, which I later learned were for pulling ammunition. We carried the less seriously wounded. In this my partner was Sergeant Paddy Jenkins and Frank Delsignore did the same with Harold Walker.'

While Lt-Colonel Otway and his men were taking the Merville Battery, Lt-Colonel Alistair Pearson and his men of the 8th Battalion were making for their objectives, the bridges over the River Dives.

Transported by Dakota aircraft, this battalion was widely scattered by high winds and enemy anti-aircraft fire. Lt-Colonel Pearson could only muster 150 men and had only one Royal Engineer instead of two troops of sappers to blow the bridges, and it was not until 1000 hrs on D-Day that the last bridge at Troarn was put out of commission after a Jeep sortie behind enemy lines.

To support the troops of 8th Parachute Battalion, landing by parachute, heavier equipment had to be flown in by glider. Sergeant Watts had begun his military career in 1934 as a bandsman, and ten years later he was flying a glider on D-Day. 'At 11 p.m. on 5 June the six gliders took off from Blakehill Farm. The C-47 Dakota tug got us to the correct area, but there was no sign of the SAS lit cross. However, we released and glided down to about 30ft above the ground and then put the large landing light on to see clearly where the telegraph poles were. We landed safely at 1 a.m. on 6 June, only losing part of a wing. About five minutes later the parachutists landed and escorted the Jeep and trailer to Troarn to blow up the bridges.' Sergeant Watts stayed with 8 Para for two days, fighting alongside the paratroopers, before making his way back to the beaches.

The Canadian Parachute Battalion, making up the 3rd Parachute Brigade, was widely scattered in the drop. Of the 35 aircraft lifting the battalion, 16 dropped their parachutists more than two miles away from the planned drop zone. The plan for the Canadians on D-Day also involved prior *coup-de-main* operations to be mounted by their 'C' Company. 'C' Company was to seize and secure Varaville, especially the two pill-boxes and a trench system that overlooked Drop Zone V, the battalion's main landing area, and a 75mm gun on the far side of the DZ must also be destroyed. Once this had been done the company was to proceed to a bridge over the River Dives and destroy it.

This battalion too had problems in the drop, as John Madden of 'C' Company relates: 'In training we had encountered defective hatch catches for the cover of the jump hole on the Albemarle. The doors had a habit of falling shut in mid-stick, so before the "off" on D-Day, I spoke to the pilot and told him that he must not take any parachutists back to England. If the hatch slammed shut while we were jumping, he was to circle round and drop the rest. Well, after the first 6 got out, the hatch slammed down. The pilot subsequently dropped the last 4 of my men, but twenty miles from where he dropped me. Of the 4, 2 were killed and 2 were taken prisoner.

'At the time I was surprised by our wide dispersal. Never mind, enough men landed on target to achieve our objective, and those who dropped astray helped to create confusion in the minds of the enemy. I am the only officer of "C" Company still alive. Two were killed on D-Day, one was killed after the Rhine Crossing, one died about four years ago.'

After 'C' Company had secured the DZ at Varaville, the main battalion drop would take place, with 'A' Company protecting the left flank of the 9th Battalion taking the Merville Battery. 'B' Company would ensure the destruction of the Robehomme bridge and HQ Company would secure the drop zone itself. However, as with the other drops that night, the battalion was widely scattered. To compound their problems they were dropped at the same time as an RAF bombing force attacked the Merville Battery. These bombers over-shot the Merville Battery and dropped their bombs too far inland, catching the Canadian paratroopers as they landed. Despite all these setbacks the Canadians managed to complete their tasks before being reinforced by men of the 1st Commando Brigade coming from 'Sword' beach.

Captain John Madden again: 'As the wind dispersed the early-morning mist, I could see a faint line in the distance, which resolved itself into the Normandy coast. It was 0500 hrs and we were a mere 1,200 yards from the beaches. I knew we were caught on the coastal strip being prepared for the seaborne invasion, and could see the flashes of gunfire from the distant warships. Following this came the roar of aircraft, bombs showered in astride and behind us.

'The entire coastline was blotted out by clouds of smoke and we scratched pitiful little holes in the earth. Five minutes after the bomb line passed inland a new terror threatened. Low-flying fighters strafed our area. One of the men had a bullet pass through the stock of his rifle as he held it between his hands. Branches were cut down all around us, yet we survived.'

While the Canadians were completing their tasks, Ernie Elvin and his pals were still trying to get to the battalion rendezvous point, having hidden in a barn all night. Once it was daylight he and the other two set off again. 'We could see that each side of the road was flooded, but our only way was to go up the road and into the water. So up the road we went and after about a mile we could hear firing in the distance and knew that a battle was taking place. We then came to a driveway leading to a large house about 400 yards away. At the house we could see what appeared to be German soldiers on guard, so it was back into the water to make our way past, hoping that we had not been seen. Fortunately nothing happened, so we made our way back to the road. About five minutes later we came across a Frenchman and his wife coming down the road.

'The only thing we could understand was that there were no Germans in the direction we were going, so we carried on for a while until we saw men moving in the distance. We moved cautiously towards them until we saw that they were Paras. They turned out to be men of the 1st Canadian Para Battalion who were about to withdraw after blowing the Robehomme bridge and using it as a road block. So into the water we went again, and holding on to the debris of the bridge, we crossed to the other side of the river and withdrew with the Canadians.

'As we withdrew we could see signs of a battle; some Paras were hanging from the high-tension wires strung from pylon to pylon, their chutes caught in the wires from which they had been unable to free themselves, and so there they had died. Late that evening we ended up at the 3rd Para Brigade HQ at Le Mesnil and were put into defence positions around the HQ. It was a very noisy night, and by midnight on D-Day I had still not joined up with my battalion. On the morning of D+1 we were loaded onto a Jeep to take a very hairy journey to the 5th Para Brigade HQ. The two brigades had not yet joined up and there were still German positions between the two brigades.

'I got back to my unit, 4 Platoon "B" Company, 7th Battalion at Ranville at about 1130 hrs on D+1. They were dug-in opposite Ranville church. In the distance I could see the wrecked gliders and the Germans were beginning to infiltrate them. We were being shelled spasmodically. I shared a trench with Private Bushell, who told me what had happened on the west side of the bridges over the Orne and the Canal. Several men were missing from the platoon, but I was back where I should have been, having taken a roundabout route, and I felt safe with my old mates.'

Not every paratrooper was an infantryman. Among the men jumping were engineers, signallers and medics. One of the medics was Lewis 'Jack' Tarr, a member of 195 Para Field Ambulance, who jumped at 9 o'clock on the morning of 6 June. 'We landed near Ranville and what is now Pegasus Bridge in the second wave. We found the glider with our Jeep and trailer and started out for Longueval and our rendezvous. There were soldiers everywhere and, quite frankly, we were all like a herd of sheep.

'Our main problem was the snipers. We were right in their line. Close by was an officer manning a machine gun. He was wounded later and I was one of those who had to go and get him in. All those around him had been killed, picked off by the snipers. There was a wood nearby, giving them really good cover and they came in after dark, moving from tree to tree, well camouflaged. The only way to bring them down was to aim carefully directly at them, which one of our corporals did – shooting a sniper right through the forehead. The sniper was, like us, only about twenty-three or twenty-four years old.'

6th Airborne Division beat off an ever-heavier series of attacks by the Germans throughout D-Day. Luckily, most of the heavy equipment had arrived by glider during the day, and with their anti-tank guns and some help from naval gunfire they were able to hold on and even improve their defences until joined in the late afternoon by two more battalions of their third element, the 6th Airlanding Brigade. Lord Lovat's 1st Commando Brigade had also arrived in the early afternoon, fighting their way from 'Sword' to arrive just two-and-a-half minutes late for the rendezvous at what is now Pegasus Bridge at Bénouville.

Philip Pritchard of 6 Commando was one of the first seaborne troops across the Caen Canal bridge. 'We went through a coastal village into open country, until we came to the Canal bridges, which we doubled across as best we could with our heavy loads. I can remember the bullets striking the ironwork of both bridges, which were not too far apart. As I ran across one of the bridges, I stopped near a dead British officer who had a Colt .45 automatic pistol attached to his neck with a lanyard. I broke the lanyard by putting my boots on it and secured the pistol in an inner pocket of my BD blouse. The pistol came in very handy later on. This officer was one of the glider party that had landed during the night and did such good work in capturing the bridges intact.'

The airlanding battalions brought with them many of the division's heavy weapons, including field artillery, anti-tank guns and even Tetrarch light tanks. Lance-Corporal Price, who had lost his PIAT while landing with the 12th Battalion, was more grateful for the heavy equipment than most. 'I was given a PIAT and joined by the other two members of my section. So, fully equipped, we made our way to Le Bas de Ranville, and took up our positions in the corner of a wood. A PIAT and three men may not seem much of a deterrent to German Tiger tanks, but on the contrary this was quite capable of disabling a tank when used efficiently. However, the main object was for the three of us to make contact with the pilot and co-pilot of a glider which contained a Jeep, a 6-pounder anti-tank gun and limber, and within an hour of setting up our position, a Jeep, gun and limber joined us, and as a crew of five we became an even more efficient anti-tank section. In fact, after a while a Tiger tank came down the field in front of us and promptly received two shells from us – one in the belly and one in the turret.

'Things were pretty hot up until then, with machine-gun fire and mortar shells landing all around. A great many lads had been killed or wounded, but so far we had been lucky.'

Bill Higgs, another glider pilot, who flew an anti-tank gun in on D-Day, remembers the tank actions. 'There was still some action in Ranville and we managed to get our gun to it, and were dug-in and camouflaged by about 2 a.m. on 6 June 1944. We encountered a Frenchman at daybreak on a bike with a long loaf of bread under his arm. When he saw my 2nd Pilot and I, with black faces and helmets he thought we were Germans and started to pull out his pass to show us. I spoke the little bit of French I knew – "*Je suis Anglais*" – and he nearly died of fright and rushed away, cycling off to the village like a man possessed.

'I had been watching the skyline area towards Caen, from where we were expecting the enemy armour to come and eventually the enemy tanks and half-tracks crossed into our right angle of anti-tank guns, with infantry extended in front of them. This is something that will stick in my mind for ever. As if someone had blown a whistle, all the guns opened up, and in a short time all the armoured vehicles were blown up or on fire. I feel sure that the enemy had no idea that we had that sort of anti-tank defence on the ground from the night landing, and I think it must have made the Germans delay sending more armour in, thus giving us a chance to secure the bridges.

'After we attacked the infantry with our Brens, the enemy withdrew, but later, having located our positions, gave us a pounding with mortars. During the tank "shoot-out", one of our gun positions came under fire, and as the anti-tank gunner had been hit, "Chalky" White got to the gun and knocked a tank out, for which he received the DCM. Poor "Chalky" was later killed at Arnhem, and I got a Mention-in-Despatches.'

Glider pilot Sgt Roy Howard was also relieved to see the glider force landing: 'At 2100 hrs on 6 June the main glider force came into the Ranville area. Our task was complete and we decided to go home, our orders being to return to the UK as soon as practicable in order to be ready to fly in a further load if necessary. We took our leave of Major Howard and walked along the road to Ouistreham, snatching as much fitful sleep as the 15-inch shells which HMS *Warspite* was pumping into Le Havre would allow. As we arrived at the beach a Ju-88 was shot down, crashing some 30 yards from us, where it continued to explode and burn for some time. Later Colonel Murray and the glider pilots from the main landing force arrived. We all waded out to the LCIs and arrived back in Newhaven at 0630 hrs on 8 June.'

As well as bringing in heavy equipment, the airlanding battalions also brought in essential items such as fuel, water and rations. One of those bringing the Airlanding Brigade was Sergeant Sidney Dodd, flying a 'Hamilcar' glider. 'On D-Day, 6 June, I was second pilot to Staff Sergeant White in Glider No. LA636. We landed in support of the gliders that had taken the bridges over the Orne and the Canal outside Caen. We were one of three "Hamilcars" that carried petrol and ammunition, the tails painted yellow for recognition. We landed safely, having to cut through poles which the Germans had erected to stop us. We didn't encounter much trouble, joined up at the bridge and when the seaborne troops arrived we were pulled out.' Sidney went on to fly at both Arnhem and the Rhine Crossing, and says: '. . . of the three operations, D-Day was the least demanding.'

The second wave of gliders flying in to the now secured landing zones carried 26 Tetrarch light tanks belonging to the 6th Airborne Reconnaissance Regiment. This was their first operation since formation in 1943, and here again D-Day did not go according to plan.

Corporal Charles Sheffield was with the Reconnaissance Regiment and recalls 6 June: 'We took off in the late afternoon, wondering what we were going to find over there. Most of us landed safely, and on leaving the glider I hitched up the three trailers to my tank. These contained petrol in the wheels and ammo in the large box between the wheels. We had very little opposition, just a few mortars a distance away, when suddenly the tank stopped. The driver did not know why so I slid out of the turret to the ground and found parachute cord and silk wound round the final drive. It was hard work cutting it off and, on moving forward, we came across the squadron leader having the same trouble.' So tangled with parachute cord were the tank tracks and sprockets that Corporal Sheffield was forced to use a blow-torch to burn it off before he could get away.

'At dawn on 7 June the regiment joined the 8th Para Battalion in the Bois de Bavent and set up a series of OPs watching the plain towards Troarn–Caen–Ranville–Escoville. We also sent bicycle patrols deep into enemy territory. Invaluable information was obtained and some very successful air strikes and bombardments by HMS *Mauritius* were directed on to enemy vehicle parks and armoured forming-up positions.'

Corporal A. Darlington was also in the Airborne Recce Regiment and recalls the preceding hours before embarking for France. 'We arrived at the airfield in the morning and were given a meal by the Air Force WAAF. We even had sugar in bowls and the best meal in years. WAAFs even refilled our water-bottles and gave us what, in the event, turned out to be a useless object – soap! This we termed the "Last Supper", and for many it was. We had been issued with a 48-hour emergency ration which when opened looked more like a child's compendium of games. Creamy-coloured dominoes turned out to be porridge with milk and sugar if reconstituted. The dice were tea, milk and sugar cubes.

'The landing was a roaring, twisting, bumping, skidding, from high speed to a dead stop, and we were all momentarily knocked out. The side door opened and the pilot looked in and shouted, "Sorry for the rough landing boys." I unstrapped, dashed out of the door to let the struts down for exit, only to find that the undercarriage no longer existed and parts of the wings were missing. The front was clear and the carrier engines were running. "All clear for exit, Sir, but the damned anchors are jammed!" I took the escape hatchet from the wall and after three or four good swipes, the carrier shot forward, the door opened and off they went. On leaving the glider, it settled down backwards and our Jeep anchor ropes were jammed also, so the hatchet came into action once more but the front edge of the exit had risen some two feet and the tail wheel was also torn off. The Jeep's front wheels could not reach the ground and we see-sawed on the edge with the chassis. I got out again, grasped the bumper so that the back wheels would drive the Jeep slowly forward, and then the front wheels would take over. I often wonder how I completed this feat of strength.'

As more and more heavy gliders swooped in, space on the landing zones ran out. Corporal Darlington continues: 'I saw two "Hamilcars" heading for the same space, and obviously they had seen each other because they tried to bank away from each other. One glider's wing tip turned the other over and it crashed sideways into the wood and the Tetrarch tank shot out of the front on impact. There was a mad dash over to it and the tank was upright, although it had somersaulted out of the glider. The crew was unstrapped and dragged out unconscious. They were strapped on the back of a passing tank's engine compartment with camouflage nets and retaining straps.

'The fields were hives of activity as gliders landed and unloaded. The problems, however, were not yet over, for as the tanks disembarked they made for cover, running over the parachutes left behind by the Paras. These 'chutes became a bigger hazard than the anti-invasion poles, for as the tanks ran over them, the tracks picked them up and they wrapped themselves tightly around the driving sprockets, bringing the tanks to a halt either by slewing the tank around or forcing it to a dead stop.'

Wally Grimshaw was present, with 6th Airborne Recce Regiment: 'I was the Troop-Sergeant of No. 1 Machine-Gun Troop in HQ Squadron. I rode a James motorcycle and led the way to the edge of the drop zone, dodging the mortar bombs which had started to fall on the DZ, as well as the odd bursts of MG fire.

'As we reached the shelter of the woods I saw one of the regiment's drop zone party, who explained that we were to rendezvous at the sawmills above Ranville. We cut through the woods until we met the main road and stopped for a quick "shuftie". We then came across a Jeep with four dead Gunners and saw they had caught a direct hit from one of the German mortar bombs. Further along the road we met some airborne medics who had some German medics working with them. I gave them the location of the bombed Jeep and a party went off to check.

'We drove through the woods and finally met up with the rest of my troop with the Troop Corporal and two pilots. I was then ordered to put out my guns as local protection, and within a few minutes engaged two six-wheeled armoured cars. After a few minutes' firing they retired down the hill, followed by one of "B" Squadron's recce troops. Our neighbours turned out to be the 1st Canadian Parachute Battalion, and I quickly liaised with them to make sure we did not receive any friendly "misses". A perimeter was being mapped out and after a few hours I went on a recce to a new position with one of the Para Battalions, the 12th I think, plus one of the Independent Para Companies. I had to select two front-line positions and one to cover the rear in case the position was overrun, because the Paras were a little thin on the ground and we had to hold this particular front.

'We used to have a "Hate Hitler" 30 minutes daily, when we fired all our weapons on our front, receiving a similar load of high explosive back in return. It was during one of these days I was wounded and back-loaded to England.'

By midnight on D-Day the 6th Airborne Division, reinforced by 1st Commando Brigade, was firmly in control of Ranville and the villages round about. Their introduction to Normandy had not been without difficulties. High winds and enemy anti-aircraft fire had broken up their aircraft and glider formations. Seven of the transport aircraft had been lost or shot down, and twenty-two gliders were missing, some having ditched in the sea. More than a third of the glider pilots had been killed or wounded and a third of the paratroopers were still missing, roaming the countryside looking for their units. The division suffered some 800 casualties, and many men had been captured.

On the other hand, all the divisional objectives had been achieved. The Orne and Caen Canal bridges had been taken, those over the Dives destroyed. The Merville Battery never fired a shot. The British Airborne and Commandos now held the heights above Ranville and had linked up with the seaborne troops. Though still thin on the ground, they were digging in to hold what they had taken against whatever enemy force would come against the eastern flank. Over to the west, in the fields and orchards of the Cotentin Peninsula, the parachute and glider troops of the two American airborne divisions were setting about the same tasks.

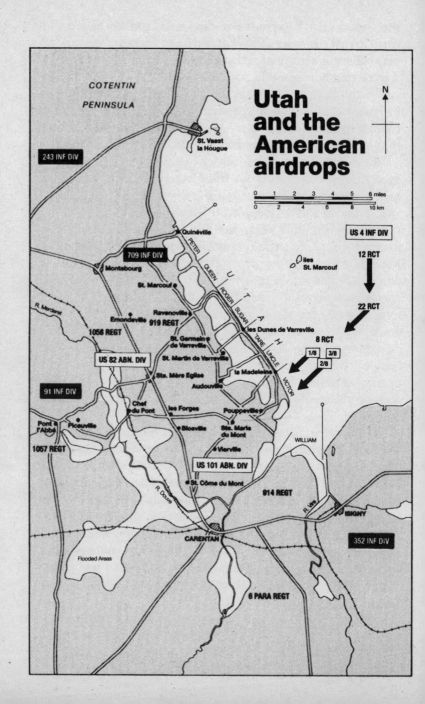

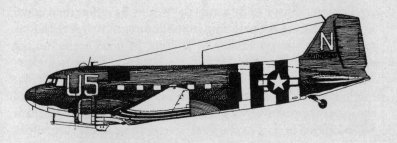

—————CHAPTER SIX—————

The American Airdrops

'Airborne, always.'
Sgt D. Zane Schlemmer
508th Parachute Infantry Regiment
82nd Airborne Division

The two American airborne divisions which flew into Normandy on the night of 5/6 June were the 82nd (All-American) commanded by Major-General Matthew B. Ridgeway, and the 101st (the Screaming Eagles), commanded by Major-General Maxwell Taylor. These divisions were to land in the Cotentin Peninsula, south of the port of Cherbourg, in support of the American seaborne landings on 'Utah', which would come in at 0630 hrs on the east coast of the Cotentin. The combined force of the two American airborne divisions was about 13,500 men.

There had been considerable controversy over the decision to drop paratroopers in the Cotentin. The area was well defended by anti-aircraft guns and the ground had been rendered unsuitable for parachute landings by flooding and the erection of anti-invasion poles in every field suitable for glider landings. A further problem was the restricted terrain.

To avoid the anti-aircraft guns of Cherbourg, the transport aircraft would have to fly across the peninsula rather than down it, thus reducing the exit time from the aircraft to less than four minutes, so the possibility of landing in flood water or the sea was very high. The British Air Marshal, Trafford Leigh-Mallory, objected to a drop in the Cotentin on the grounds that the losses would be too severe, perhaps up to 70 per cent of all the men dropped. He was eventually overruled, though the plan was modified in part to allow for at least some of the difficulties he anticipated. The wild card here as elsewhere was the weather.

Ideally, for a successful drop paratroopers require a flat, open plain, without rivers, trees or man-made obstacles. The aircraft have to fly across this plain below 1,000 feet, upwind and at as slow a speed as possible, certainly not faster than 120 m.p.h., while the troopers jump out as speedily as possible, one after the other. The faster they can get out of the aircraft and the slower the aircraft is going at a low height, then the closer the troopers will be when they arrive on the ground, enabling them to assemble quickly in orderly groups and set about their tasks. This close grouping is particularly important when the drop is made at night. A parachute drop is simply one way of getting an infantry battalion into action. It is not supposed to scatter individual soldiers all over the landscape.

Up to this time the two American airborne divisions had had quite a different war. The 82nd, which contained the 505th, 507th and 508th Parachute Infantry Regiments (PIR), had been in action in Sicily where they had been severely scattered in the drop and had a very bad time. They later fought at Salerno on the Italian mainland. The 82nd were an experienced and fully trained formation which had received plenty of reinforcements and had plenty of know-how to back their training. The 101st, or the 'Screaming Eagles' as they came to be called, were a new formation made up of the 501st, 502nd and 506th Parachute Infantry Regiments, and their men would be going into action on D-Day for the first time. Each division consisted of three regiments, each of three battalions, roughly the equivalent of a British brigade, supported by airborne artillery, engineers and medical units. Their heavy equipment was carried in American

CG-4A 'Waco' gliders, or in British 'Horsa' gliders, for in the American as in the British airborne forces, men and equipment were delivered to the battlefield by glider as well as by parachute.

The German forces in the Cotentin Peninsula consisted of three infantry divisions, the 709th in the east, the 91st in the centre, and the 243rd on the west coast. The 709th and 243rd were second-rank formations, with plenty of men, although short of transport, but the 91st had received special anti-invasion training and equipment. The most formidable unit in the Peninsula was the German 6th Parachute Regiment, three battalions of tough and well trained young men whose average age was seventeen-and-a-half. These were commanded by a veteran paratroop officer, Colonel Friedrich August von der Heydte, hero of the German parachute assault on Crete in 1942. There was also a scratch tank formation, Panzer No. 100, equipped with obsolescent French tanks.

The 82nd's task on D-Day was to land around the small town of Ste-Mère-Eglise to seize and hold the crossroads there, and then seize or destroy the bridges over the River Merderet to secure the western flank of the invasion. The task of taking Ste-Mère-Eglise was given to the 505th Parachute Infantry Regiment of the 82nd, while the other two regiments were to drop on the flat plains beyond the Merderet. The Germans had broken dykes and sluices and allowed this river, like the Douve, to flood the surrounding fields to a depth of two or three feet, but surface weed had concealed this fact from the reconnaissance aircraft and from the invasion planners. The parachute drop would take place about 0100 hrs on 6 June and the gliders would arrive two hours later, bringing in field artillery and the vital anti-tank guns.

The 101st Division was to land further south, north and east of Carentan. Their task was to capture that town and seize four landward exits of the high causeways across the flooded ground behind 'Utah' beach. This belt of flooded land was some two kilometres wide and thickly planted with mines. Even with flail tanks, clearing paths through these minefields from the beach would take hours, if not days, so seizing the causeways was vital. This task was given to two of the 101st regiments. The other regiment, the 506th, was to advance on Carentan, seize the bridges over the Douve, and so secure the southern half of the Cotentin against enemy counter-attacks from the mainland of Normandy.

The American paratroopers would take off from airfields in southern England at about 2200 hrs on 5 June and fly a circle route to their drop zones, crossing the Channel to approach the narrow Cotentin from the west, flying in north of the Channel Islands and across, rather than down, the Peninsula. Britain was on Double Daylight Saving Time in 1944, so it was still broad daylight when their aircraft, the robust C-47 Dakotas, lurched heavily into the air and flew west towards Brittany.

Coming in from the west and flying across the Peninsula with the prevailing wind meant that the aircraft would be over the land for barely ten minutes and over their drop zones for less than four. The men knew that anyone jumping late stood a fair chance of landing in the sea. If the troops were scattered in the drop they might never find each other in the dark, enemy-held countryside on which they were to descend. Some confusion had been anticipated and every American trooper carried a small tin 'snapper', which made a 'click-clack' noise, rather like a cricket, to help them locate one another in the dark.

The Allied planners were well aware of these potential problems. Prior to D-Day the Americans held a series of night exercises, with mass parachute drops, to train the pilots in their duties and to rehearse all the pathfinding and drop-zone in- dicating techniques. All airborne divisions included pathfinder units, small bodies of highly trained men who would drop ahead of the main body to locate the drop zone and mark it accurately with lights and radio beacons in order to bring the main force in on their correct DZs. The exercises in England went reasonably well, and no real problems of drop-zone marking were expected on D-Day. Unfortunately, it is never possible to reproduce the nervousness and excitement generated by an operational drop, and the event itself was to confound all these hopes.

One problem the planners had anticipated on D-Day was the risk of aircraft collision. On D-Day there would be literally thousands of aircraft milling around in the skies over France, and it was far more likely that they would run into each other than into the much depleted Luftwaffe. A hundred thousand gallons of whitewash and twenty thousand paint brushes were supplied to ground crews in all the Allied air forces, and on 3/4 June three broad white bands were painted on the wings and fuselage of every bomber, fighter, parachute aircraft, transport plane and glider in the Allied command.

The delay in launching the invasion came as no surprise to the US airborne troops waiting on their air bases in southern England. They could see the wind bending the branches of the trees and whipping out the windsocks on the airfields. The wind was still blowing strongly at the North Witham Airfield, near Nottingham at 9 p.m. on 5 June, when the pathfinders of the 101st Division emplaned. The men were heavily loaded, carrying in addition to their normal equipment the pathfinding Eureka radios, beacons, lights and batteries. Some of these men had the additional task of reconnoitring routes from the drop zones to the various regimental objectives, which would make for swift deployment when the main force arrived. One example here will describe what happened to the majority of 101st's pathfinders on 5/6 June.

The pathfinders for the 502nd Regiment, 101st Airborne, had to find a route for their regiment from their drop south of Ste-Mère-Eglise to a battery of coastal guns near 'Utah', which the regiment were to knock out before dawn. They took off at 2200 hrs on the night of 5 June and had a quiet, almost uneventful flight out to the west coast of the Cotentin. There they ran into the first difficulty. Low cloud and fog prevented the pilots from spotting any positive spot on the ground to check their navigation on crossing the French coast. The pathfinders were therefore dropped two miles from their correct location, which was, under the circumstances, not too bad. They duly set up their equipment in open fields near Ste-Mère-Eglise, and awaited the arrival of the main force. Time passed, and nothing happened.

For the next two hours the pathfinders waited in the darkness as aircraft streamed overhead, listening to bursts of machine-gun fire and watching the odd flight of tracer as the now-alert Germans began to investigate the appearance of groups of

parachutists. Shortly after 1.00 a.m., however, the deep drone
of hundreds of engines announced the arrival of the main force,
and all eyes turned to the sky where confusion seemed to be
reigning.

Aircraft were appearing over the drop zone from all points of
the compass, and as the 101st's pathfinders ran out to meet the
men landing, they were more than a little disconcerted to
discover that the regiment now descending on their drop zone
was not the 502nd of the 101st but the 505th Parachute Regiment of the 82nd Airborne Division. Something had gone
seriously wrong.

Among those parachuting into Normandy that night was
Leslie 'Bill' Kick, serving with the Headquarters of the 82nd
US Airborne Division. 'About 200 of us, called "special
troops", were directly under Brigadier-General James M.
"Slim Jim" Gavin, the Assistant Division Commander. We
were to go in with the 508th Parachute Infantry Regiment. The
General got us together and gave us a quiet talk, after which I
believe we would have gone to hell with him.

'On the evening of June 5, we were lined up by plane loads
(sticks), getting ready to load into the C-47s. My stick was next
to one from the division's engineer battalion. A friend, Bill Yeo,
was next to me in that stick. Bill looked pretty bad, shaking and
obviously not his cool, easy-going self. I asked him what was
bothering him and he said something like, "I'm not going to get
through this one." I told him to relax, that we were both going
to get through it because we were both too mean to die. Several
days later, his First Sergeant told me that he got it the first day,
right between the eyes.

'The jumpmaster of our stick was Captain Whitley, whom I
did not know, but he may have been a newcomer to the HQ
staff. I was placed in the middle of the stick, with the job of
hitting the strapped toggle switches to salvo the equipment
bundles. It was still daylight when we took off, as Double
British Summer Time was in effect, two hours ahead of Green-
wich Time.

'Much of the flying time must have been used to get into the
planned formation, and it was not a comfortable ride. In
addition to the clothing, I had a .45 pistol with 3 clips, M-1

Garand rifle in 2 parts in a scabbard, trench knife on leg, 1 Gammon grenade, 1 'P' grenade, 2 fragmentation grenades, 2 bandoliers of rifle ammo, musette bag, pack harness, 3 days' D-rations, first-aid packet, canteen, switchblade knife, message book, pencil, escape kit, main and reserve chutes. All this was strapped, pocketed and tied on at take-off. There wasn't much room left for breathing. As a consequence there was some vomiting along the way, which gave us slippery footing. There was very little talking, no ditties were sung, no smart-ass remarks as were heard during practice jumps.

'As we approached the Normandy coast we were given the "Stand up and Hook up" order by Captain Whitley, so that we would be ready for any emergency. Shortly before we got the "Go" the tracers started going by the door and windows, but no lurching as at Sicily. It was quite a spectacle. Then we were going out, slipping on puke but keeping our balance by holding tight to the static line snap. There I was, hanging from a nicely opened 'chute, sharing the air with a whole lot of tracers and a whole lot more that weren't tracers. I remember thinking that I couldn't possibly get to the ground alive, so I kept slipping air front and back to hurry my descent.

'In the moonlight it looked like a nice smooth meadow to land in, but instead it was a splash. I couldn't get my leg straps unbuckled, so I cut them with my trench knife. The wind was blowing the 'chute and I took in a lot of water before I got myself cut loose. I was close to drowned and was having a tough time – standing in chest-deep water – getting my rifle together. A voice said, "Let me help you, Kick." I found out weeks later that the voice was that of Paul Wells.

'Several of us got to a railroad causeway which cut through the swamp, an inundated part of the Merderet river flood plain. We followed the railroad until we got to a road. At dawn, along came a German motorcyclist. Several of us fired, and we figured it would have taken three strong men to carry him to a grave with all that lead in him. He was being followed by a staff car which managed to turn around and get away. We sent a few rounds at it but there were no observable results. We had been unable to recover any of the equipment so all we had was our personal stuff. We were all soaked, and all that clothing held a lot of water for a long time.

'My first laugh of D-Day was seeing my buddy, Cliff Hieta, making a vest out of a piece of 'chute to help keep him warm. He had previously picked up malaria in Sicily, and I think a relapse was setting in then, because a few days later it hit him hard. We tried to take a German roadblock but didn't have much success. A few guys got hit. I helped a casualty out of the mess. Somehow he had got mixed up with us, as he was from the 505th in the other division. He had a nice clean hole in his leg and seemed happy about the whole thing. No shock there! Later we met up with our Divisional Commander, Major-General Matthew B. Ridgway, and Brigadier-General Gavin, who we had jumped with, and about a hundred others. The enemy got us pretty well located – they were good – and gave us a bit of hell with mortar and small-arms fire, including snipers. We had a few prisoners – as I remember, about twenty – including a few officers of field grade.

'I was given the job of setting up part of the perimeter defence, so I was kept busy. A sniper missed me with two rounds. I went looking for him but all I found was a makeshift ladder in a hedgerow tree that he had evacuated. Mortar fire came in hot and heavy that night, but the drainage ditches in the hedgerows gave good cover so the casualties were nil, as far as I knew.

'All in all, it wasn't a bad day for our plane-load. We all made it and I considered that a miracle of some sort.'

Leslie Kick was right. Many American paratroopers were not so lucky. Many men were not descending on marked drop zones at all but simply jumping blindly into the night. The 101st Division, instead of landing in four tight groups, were scattered over 300 square miles of Normandy and some troopers landed over 30 miles from their correct drop zones. Many, too many, jumped into the marshes or the sea. All over the Cotentin, poor visibility, high winds, anti-aircraft fire and bad luck combined to confuse the American airborne operation from the outset.

Jack Schlegel, now the Chief of Police in Shandaken, New York, was then with the 3rd Battalion of the 508 PIR. 'As D-Day approached, training took up almost all our time, and on

June 4/5 we moved to an airport for the jump. I carried a carbine, tripod for the 30-calibre machine gun, grenades, Gammon bomb, ammo, shovel, gas mask, Mae West, C-rations and all the other items that were needed. We all needed help to get our 'chutes on, and two Air Force men assisted each trooper into the C-47. Our plane had 2 rows of 12 – putting 24 paratroopers, supply bundles and the air crew into the C-47. I cannot recall any laughter or joking on the flight except for the slop bucket being passed up and down the plane. Many threw up when the bucket was passed. I was the twenty-fourth man on our stick and sat next to the plane's radio man, who happened to live in the same area of the Bronx as I. He lived only three blocks from my house and we talked practically all the way over.

'As we approached our area to jump, some of the paratroopers from HQ 3rd Light Machine Gun Section were dozing when a line of tracer bullets cut through the length of the fuselage of the C-47 causing the men sitting on either side to pull their feet in closer. No one was hit, but it got their attention fast so that everyone was fully alert for the next surprise – a direct hit on the left engine. Immediately, Lt John Evans yelled, "Stand up and Hook up!" It didn't take any urging for the paratroopers to obey that order, as the plane was struggling to remain airborne. No sooner were we in place when a third hit took off part of the right wing. The plane tilted down and to the right. Lt Evans yelled, "GO!" and led the way. That was the last time anyone ever saw or heard from Evans. I recall that I was the twenty-fourth man and last to leave the plane, and remember how the plane was going down. I moved as fast as I could to get out and, after baling out, saw the plane go up in a ball of fire.

'I dropped in an open field amongst some cows and, with difficulty, shed my parachute and quickly found two or three other men of the 508th. Chick Miller remembered that I asked him to help read a map. We used a flashlight under a raincoat to study the map, but we could not get our bearings. Seeing a farmhouse with a faint light inside, we decided to seek information from the local Normans.

'I banged on the door until a frightened, elderly couple timidly opened it just enough to peep at the paratroopers outside. "*Je suis Americain*," I announced in schoolboy French, which was effective enough to calm the fears of the startled Normans, as they invited us inside. Using sign language, French, German and American English, we troopers learned we were near Picauville and our hosts were Monsieur and Madame Le Comte. The Le Comtes served bread and wine to the paratroopers as we sat around the dining table and planned our route. As a parting gesture I gave my paratrooper wings to Madame Le Comte as a remembrance.

'Our group started on our journey to find other members of our unit. A short while later, while walking along a road flanked by steep hedgerows and a farmhouse, we heard vehicles approaching. Two motorcycles with Germans approached and were killed by our unit. Upon hearing more sounds of approaching vehicles, we crossed a hedge and headed towards what we thought was Ste-Mère-Eglise. We were actually lost and walking in circles. About daylight, our group came upon a bullet-riddled German staff car rammed up against a stone wall and three dead Germans in the road. One of the dead was General Wilhelm Falley, CO of the 91st German Infantry Division, who had been killed earlier by Lt Malcolm Brannen of the 82nd. In examining the car, I found a package which contained a large swastika banner, the command flag of Gen. Falley which normally flew over his headquarters. This flag now hangs in the Airborne Museum at Ste-Mère-Eglise.

'Some time during the morning, Lt Bodak's group and my group came together, running into machine-gun cross-fire, when about nine of us made a break through a hedgerow. The group remaining with Bodak was totally surrounded. One of the paratroopers with Bodak translated the words of the German commanding officer: "You have three minutes to surrender or we will sweep the ditch from both ends, and there will be no chance of anyone surviving." Lt Bodak then gave the order to surrender.

'My group fled towards a barn. As we entered the barn door three Germans were trying to get out of the same door. The paratroopers grabbed the Germans and pulled them back inside as prisoners. While the prisoners were guarded in a small room, I slipped away alone to another part of the barn. I pulled up a loose board in the floor, stuffed my package of loot containing the German flag under the floor, replaced the loose plank and covered it with straw. I recovered this after the war.

'With our prisoners as insurance, we troopers left the barn safely. After travelling a few hundred yards, we came face to face with a German tank which fired its big gun. A shell exploded just behind the group, wounding many. One of the prisoners, although bleeding from his wounds, jumped up and waved cease-fire gestures to the tank commander. The insurance paid off. The tank commander decided to take prisoners rather than finish off the Americans.

'After capture I recall walking several miles to a château where there were about 250 prisoners – American, British and Canadians. The next day we were loaded on about ten unmarked German trucks with canvas covers and moved in convoy toward St Lô. About noon, Allied planes strafed the convoy and I estimate that 30 or 40 of our men were killed (many from the 508th). Over 80 were wounded. All of us pitched in to help with the dead and wounded. I remember moving three from my own company with the dead and placing Lt Bodak with the wounded. He was hit with a large-calibre shell in the spine and never walked again. So ended D-Day.'

One of the German soldiers now in action against the American paratroopers was Sergeant Rainer Hartmetz, whose battalion had been brought up from Brittany. 'Behind Pont l'Abbé we were stopped by a corporal of our Heavy Company, who directed us into an orchard. A half-track for our anti-tank guns was riddled with bullets and smeared with blood. The corporal was very excited and hurried us to make ourselves ready for combat. He hardly answered my question about the dead paratroopers we had seen hanging by their 'chutes on trees and poles and chimneys. "Hurry up," he said. "They are plastering each ten minutes this place with naval artillery, and the companies are in contact with them. They are 'Amis', you know." Crossing the road, I heard him shouting after me, "And take care!"

'A rifle squad had twelve men and our battalion had the machine pistol No. 43, which was issued in Russia and the soldiers were enthusiastic with that weapon. We had the rifle 98K for snipers and every soldier had hand grenades and additional ammunition for the Spandau. Magnetic mines and

Panzerfausts had been distributed over the squad, but one of the most important pieces of outfit was the short infantry spade. Without the spade a German infantryman felt naked. We'd learned digging fox-holes in Russia, and you know the word, "Sweat saves blood". Besides that, the spade was an excellent weapon for man-to-man fighting, for it was sharp and handy.

'After some hundred metres we met about forty German soldiers along the road. They were very young – perhaps seventeen (I was nineteen) – some were wounded and supported by their comrades with a sergeant beside. When he saw us he addressed us. "They're recruits. We had a night training when they jumped into us. We had only blank cartridges." He had tears in the eyes and started sobbing.

'I never had interest to look at killed men, but this time we stopped to see our new adversaries. They had lost their helmets so we could see their uncovered heads with that crew-cut. We had been told that American troopers were convicts who had volunteered for the Airborne, but these couldn't be convicts, and when I saw that I felt better, knowing we had to fight against soldiers and not against criminals.

'The quietness became interrupted by the noise of rifle-fire and bursts of machine guns, and we could distinguish the American bursts from the German Spandau and figure out the direction of it. We hardly started digging our fox-holes when a salvo of artillery shells exploded between us, and one of the riflemen was hit, and the next problem was to locate their snipers. I heard a noise like a slapping in the face, and Willy came down in the hole, the face covered with the hands, through which poured blood.

'We were sitting behind the hedgerows, not having seen an enemy soldier or fired a round, and had two casualties. I crawled over to Gottlieb, my assistant squad leader, and discussed how to tackle the snipers. This sniper was sitting in a tree, probably tied in, so I gave the order to some of our boys to observe the trees if there would be any movement, and we stayed there for two hours, but nothing happened. The night and the darkness came.'

Howard Huggett of North Carolina was in the 326th Airborne Engineer Battalion of the 101st Airborne Division. His aircraft had been hit by anti-aircraft fire soon after crossing the French coast and the 600lbs of C-2 explosive on board was now on fire. 'With the plane on fire, in a dive, the pilot and co-pilot slumped forward and the crew chief unable to determine our position, I gave the order to go. I estimated our altitude at between 350 and 400ft. When my 'chute opened it seemed I had two oscillations in the air and then I hit the ground hard somewhere in France, not sure of my location.

'While lying on my back in the middle of a field I readied my weapon, checked the direction of flight of the aircraft and removed my 'chute ready to engage the enemy – which turned out to be a big white horse. I could see that the plane had crashed approximately one kilometre away in a south-easterly direction. I collected my gear and proceeded to the edge of the field and started down the hedgerow to collect the jump stick. From the amount of firing it was obvious that a sizeable German force was between me and the men who had jumped with me and joining up was going to be a real problem. As I started down the hedgerow I saw an enemy patrol on the other side so I held my position to let them pass and then proceeded to get into position for a fire fight. I then back-tracked, hoping to find someone from my group and I even used my "cricket" to try and contact someone, but to no avail. I then surmised that the men in my stick had landed among enemy troops and I had landed on the fringe of the enemy bivouac.

'As daylight approached I could hear artillery to the north, and I started making my way towards the sound. I could hear German troops and vehicles moving around on roads and paths so I thought it would be safer to move in the hedgerows. It was now daylight and I was lost and alone, except for the enemy. By this time exhaustion was overtaking me. My cover was adequate in the hedgerow and I didn't resist the temptation to close my eyes and try to cat-nap.

'The sounds of battle seemed to have intensified so I decided to try and find some friendly troops in the area. When D-Day ended on 6 June 1944 I was lost and alone, not knowing if the beach landings had taken place, or even if I would be around for my twenty-second birthday just ten days away.'

John G. Kutz from Easton, Pennsylvania, was a demolition

man. 'My assignment for D-Day was to destroy two wooden bridges over the Douve river north-east of Carentan. We were briefed for our mission at Exeter and prepared our equipment, which included in my case, 60lbs of C-2 explosive, a roll of primer, a roll of safety cord, 12 blasting caps, a Hawkins mine, plus rifle and so on. It took two men to get me into the plane, a zebra-striped C-47.

'We flew close to the water over the Channel and the plane pulled up to about 600–700ft over the coast of France when the flak and ground fire started coming at us. It looked like a giant Fourth of July celebration. I jumped out of the plane in the middle of all this, and landed in the Douve river.

'Fortunately, I landed close to shore, and pulled my equipment in. Then I took a rest for about five or ten minutes before carrying all my equipment through a flooded area, close behind three German soldiers moving a German artillery piece. Then I met my sergeant and six of my buddies. As we headed for the bridges we kept picking up more men and had a few fire fights, and we also blew up high-tension and underground cables on the way, getting to the bridges just before daylight.

'We could not prepare the bridges for demolition in the daylight because of enemy fire, but we prepared them as soon as it got dark, and the bridges were under mortar fire when we did it.'

George Rosie of Highland Park, Illinois, was with the 506 PIR in the 101st Airborne Division: 'Through broken clouds and a bright moon we headed for the coast. Over the Channel we could see hundreds of boats starting towards the south, and in every direction were planes. About 1.00 a.m. on June 6, one of the guys yelled, "There she is boys." We all knew what it was – the coast of France. About nine minutes to the drop zone. Flak and machine-gun tracers could be seen to the right and left. It looked like the Fourth of July. About that moment a plane on our right blew up, hit the ground in a large ball of fire – 18 to 20 men wiped out. This was no Fourth of July celebration. Welcome to the real war.

'The red light in the door came on. We stood up and hooked up. Then came the green light and we were out the door. Quite a struggle because of all our equipment. Someone fell down and had to be helped up and out the door. I don't know how high our plane was, but I'm sure it was very low because I remember swinging about twice and then landing in the middle of a road. I could see a man and a woman standing in the front yard of a house just beneath me. I took about two steps and went head first through a wooden fence, knocking out two teeth and cutting my lip. I rolled over, tried to get my carbine out, couldn't, sat up, and the man and woman were gone. I finally got out of my harness – those snap harnesses were a bugger to get out of – pulled my folding stock carbine out and could hear some soldiers coming down the road. I started up a hedgerow but it felt like someone was holding me by my belt. I stopped, tried to move again – same thing. I found the shroud lines from my parachute tangled up in the fence. I could hear the boots getting closer and closer. I finally got the shroud lines unhooked, climbed to the top of the hedgerow, fell over on the other side, and in about a minute 35 or 40 Germans came marching past. I could have reached out and touched them. Being alone behind enemy lines is a unique, indescribable feeling. You just feel so helpless, so alone that there is nothing in your life you can relate it to.

'After a while I ran into John Gibson, our medic, and Charles Lee, one of our 81mm mortar men. It was as if I had found a long-lost brother. It was the greatest feeling in the world. We could hear a German machine gun firing in our area and small arms a bit further away. Later I looked up and there was a C-47 at about 800ft with the left engine on fire and troopers baling out. Flames were streaming alongside the plane right by the door. The plane was flying in a kind of semi-circle, and at about 600ft it was coming straight at us and the troopers and the crew were still baling out. The last one baled out at not more than 200ft. The plane went right over the top of our heads, hit in the enjoining field and burst into a thousand flaming pieces that lit up the whole area. From the direction of the crashed plane four men came running towards us. When they got near the ditch we discovered they were from our plane: Phil Abbie, Francis Swanson, Leo Krebs, and Ronzani. The downed plane had hit right in the area where they were hiding and damn near got them.

'We now had a small army of seven. We decided to head for the river and the bridges which were part of our unit's objectives. We stuck to the ditches and hedgerows for concealment. When we got down near the river we had to cross a field. Abbie was our scout. As he came out on the road with Ronzani just behind him, daylight was breaking. There were approximately 100 Germans who were concealed in the field on the other side of the road. Fifteen or twenty of them stood up with their machine pistols and shot and killed Abbie and Ronzani. Seven men against a hundred was a hopeless position. In no time at all they had us surrounded and captured. Charles Lee crawled to the left and got away into a wooded area. A short time later they had four of us who were not wounded lying in a shallow ditch with our hands over our heads and a guard with a rifle on either side of us. Lee began shooting at the guards from about fifty yards away where he was hiding. I told Leo Krebs I had a hand grenade in my jumpsuit pocket the Germans had missed. I told Leo if Lee hit one of the guards, I was going to try and get away, but the Germans circled around Lee and killed him. Later, when they moved us out, I left the grenade lying in the ditch.

'All this took place years ago, but when you start thinking about the day you lost Abbie, Lee and Francis Ronzani it is still very difficult to talk about. After we were captured, Gibson and I had a chance to check out Ronzani. I don't know how many times he was hit through the chest – 3, 4, 5, 6. I'm sure he never knew what hit him. When I returned to the States after the war and visited his mother and father, one of the things that seemed to be of great relief to his parents was that Francis had not suffered.

'When we were first hit and pinned down in that field, strange things went through our minds. Bullets flying all over the place and Leo Krebs remarked, "God, these guys are lousy shots." During the short time we were exchanging fire with the Germans there was a German officer running, back and forth on the road in front of us. Krebs said, "What the hell is wrong with that guy? Is he nuts?" Leo and I both shot at him and he went down. Later, after we were captured they had us carry him on a shelter half back to the farmhouse where they were quartered. He was the first dead man I had ever touched. When we picked him up to put him on the shelter half, he broke wind and was making sounds like he was still breathing. As far as I could tell we had hit him several times in the chest area and I knew damn well he was dead, but those weird sounds really gave me the creeps.

'With my broken teeth and a swelling knee that I had injured when landing on the road and the sheer fear of being a prisoner, there was no sleep that night. I would open my mouth to breathe and the raw nerves from those broken-off teeth just killed me. In the morning, Leo Krebs, who could speak German, talked to one of the guards and an older soldier who might have been a cook or something came over. He had an old rusty pair of pliers. They sat me down on a bale of hay with Swanson and Krebs holding my arms and this old German started towards my mouth with these pliers. His hands were shaking and at the first grab he got the remaining portion of the first tooth and a hell of a chunk of my gum. I felt pain like I had never felt in my life. The second time his hand was shaking even harder. On his first attempt he didn't get the other stub out but did on the second try. It hurt like hell but at least the pain of the raw nerves was gone. Talking about this brings back memories that have been stored back in the furthest reaches of my mind that I haven't thought about in years.'

D. Zane Schlemmer, who now lives in Hawaii, was a nineteen-year-old sergeant in the 2nd Battalion, the 508th PIR, 82nd Airborne. 'I was a forward observer for an 81mm mortar platoon. My biggest memory of the night of June 6/7 was the struggle to stay awake. I had taken Benzedrine but the lack of sleep and constant staring at the grazing Normandy cows caused me to hallucinate – and I think that German patrols were roving out there. I spent the night swapping a hand grenade from hand to hand. How I slept when I finally got to sleep the next morning!

'Before the jump, my battalion assembled at Saltby airfield, under high security. We drew combat-scale ammunition and I had an M1 Garand 300-calibre rifle, for I was to be a front-line observer, and I was trying to look as inconspicuous as possible. I also had fragmentation grenades and a Gammon grenade – an English grenade that was a cotton sock filled with plastic explosive. These were ideal for attacking vehicles and we called them our hand artillery. However, they were also popular because the plastic explosive was ideal for lighting fires to brew coffee or K-rations in our fox-holes, so as time went on the grenade got smaller. We also had anti-tank mines. We were really loaded, but everyone drew more, as much ammo as we could carry.

'We cleaned and re-cleaned our weapons, sharpened and re-sharpened our knives, checked and re-checked our equipment. We then went into sand-table sessions showing our objective. We were told that we should jump regardless of circumstances, and were not under any circumstances to return with the aircraft. The places on the map eventually got their French names, like Pont l'Abbé, and we were finally told that our objective was Normandy, France, and that our task was to block all German advances onto the landing beaches.

'As you know there was a 24-hour delay, but finally about 8.30 p.m. on June 5 we assembled by our aircraft in "sticks". There were eight men in my "stick". We had a relief stop because once we had our equipment on it was impossible to relieve ourselves. We blacked our faces, donned our equipment and our chutes, and were pushed or hauled onto the planes. The mood was nervous chatter to real quiet, but camaraderie prevailed. I chewed an entire pack of gum after departing.

'June 6, 1944, 0001 hrs found us approaching the English Channel. After some time we banked left over two small islands, and then over the coast of France. We then ran into cloud which really concerned us. This suddenly cleared and we started to receive German flak and small-arms fire. When it struck the aircraft it was like gravel on a tin roof. I thought only of getting out of the plane as quickly as possible and of what I had done to get myself in this situation – then the green light came on and out went the stick.

'The sky seemed alive with tracer, red and green and pink, floating up and snapping past. In the distance to the east I could see a sizeable fire, a house in Ste-Mère-Eglise, though I didn't know it at the time. We had jumped anyway, and I hit in on an apple orchard and got some bruised ribs. I cleared my harness, put my rifle together, but I could not find any sign of life except some firing from down the road. Our stick leader had been immediately captured and was later killed by our own aircraft in a strafing attack. Another aircraft, flaring like a comet, crashed in a field nearby and I thought of the troopers on board. I later saw a C-47 down on the marshes of the Merderet river. The area into which we had jumped was occupied by the tightly disciplined 91st German Division, and they occupied most of the farms. We were also surprised at the immense size of the hedgerows. No one had told us about the flooded marshes. I had no idea where the hell I was and I could not find my stick, but I was alive.

'I laid my anti-tank mine and headed off in a southerly direction. Near the edge of the next field I came across a sergeant in the 101st, who was just as bewildered as I was as to where we were. We were both far from where we should have been. We then heard firing from the south-east and decided to head there and came across a road running east–west. We crossed a causeway to a masonry bridge and then to an intersection, so I knew we were near Chef du Pont, which meant I had landed some one-and-a-half miles south-east of our drop zone, which wasn't bad compared with others, but it meant I was on the wrong side of the Merderet river. The sergeant from the 101st decided to march on alone to find his division and I turned back to find mine.

'There was sporadic small-arms fire everywhere. As I reached the edge of the marsh I heard a glider crash into the trees nearby. Soon after, by using the "clicker" I met three troopers, two of whom were already hurt, one with a broken leg. We concealed the two wounded and the other came along with me.

'At dawn we left the road and kept to the fields, scouting the Germans like Indians in the West. I never entered a farmhouse during my time in Normandy. We eventually met other troopers waiting to ambush the enemy; every field was a separate battleground. The Normandy cows would stare at anyone in the fields and I still have a warm place in my heart for those big Normandy cows.

'By mid-morning on D-Day many more troopers had assembled and we found we had no mortars, few machine guns, little medical supplies, few medics for the wounded. However, we did have our personal weapons and we managed with them. We assembled on Hill 30 which overlooked the marsh I had crossed that morning, from which we could, theoretically, control the causeways across the Merderet. I was positioned in an outpost and I spent the time here with Lt-Colonel Shanley's group. I preferred the outpost as there were too many men we could not help inside the perimeter. It was difficult to listen to their cries. We had no re-supplies of any kind but the lack of medical supplies was felt by everyone. Later we could call up 75mm fire to break up German attacks on our position.

'June 6, 1944 at 2339 hrs found me very weary but very alive, dug-in with a parachute in my fox-hole, which was very warm and very luxurious. We did not know if the invasion had succeeded or not, but we stayed there for five days until the seaborne troops came up. Our Chaplain was killed while attending to our wounded. I was wounded in July and the fourth of July found me on a hospital ship bound for an English hospital. They had to cut off my bloody, stinking jumpsuit, which I had worn continuously for 29 days, but I insisted that they let me keep my jump boots.'

Of the 2,056 men of Zane Schlemmer's 508th Parachute Infantry Regiment who flew to Normandy on 5 June, only 995 returned to Nottingham on 14 July.

Scattered widely across the Cotentin countryside, the American paratroopers were making the best of a bad job. They cut telephone wires, ambushed enemy transport, attacked the Germans wherever they found them and slowly made their way towards their objectives, joining up with other paratroopers as the night wore on. None of this was easy and even the glider-borne forces suffered from the confusion.

The great advantage of gliders, apart from their ability to lift heavy equipment, lay in the fact that they could put down men in organized groups, but even here things went wrong. The first glider to land, carrying Brigadier-General Don Pratt, Assistant Commander of the 101st, landed perfectly on a well marked landing zone. Unfortunately the glider ran across the marking lights, totally destroying them, and crashed into a wall. General Pratt was killed, and the other gliders, landing in the pitch dark, also crashed, with heavy losses among the passengers and crews. General Pratt was the first American general to die in France.

Milton Chadwick was with the Glider Field Artillery of the 82nd Airborne. 'On June 6, 1944 I was a sergeant in charge of a howitzer section. We flew into Normandy in a British "Horsa" glider. We left England at 9 p.m. on June 6, but I cannot remember the name of the airport. We crash-landed at 11 p.m. near Ste-Mère-Eglise and our glider was literally torn to pieces. If we had not been well belted in I am sure some of us would have been killed but as it turned out all five of us walked away. Our equipment was salvaged although only 4 of the 6 howitzers were usable. It worked out well, however, as in the event there were only enough men left to man 4 guns anyway. During the battle our combat team was given the task of capturing Hill 95 and Hill 131, which are the highest points in that part of Normandy.'

Arley Goodenkauf of Table Rock, Nebraska, was a corporal in 'B' Battery, 377th Parachute Field Artillery Battalion, 101st Airborne Division: 'Our division had arrived in Liverpool, England in mid-October 1943 and were quartered in the little village of Wickham, near Newbury, Berkshire. We probably had the longest passage across the Atlantic of any army group, taking 45 days to make the journey from New York.

'I landed outside Montebourg, north of Ste-Mère-Eglise, instead of at St Martin de Varreville, just in from "Utah" beach, which was our designated drop zone. We had our first action just outside Le Ham early that morning, after we had stopped and destroyed three or four German ammunition trucks. During the next three days, we were involved in several skirmishes, usually against superior numbers and weapons. We had only carbines and grenades. Out of the twelve 75mm howitzers in the battalion, only one was ever recovered and put into action. On about June 9 I was wounded and taken prisoner, and remained in Germany until January 31 when I escaped during the POW evacuation. With several friends and with some assistance from the Russian Army, I made my way to Odessa on the Black Sea and eventually back to the American army at Naples.'

George Maruschak of Chicago, Illinois, who had performed

in the airborne concert party in England, was a sergeant in the HQ Battery, 320th Glider Field Artillery, 82nd Airborne Division. 'My Army Serial Number was 36526691. It's funny that I still remember my ASN, because when I call one of my children I have to look up the number on our Rol-O-Dex!

'We were given an introduction to the "Horsa", a giant British glider, made completely of plywood, which made our "Waco" gliders look like toys. We left the airfield shortly after 2300 hrs on June 5. We sat a little behind the pilot's cabin, five on each side, directly above the single wheel of the three-wheel landing gear.

'We were cut loose and the glider was dropping quickly at a 45-degree angle – a great crash and the nose hit the large hedgerows – the single wheel broke through the bottom and separated the ten of us. We couldn't cut the six cables because the back was about 20ft in the air. Our main concern was how to get the Jeep and trailer out. An axe was part of the equipment on the glider, and one wing was touching the grass on the field. The other was way up, high over the road. The best place was at the door. We didn't want to chop, not knowing where the enemy was, but we had no choice. It took hours but we got the job done.

'We found another glider and the guys who were in it. It had one 105 howitzer and two rounds of ammunition. We put the howitzer on the road facing the direction we thought the enemy would be coming from. At dawn we met my major, who was happy to see us, but was worried as to what had happened to the rest of the battery, and he wanted me (from memory) to start making up our MIAs (Missing-in-Action).

'Looking around, we finally reasoned that we were on the wrong side of the church at Ste-Mère-Eglise. It was June 7 before we were reunited with the rest of the guys from the HQ Battery, and 28 days before we were replaced by infantry divisions. We moved back towards the beaches, and Boy! ... it sure was great to remove the impregnated underwear, to wash and shave, and to relax. The Red Cross was there to hand out just what most of us wanted most – a toothbrush and toothpaste. As for me, I would have preferred a beer and a shot of booze.'

'Stub' Storeby of Avenal, California, was in the 326 Engineering Battalion, 101st Airborne. 'As we started exiting the planes the sky was full of red tracer, and when my parachute opened I lost all my equipment, including my rifle. I landed in a bomb crater about 10ft deep, with only a trench knife strapped to my leg and some explosive caps taped to my armpit. Climbing out of the crater I was challenged by Harold Conway, who had a rifle pointed at my head, and I used my D-Day "cricket" to give the counter-sign. A few minutes later, Harold was hit in the groin by a bullet. I gave him sulpha powder and put him in some brush. He kept his grenades and gave me his rifle.

'I then located more of my platoon and we stayed in the hedgerows and watched the other paratroops and gliders land, while the Navy was shelling everything, especially towards our objectives at Carentan. We also found an equipment bundle with a machine gun and ammo, and at daylight my lieutenant told me to shoot up a farm where the enemy were holed up. After some corrections I managed to silence the Germans, and later that day I got another German on the far side of the hedgerow. I crawled over and examined him, taking his insignia and wallet. I still have his photos today but I saw his face every night for months. We spent the rest of D-Day assembling more and more troops for an assault on Carentan and waiting for the troops to come up from the beaches – and that was my D-Day.'

Captain Harold A. Shebeck of Minneapolis, Minnesota, was the Assistant Supply Officer and Graves Registration Officer with 325th Glider Regiment, 82nd Airborne Division: 'About May 27, the 82nd Airborne left our area around Leicester for the south of England. Of course, at this point we did not know when D-Day was, but we obviously knew it was imminent. When we left the train at a small town I noticed that the name of the town was Honiton in Devon, about ninety miles west of Southampton. At this time thousands of troops were making their moves to staging areas all over southern England.

'We were directed to our gliders and now began the job of loading. The glider to which I was assigned carried a Jeep, my driver, the Regimental Transportation Chief who was staff sergeant and myself as well as some assorted ordnance items. The gliders had to be loaded very carefully and heavy equipment lashed down very securely, because a shift of only four inches by a Jeep or cannon could send a glider into a dive, from which it could not recover. I sat in the Jeep and as we left the ground and began passing over the villages and towns of southern England, people filled the streets, waving from doorsteps or wherever they happened to be.

'My driver was now lying on the floor under the Jeep and vomiting as he suffered from a good case of air sickness. It might sound impossible to believe, but I soon began dozing, which I did intermittently once we were well underway. The Cherbourg Peninsula is only twenty-five miles wide, so it only took a short time to cross. Excellent timing, therefore, was vital in cutting the glider loose from the tow plane. Too early or too late and the gliders would land in the Channel.

'Now we began to see all the "welcoming" devices the Germans had erected in most of the fields in Normandy in anticipation of an airborne invasion. Poles, somewhat smaller than telephone poles, had been set up with wires strung between them, booby-trapped, to cause gliders to crash-land. Ditches had been dug about 6ft deep and 12ft across to cause a smash-up even if a glider was able to land in an open field.

'The Germans were aiming their fire at the tow planes, but were often late and were hitting the gliders. Machine-gun, artillery and small-arms fire was now coming up from barns, houses and German firing positions in scattered locations. In the glider we tried to make ourselves as small as possible, elbows close to the body, knees pulled up to chest and head bowed down. Now it was time for our pilot to cut loose from our tow plane. The pilot was desperately trying to slow the speed of the glider, which was now about 50 or 60 miles per hour. We came across the top of a hedgerow, knocked the wheels off the glider, crash-landed, and came to a stop about 4 miles inland from "Utah" beach, in the general vicinity of Ste-Mère-Eglise and the smaller village of Chef du Pont.

'Miraculously, no one was hurt. As we hit the ground I felt a terrible pain in my back and thought my back was broken, but I was able to move my legs and I knew I was lucky. I was concerned that the Jeep had been damaged, but luckily it was not, and we manhandled it out of the glider. My driver had recovered from his air sickness in a hurry what with the noise, dust, smoke, confusion and small-arms fire from snipers in the area. Our regimental mission was to assist in seizing and holding the main road up through the peninsula to Cherbourg.

'Here I think I should mention some of the things that led to the glider crack-ups in the landings. First, the fields were often smaller then they appeared on the photos and the sand-box models. The hedgerows which surrounded most of the fields in Normandy were often much higher than they appeared in the photographs, in some cases 20ft high. The result was that the pilots misjudged the height as they came in for a landing, and this caused a great many crashes, including ours. There were poles and ditches, and maps were not always accurate.

'Some gliders broke down before we even left England, and I was told that at least two came down in the Channel. I have been told that obstacles caused 50 per cent of the smash-ups in Normandy and enemy action the other 50 per cent. In all my time in Normandy, I only saw one glider that looked as though it could be used again, providing it could have been towed aloft – otherwise they were in various stages of destruction.

'Not long after our landing, I approached a smashed glider in which I saw the pilot slumped dead over the controls. No one else was around, and in the pilot's kit bag I found several oranges and a half-pound bar of chocolate, which I retrieved. The oranges were priceless in England and I savoured the chocolate for several days by eating a small square each day. It was permissible to take foodstuffs from the dead but everything else, obviously, was left for Graves Registration action.

'Shortly after I ran across the dead glider pilot, I found the Graves Registration Service people in a field where they were already in operation in a smashed glider. Bodies were gradually being collected and taken to a large field near Ste-Mère-Eglise, where the first American cemetery was being established. Here, row upon row of bodies were already being laid out. German bodies were being transported to their own cemetery which had been established by our GR people a few miles north-west of Ste-Mère-Eglise in the vicinity of Montebourg. I happened to be in this cemetery when a truckload of bodies arrived. Bodies were being hauled in GI two-and-a-half-ton trucks, with a couple of German prisoners to do the unloading. When the truck stopped, the front end was alongside what looked like a black, burned tree stump. As I looked at this "tree stump" more closely, I realized that it was the burned torso of a human body from mid-section to the knees, which had previously been brought in for burial.

'There were two things that were invariably found on nearly every German enlisted man, and these were a head of a partly eaten cabbage, and a loaf of dark rye bread.

'We had a young lieutenant in my regiment who was a company commander just promoted to captain a day or two before D-Day. He had not obtained captain's bars and had affixed two strips of white tape to the shoulder straps of his field jacket to denote his new rank. In my hurried travels an excited French farmer told me that there was a dead American officer in his barnyard. I found the body lying face down and I noticed the strips of tape on his shoulder straps before I turned him over.'

The more obvious landing zones had been quickly identified by the Germans, who added to the confusion on the drop zones by mortar fire and machine-gunning. All the 101st drops were from aircraft of the 9th US Airforce Troop Carrier Squadron and General Maxwell Taylor flew in the lead aircraft of his division to make his fifth parachute jump. On the way to France the general slept on the floor of the aircraft, a feat that was much admired by the other troopers in the aircraft, but as soon as his aircraft crossed the coast of France, the general led his men out into the night.

This sudden arrival of the American Airborne was a great surprise to the Norman villagers. André Heintz recalls one story: 'My great-aunt lived in what was going to be one of the drop zones for 101st US Airborne, at St Côme du Mont, near Carentan. The night before (5 June) the Germans asked the farmers in the area to bring in the cattle as they were going to have manoeuvres with live ammunition. That had happened before and the Germans always had manoeuvres in one part of the country or another to keep their men in shape.

'So when the family – my great-aunt over seventy, her son, and the old maid – heard quite a lot of noise during the night they didn't think at first about the Landing, but since more and more planes kept coming over and more noise could be heard towards the coast, they got scared. There were no shelters in the area so they chose the dark passage in the middle of the house on the first floor to take refuge.

'When, early in the morning, they dared at last to look through the windows, they saw an amazing sight. The fields there extend very far, as it is the open country by the marshes – that part was not flooded and there were no hedges to obstruct the view. There were parachutes all over the place, like huge flowers of all colours – red for ammunition, yellow for supplies, blue for medical supplies, white (very few) – the parachutist's second chance, a lap-pack parachute – and then the main camouflaged ones, mostly green, for the men.

'Unfortunately they also saw that a man whose white parachute had not opened had been impaled on the gate; the twisted white parachute lay beside him on the ground like a shroud, a trail of blood also came towards the front door, and probably a wounded soldier had tried to seek help. My family felt bad that from their dark passage, with all the noise outside, they had not been aware of him. A parachute was hanging from the roof, and obviously the man had slid down the ropes. Another one had apparently broken through the roof of the farm next door. Altogether eighteen men had dropped down in the grounds around the house.

'The battle lasted three days, sometimes with the Germans, sometimes with the Americans. Every time a new group of Germans came they would kick the corpse of the American killed in front of the house, turn him over and search his pockets.

'After the front door had been broken open with a hand grenade by an American Para, the family couldn't stay there any more. The Germans and the Americans chased one another through the house. It was a big place with two staircases, six different entrances, and it had become unbearable. The family couldn't even cook; every time they lit a fire (there was no gas or electricity then) the smoke through the chimney would bring a volley of shots through the windows. Whoever was outside, whether German or American, thought there were enemies inside. The family then decided to try and reach the tool shed at the end of the garden, but as they didn't have any helmets they wore copper saucepans on their heads and crawled across the garden with mattresses on their backs.

'When they came back to the house they found a dead German on one of the beds upstairs. He had written something with his blood on one of the mirrors, but it had dried off and could not be deciphered. The mother of the farmer next door had been killed and they had to bury her in the garden as no proper funerals could take place at this time.

'The day after the battle was over, Colonel Howard Johnson, who had been in charge of a special mission, holding a lock in the middle of the marshes, came and visited the house, explaining that he had fallen into the garden that night of 5/6 June. As he was coming down he had noticed, thanks to the tracer bullets, that he was being shot at by some Germans in the field opposite the house. Once on the ground he feigned death and then crawled towards the Germans and killed two in their slit trenches.'

On landing, General Maxwell Taylor of the 101st Airborne found himself commanding not 6,000 fighting men, but completely alone. The bulk of his division was dispersed over a wide area, generally south-east of Ste-Mère-Eglise. A further 30 per cent of his division fell outside this area, and most of these were quickly rounded up by the Germans. General Taylor's first encounter in Normandy was with a solitary trooper from the 501st Regiment. They were so pleased to see each other that general and GI hugged each other with delight in the darkness. The general and his sole subordinate then encountered Brigadier-General Anthony McAuliffe, who commanded the divisional artillery, but by dawn, only 1,100 of the 6,600 troopers in the 101st had rejoined their units.

The first organized group General Maxwell Taylor encountered was a small group from the 3rd Battalion of the 501st Parachute Infantry Regiment led by Lt-Colonel Ewell. Ewell had an uneventful jump, although his battalion was widely scattered, and like most of the other men, he didn't know where he was. General Maxwell Taylor took command of this detachment but it was some hours later before he located their position by the church at Ste Marie du Mont on the eastern Cotentin. This was near one of the causeway exits from 'Utah' beach, which was actually the objective of two battalions of the 506th Regiment, but since neither of these had been dropped on the right spot, General Taylor decided to lead his scratch formation to the attack, and capture the causeway exit.

The two battalions should have had 1,200 men for the job. General Taylor's force consisted of the 40 available men of the 3rd Battalion of the 501st, and 45 members of the Divisional Staff. Most of these were officers. The group contained two generals, a chief of staff, two colonels, a major, several captains and eight lieutenants. 'Never,' remarked General Taylor, wryly, 'have so few been commanded by so many.'

Lt-Colonel Ewell was placed in command, and the force made their way south, against light opposition, towards Pouppeville, collecting more men as they went. By the time they reached Pouppeville they had grown to about 150 men, from all parachute regiments and of both divisions. The group had 18 casualties in the fight for Pouppeville, but they took the village and 35 German prisoners, and so, just after dawn, secured the landward exit of the causeway.

On that wild and windy night in 1944, the US paratroopers were in action all over the Cotentin Peninsula of Normandy. The men might be dispersed, lost and confused, but they were not dismayed. They still had weapons and ammunition, and they were determined to make a fight of it. They cut telephone wires, shot up patrols and set up ambushes along the roads. One of these caught and killed General Falley, Commander of the German 91st Infantry Division, who was returning from an anti-invasion exercise in Rennes. In addition, using scratch forces like the one collected by General Maxwell Taylor and Lt-Colonel Ewell, they took their objectives. One of these was the small market town of Ste-Mère-Eglise, a target for the 82nd Airborne Division.

Ste-Mère-Eglise had been having a disturbed night even before the invasion began. A fire had started in the main square which called for the presence of the town fire brigade, while most of the town's population turned up as spectators. Thus distracted, the assembled French and Germans hardly heard the drone of engines as the parachute aircraft arrived overhead.

It was the sight of descending parachutes, each lit red from the fire, each with a man dangling below, together with the sudden bursts of fire from the German garrison, that alerted the startled citizens to what was happening around and above their little town.

The men now descending on Ste-Mère-Eglise were from the 3rd Battalion, 505th Regiment of the 82nd Airborne, commanded by Lt-Colonel Edward Krause. The dropping of men on the town centre was another accident, for the drop should have been in the surrounding fields, and those who landed in the town paid for it with their lives. One actually fell into the fire, and others landed in the trees around the square or fell heavily onto the stones. One, the most famous paratrooper of all the D-Day men, landed on the church tower in the centre of the square, then slid down the roof to hang suspended by his parachute rigging lines from the edge of the tower.

This was John Steele, a trooper in the 3rd Battalion of 505th. Private Steele wisely decided to sham dead, and hung limply in his harness while gunfire whipped across the square below, some of the fire coming from a German machine gun set up on the church roof a few yards away. A member of this gun crew eventually suggested they haul up Steele's body and relieve it of chocolate and cigarettes, only to discover that Pfc John Steele was very much alive. Steele was taken prisoner about 0430 hrs, just as dawn was breaking, an hour before his comrades took the town. He spent the rest of the war in captivity, dying in Kentucky in 1969.

The 82nd Division had a generally better drop than the 101st. Most of the 505th Regiment landed on the drop zone near Ste-Mère-Eglise and by 4.00 a.m., with the assistance of men from the 2nd Battalion, 505th, under Lt-Colonel Ben Vandervoost, the 3rd Battalion of the 505th had taken Ste-Mère-Eglise and cut the Cherbourg–Carentan road. The 1st Battalion of the 505th had a much worse time during the drop, and most of their heavy equipment went astray. The 82nd were supposed to land astride the River Merderet and as the area around this river had been flooded, many men who dropped accurately fell into floodwater at least 2 to 3ft deep. Under normal conditions a fit man could simply stand up, wet but unhurt, but when carrying up to 100lbs or more of equipment and ammunition and tugged over by the collapsing parachute, some found getting up too difficult, and therefore drowned.

Milton Chadwick of Upper Sandusky, Ohio, flew in with a glider formation of the 82nd Airborne. 'As for problems we had in the Normandy landings – they were many. My howitzer section and I flew in a "Horsa" glider. We had to land on a strange field since our original field was staked by the Germans. It was 11 p.m. and of course dark. Our glider hit the ground so hard that it disintegrated. After all the noise was over the first thing I heard was our pilot swearing. He was angry because he had made such a poor landing. Because of the condition of the glider we had trouble getting our equipment out – a Jeep and a howitzer.

'Our section had two axes as part of our equipment. In trying to unload I asked my corporal for an axe. He handed me one and I promptly broke the handle. I asked for the other axe and broke the handle on that one also. For the remainder of the war his favourite joke was, "Hand me that other axe."'

The 82nd had one great advantage in that they were quickly able to find their position in the ground, for the Cherbourg–Carentan railway line on its embankment above the Merderet made a perfect landmark. The Divisional Deputy Commander, Major-General James Gavin, dug his first fox-hole beside the road above the Merderet, where it remains to this day. He was then able to group the surviving troopers into sufficient strength to disperse or repel any counter-attack the Germans could make against them from beyond the river.

The German reaction to the paratroop landings was, in fact, surprisingly and mercifully slow. Had they reacted more quickly, the two American divisions might have been severely mauled, but the scattered nature of the landings gave the Germans nowhere to aim at. The Americans were everywhere, and the paratroopers, facing up to the situation in which they found themselves, took the initiative and held on to it. When the Germans finally realized what was happening, they found it difficult to mount a co-ordinated counter-attack against the large but scattered forces now harassing their positions.

Fighting by squads, platoons and companies, the American

paratroopers overran the Cotentin. This was fighting in which time was on the side of the Americans, for at dawn the sea invasion must come, and by their guts and fighting ability they had already made its success certain. Soon after dawn, the men of Lt-Colonel Ewell's small force near Pouppeville saw a tank advancing towards them down the causeway. Playing safe, they greeted it with a few warning shots, at which it stopped and displayed a yellow recognition flag. Other men, infantrymen, then appeared from beside the causeway, also waving yellow flags, and the paratroopers were very glad to see them. These were men of the 4th Infantry Division, and they had come from the sea.

When they re-assembled in England after D-Day and counted the cost, it was found that the American airborne divisions had suffered about 20 per cent casualties on D-Day. Half of these were men killed or missing. This was bad, but nothing like as bad as the 75 per cent casualties forecast by Leigh-Mallory. Only 20 parachute aircraft had been shot down out of more than 800 employed on the night of 5/6 June. The paratroops did not take all their D-Day objectives, for Carentan was not taken and the bridges over the Douve were still held by the Germans, but they had done very well. In spite of their misfortunes and the odds against them, the 82nd and 101st Airborne had given the 7th Corps of the US Army a foothold in France and a bridge-head in the Cotentin, from which Cherbourg could be quickly reduced, though there was a lot of hard fighting ahead before Cherbourg fell on 26 June. Above all, though, they had assured the success of the landings on 'Utah' beach. For 13,000 troopers, sorely harassed and scattered at the start of their adventure, that was an achievement indeed.

CHAPTER SEVEN

'Utah'

'We'll start the war right here.'
Brigadier-General Theodore Roosevelt
Deputy Commander, 4th Infantry Division,
Utah Beach, 6 June 1944

Midnight had come and gone. On the heights east of the Orne and in the close-knit fields of the Cotentin, men were fighting and dying, but elsewhere along the Normandy coast all was quiet. Had Field Marshal Rommel been at his headquarters at La Roche Guyon on the night of 5 June when reports began to come in of parachute landings astride the Orne and south of Cherbourg, his eyes would surely have strayed watchfully to the 40 miles of coast between the two. The image is so clear that it is possible to visualize him standing by the map-board, his hand moving over the surface and hardening into a fist which smites the Calvados coast as he says, 'Here!'

Rommel's action at the map-board is imaginary. Rommel was in Germany on 6 June 1944, celebrating his wife's birthday, waiting to see Hitler and get permission to move his Panzer divisions closer to the coast. He had been lulled into absence by

the weather forecasts and the Channel gales. Those same forecasts had allowed some of his commanders to snatch some leave
in Paris and others to attend an anti-invasion map exercise at
Rennes. Even so, someone should have studied that map and
drawn the obvious conclusion; that seaborne landings in the
centre must surely follow these widely separated airborne assaults. If anyone reached that conclusion, little was done about
it. All was still quiet at 0630 hrs on 6 June 1944, when American
infantry from the 8th Regimental Combat Team of the 4th
Infantry Division began to come ashore on 'Utah' beach on the
east coast of the Cotentin.

Utah' beach lies six miles east of Ste-Mère-Eglise. It is a
smoothly shelving, open beach, some ten miles long, of compact
grey sand, firm and free from natural obstacles. A mile offshore
lies a small group of rocks and islands, the Iles St Marcouf. At
the rear of the beach lie sand dunes which run up to twenty feet
high in places and behind them a low sea wall which carried a
narrow coast road. Beyond the dunes and the road the land is
low-lying and marshy.

In 1944, this area had been flooded and mined for up to two
miles inland, as part of Rommel's anti-invasion preparations.
Passage across this mined marsh depended on narrow causeways which, in peaceful times, give the villagers access to the
beach. There were five of these, leading from the beach to
the villages of Pouppeville, Hebert, Audouville, St Martin de
Varreville and St Germain.

In the original plan, the inland exits from these causeways
were to be seized by the airborne forces, and if they did their
work well the beach defences could be quickly overwhelmed
and the Americans rapidly debouch across the peninsula, well
on the road towards the capture of Cherbourg.

The troops landing on 'Utah' were from the US 4th Infantry
Division (the Ivy Leaves), commanded by Major-General Ray-
mond O. Barton. This division formed part of General Lawton
Collins's VII Corps. They were carried in a force of ships, Task
Force 'U', commanded by Rear Admiral D. P. Moon, USN in
the Force HQ ship, the USS *Bayfield*. This force contained,
apart from troopships and landing craft, the US battleship
Nevada, the 15-inch gun British monitor *Erebus*, 2 US cruisers,

the USS *Tuscaloosa* and *Quincy*, and 3 British cruisers, HMS *Hawkins*, HMS *Enterprise* and HMS *Black Prince*, as well as 8 destroyers and the Dutch gunboat *Soemba*.

The Germans had three infantry divisions in the Cotentin, but 4th Infantry were to be chiefly concerned with the 709th and 243rd Infantry Divisions, which occupied defences on the east coast of the Cotentin. Fortunately, they were already engaged in attempting to swat the myriad bands of roving American paratroopers, and while they were thus distracted, 4th Infantry came ashore.

The infantry would be led ashore by the 8th Infantry Regiment (Colonel Van Fleet), with the 3rd Battalion of the 22nd Infantry attached, followed seventy-five minutes later by the 22nd Infantry (Colonel Tribolet), and on H+4 by the 12th Infantry (Colonel R. P. 'Red' Reeder). The assault would be supported by thirty-two DD tanks and a small amount of specialized equipment, mainly bulldozers, to clear the beach obstructions and deal with the beach defences.

The 709th and 243rd were composed largely of 'stomach' battalions, infantry considered fit only for coastal defence work, plus a small proportion of Russian and Georgian troops. The 243rd had, in theory, become an attack infantry division, when the men had been supplied with bicycles and some motor transport. There seemed to be no insurmountable problem to the Allies here, but early in June, Intelligence had reported that the formidable 91st Division, well trained in anti-invasion tactics, had arrived in the area and the possibility of some tough opposition grew stronger. The 91st Division had already suffered a major setback just after midnight when their divisional commander, Lt-General Wilhelm Falley, was ambushed and killed by Lt Malcolm Brannen of the 82nd Airborne.

Task Force 'U' sailed from ports in the west of England. Arthur McNeil was a nineteen-year-old signalman in LCT 2440, part of the British 104 LCT Flotilla, and recalls taking the Americans to France: 'I arrived in Brixham on the Saturday morning and from the railway station which stood above the harbour I looked down on an amazing sight. Both the inner and outer harbours were so full of LCTs that the water could hardly be seen. All the craft were covered with camouflage netting but it was obvious that they were all fully loaded. On reporting to the Flotilla Officer in his makeshift office on the quay, he asked me if I was ready to tackle the biggest job of my life, but before I could reply he had assigned me to LCT 2440 and I was aboard within the hour.

'My new craft was a Mark 5 LCT – American-built and shipped over the Atlantic in sections aboard cargo ships to be assembled in UK ports. The Royal Navy had 5 flotillas, each of 12 craft. Thus, it had 60 of the 500 which were built. It is possible that some "Overlord" planner felt that since we were American-built, we should have the honour of carrying American soldiers on the great day.

'Our ship, together with scores of others lying at Brixham, had loaded during the previous week at "hards" – man-made concrete "beaches" – on the River Dart above Dartmouth. Our Americans were part of a unit of US Army Assault Engineers and they were in three half-track vehicles and a Jeep. The vehicles were loaded with high explosive for clearing obstacles on the beach or further inland. There must have been about 20 GIs aboard and they outnumbered the ship's company by about 2 to 1. They took the view – rightly, I suppose – that this was what the craft had been built for, so they made full use of our messdeck and "heads" facilities – and later, when we were underway and most of us closed-up at defence stations, they used our bunks. Nothing was sacred! They were quite the opposite of the archetypal GI and we were all good friends – perhaps the fear of what might lie ahead brought us closer together.

'As we left Brixham in the late evening of the Saturday to form up in Torbay, I was on the bridge with the Skipper, Sub-Lieutenant Walter Webb RNVR, and an American officer. As we cleared the harbour, the Skipper called down the voicepipe to the Cox'n, "This is it, Cox'n, no exercise this time." He then gave me copies of the two Orders of the Day – one from General Eisenhower and one from the Naval C-in-C, Admiral Ramsay, RN – to distribute to the ship's company. The American officer did the same, handing copies of General Eisenhower's order to his soldiers. We were told that they were being handed personally to each member of the assault forces but that they would be read out to the follow-up waves. For that reason, I treasure my own copies.

'We formed part of Force "U", the assault force bound for "Utah" beach, the most westerly beach on the eastern side of the Cherbourg Peninsula. Force "U" had loaded at the Devon and Cornwall ports and had, therefore, the longest sea crossing by landing craft. The latter point is worth bearing in mind because many of the troops were carried in liberty ships and the similar victory ships which had been adapted as troopships for the invasion. The soldiers then transferred to landing craft a short distance from the beach. In leaving on the Saturday evening, we were scheduled to arrive at the assembly area off "Utah" after dark on the Sunday night. The crossing followed a dog-leg course at about six knots. LCTs were slow and cumbersome craft and not the best of sea boats.

'During Saturday night and Sunday morning the weather became steadily worse and, as we all know, H-Hour was postponed for 24 hours until Tuesday 6 June. For most of the Allied force this simply meant remaining in harbour for another 24 hours and nerve-wracking as that was, at least they had the relative comfort of calm water. Force "U" was already at sea and that made for problems – one of which was the formation of the convoy. Normal convoy formation consisted of a number of quite short columns of ships, never more than nine, although there could be a large number of columns. The object of this was to protect the flanks of the convoy against U-Boat attack. Because Force "U" had a vast number of craft, normal convoy formation would have led to an impossibly wide convoy, so we were in three long columns with a vanguard of minesweepers in an arc ahead of the convoy and escorts of every kind patrolling the flanks. Our craft was near the front of the centre column and as one looked astern, the columns seemed to merge into a solid line stretching right back to the horizon – an optical illusion, no doubt, but there were a lot of ships.

'When they landed, our GIs would have been at sea, a very rough sea, in a small craft, for over 60 hours. They had the longest and roughest sea crossing to Normandy of the entire assault force. Our hearts went out to them. At least we were more used to being at sea and we did not have to go ashore and fight.

'On the Monday afternoon, one of the GIs, a youngster of about my own age, lifted himself off the quarterdeck guardrail where he was trying to be sick. "Hey, Limey," he said. "Have you ever been in combat before?" I could only say that I had been in many air raids but I tried to reassure him by saying that the reality was not as bad as the apprehension. He said, "Well, I don't care how bad it is, it can't be any worse than this lousy boat and this lousy weather."

'We arrived at the assembly area east of the Cherbourg Peninsula after dark on the Monday evening and the weather seemed to be moderating – perhaps because we were now in the lee of the land. When dawn broke the sight was amazing. By now the heavy ships had arrived and the bombardment had begun. Battleships and cruisers were firing their main armament and they were being assisted by LCT(R)s – LCTs modified to launch thousands of rockets from launchers covering their tankdecks. The noise must have been deafening but our own engines and those of the craft all round us were noisy diesels, so the sound of the bombardment was rather dulled.

'As the LCTs of our flotilla formed a line abreast for the run into the beach, there seemed to be little opposition. As it turned out, "Utah" beach was indeed the quietest of all five Allied beaches – perhaps because it was over a mile south of where it should have been. The last thing I remember the American officer saying before he thanked us and left the bridge to join his men was that the run-in to the beach was quieter than some exercises he had taken part in. In any event, the only resistance was some mortar fire and light shelling. We could see the explosions in the water but none of our craft was hit. Just as well, in view of the explosives we were carrying! Neither were there any wrecked landing craft on the beach from earlier waves. We were quite proud of the fact that we gave our American friends a dry landing. The water barely reached their axles.

'When we started our approach to the beach, I hoisted our pennants – our number – and an additional White Ensign at the yard-arm (we always flew it at the gaff at sea). The additional one was our battle ensign and we explained to the American

High tide on Juno Beach: the Canadians come ashore.

4th US Infantry Division land on Utah.

The Commanders. Left to right: Montgomery, Eisenhower, Tedder.

S/Sgt Wallwork, Glider Pilot Regiment.

The glider pilots. Left to right: Lofty Lawrence, No. 4 Glider; Roy Howard, No. 6 Glider; Len Guthrie (at back); 'Shorty' Shorter; Pete Boyle (at back); Stan Pearson, No. 5 Glider; George Chatterton (back to camera).

*S/Sgt R. A. Howard D.F.M—
B Squadron, Glider Pilot Regiment.*

*Pfc John Robert Slaughter, Company D,
116th Regiment, 29th Infantry Division.*

*Captain H. A. Shebeck,
82nd Airborne Division.*

*Guillaume Mercader, Chef de la Résistance,
with General Koëning at Bayeux,
14 June 1944.*

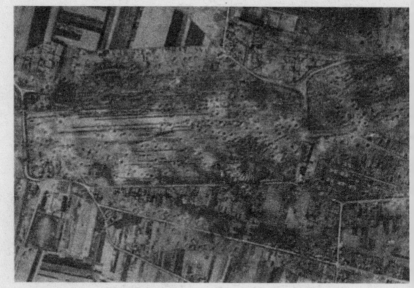

Preparations: the bombing of railways.

US infantry train on Dartmoor, England.

Transport aircraft and gliders in D-Day markings wait on an English airfield.

Troopers of the 508th Parachute Infantry Regiment on a training jump in England, April 1944.

Aerial reconnaissance before D-Day over the beach obstacles near Arromanches.

Bombardment warships sail for Normandy.

Canadian infantry wait offshore in LCAs (Landing Craft Assault).

Sword Beach, 0830 hours. British tanks and infantry under fire.

'The Killing Ground': Omaha beach, with obstacles and bunkers, 7 June 1944. 3,000 men were killed here on D-Day.

Troopers of 508th Parachute Infantry Regiment in Normandy. Left to right, standing: Privates W. L. Lamberson, A. J. J. Grindo, E. F. Wenzel, W. L. Ulrich, G. W. Womack; kneeling: Privates S. Smith, H. Pubal.

officer that it was customary in the Royal Navy, when going into battle, to fly as many battle ensigns as possible so that if one was shot away there would, hopefully, always be one still flying. The "battle" hardly seemed to justify our ardour. Having said that, I marvelled at the composure of our First Lieutenant, Sub-Lieutenant Jack Lathan RNVR. His beaching station was on the fo'c'sle to the right of the ramp down which the vehicles drove onto the beach. He had with him one of the able-seamen, "Dolly" Gray, whose task was to take soundings with a pole marked off in feet. These were relayed by the "Jimmy" to me by telephone and I called them over to the Skipper. The bridge was at the after end of the craft and the "Jimmy" and "Dolly" looked awfully exposed at the bow.'

Herb Stamer of Appalachin, New York, was then serving on LST 47, bound for 'Utah'. 'One hundred and seventy-three US-manned LSTs took part in the invasion, and only five were lost, and none on 6 June. On board our LST was a special service force of 40 underwater demolition men (UDT men). After the initial assault there were only 13 of the UDT men alive, and only 2 were uninjured. At H−2 we loaded the small boats with the demolition teams and they went ashore to do their jobs. Our H-Hour was set at 6 a.m. and proved to be everything it had been billed to be. The battleships began their barrage, minesweepers approached close to the shoreline, and the movements of troops landing in the heavy seas made it very difficult for the small boats. Two of ours breached-to and were swamped while landing. When the tide rolled back later we could see the red-iron railroad ties and crosses which made up the beach obstacles.

'We picked up 1,087 German prisoners, including a French woman who had been collaborating with the enemy. The crew members gave up their cots so the wounded could have a place to rest, and the officers gave up their quarters to the captured SS troopers, who were all tall, blond, tough as nails, and arrogant. In the tank deck, the majority of prisoners were kept with a clear space down the centre, where guards watched with machine guns.

'We returned to Normandy many times, perhaps 20 in all, before we left this area and sailed for Africa.'

Robin McGarel-Groves was a Royal Marine gunnery officer on one of the support ships, the cruiser HMS *Enterprise*. 'Back in mid-May, the Padre, the Rev. P. Husbands, had organized a sweepstake on which day was to be D-Day, and I had drawn 5 June; but as I was sworn to secrecy I could only gloat privately over my potential winnings.

'Once we had rounded Land's End the weather got steadily worse and we felt sympathy for the unfortunate soldiery exposed to these unfamiliar elements. It also looked pretty tricky for those in small craft and particularly the Duplex Drive (DD) tanks, which had a canvas screen superimposed on them but with only a foot or so freeboard. It came as no surprise that all convoys were ordered to reverse course and that D-Day was postponed from 5 June. There went my sweepstake winnings.

'Eventually the signal was received that D-Day was to be 6 June. What a way to spend my twenty-fourth birthday! We managed to arrive at our allotted bombardment position where we commenced firing just before 5.30 a.m. First a series of ranging shots to make sure we had found the target, and then a series of rapid broadsides, with small corrections to ensure that the whole length of the beach and village of St Martin de Varreville and its defences were covered. It all looked most effective. Intelligence had indicated that there were two German 15-inch guns on the coast, within whose range we lay, and the plan was that these should be knocked out previously by the RAF or US Army Air Force. Fortunately this had happened, as we received no trouble from them. We ceased fire a short while before H-hour at 6.30 a.m. when the beach was engaged by LCRs using 1,000 2-pounder rockets fired in 3 salvos.

'The firing of these LCRs was most spectacular as the whole craft seemed to erupt. One did not envy the crew of these LCRs, who must have been mildly fried to say the least. The effect on the beach was equally spectacular as the entire area seemed to explode, literally drenching the beach with explosive, to the extent that it seemed hardly possible for anyone to survive.

'Due to all the smoke and dust from explosions on the beach, it was not possible to see much of what was happening. Anyway, even if we could have seen what was going on, we would have realized that the landing actually took place some mile and a half from the planned position. This was caused by casualties among the guiding craft. Landing on the wrong beach produced an immediate bonus as this beach was lightly held and the troops got ashore with very few casualties.

'Having carried out our pre-allotted task, we were now available for target opportunity with our fire controlled by aircraft spotting. I can still remember our call sign on radio. We were "Queen Easy Dawg" and our spotting aircraft, piloted by an American with a lovely Texan drawl, was "Nan Tare Rahger". Our Texan friend designated a target and ordered us to fire one round for him to apply the appropriate correction to get us on to his target. This being achieved he instructed us to "Fire for Effect". This meant a six-gun broadside, followed as quickly as we could by two similar broadsides. In order for him to spot we gave him the word just before the salvo was due to land. He dipped his wing so he could see and then gave us the appropriate instructions or correction. He and his successors kept us busy for the rest of that day and into the dusk. For once our own aircraft were everywhere, and on that first day we hardly sighted an enemy aircraft.

'One problem, however, did start to emerge. The Germans had laid a number of oyster acoustic mines, which exploded under a ship, triggered by the noise of its propellers. These mines lay on the bottom and were not swept by normal sweeping methods. Quite near us, the American destroyer the USS *Corry* struck one of the mines or was hit by shellfire, broke in two and sank quite quickly. Fortunately there were few casualties, and the survivors were picked up quickly by the many returning small craft, going back empty to fill up again. An American pilot vessel and several landing craft in our area suffered a similar fate and there were casualties on the other beaches from these mines, until a dead slow order was given for all movements in the immediate area of the beaches.'

The first men ashore were 132 men of the 4th and 24th Cavalry, who landed on the offshore Iles St Marcouf, which they found heavily mined but otherwise deserted. Meanwhile, as the troops trans-shipped into their landing craft, 247 Marauders of the 9th US Air Force began to bomb the beach and at about 0530 hrs the warships of Task Force 'U' began to fire on the shore defences and batteries.

The assault was supported by 33 LCRs or LCGs to give close support on to the beach, plus 32 DD tanks. The DD tanks were launched close in at only 3,000 yards from the beach, and 28 made it ashore, though they arrived fifteen minutes after the infantry. The first infantry wave, of 2nd Battalion, 8th Infantry in 20 LCVPs, got ashore quite unopposed and, highly delighted, were waving their rifles in the air and cheering as they ran across the beach towards the dunes. They had not quite reached them when it became clear that something had gone wrong. The 4th Infantry Division had landed in the wrong place.

One of the ships going ashore that morning was commanded by Joseph Suozzo of Oceanside, California. 'I participated in the Normandy invasion as Officer in Charge of LCT 2310, beaching her on "Utah" beach at H Hour + 6 minutes. On May 10, 1944 I had been given command of LCT 2310, and went to Tilbury Docks to pick up the craft and crew. We became part of the Commander Gunfire Support Craft, Eleventh Amphibious Force. On June 1, 1944 we loaded three Sherman tanks and proceeded to Salcombe where we were berthed in mid-stream until getting underway for the invasion.

'Early on June 6, we arrived at the departure point. About 15 minutes before hitting the beach, Allied planes passed overhead and proceeded to saturate a strip of the landing beaches with bombs. Smoke, debris and dust obscured our view of the beach so badly that we couldn't see the beach for some time. We ended beaching some 300–400 yards further south than planned. It finally started to clear somewhat in the last 300 yards of our approach when we came under fire from an 88mm cannon in one of the pill-boxes on the beach. The profile of the beach was flat with no significant features and so we couldn't determine where the gunfire was coming from.

'Despite the gunfire, we did put the three Sherman tanks on the beach. They did not fire during the landing and I never did find out why. The wheel-house structure took one hit and both the helmsman and the engine man were wounded. Other damage was a hit to the winch, disabling it with 300ft of anchor cable out. Another hit the rudder cable, severing it with 30 degrees right rudder on and one hit in the engine room, disabling the starboard engine. We were able to back off after cutting loose our anchor cable and then jockeying the engines between forward and reverse to try and compensate for the loss of steering. All in all we took ten direct hits from 88mm and mortar fire. We were able to get a tow from a British LCF to the staging area five miles or so off the beach, where we remained until one of our LSTs towed us back to Portsmouth.' Joseph M. Suozzo was awarded the Silver Star for his action on D-Day.

Walter Schaad of Marietta, Ohio, went ashore on 'Utah' in a tank. 'On the morning of D-Day I woke up in the bottom of the tank, then I crawled on to the top and sat down to wait, and before long I was able to make out the beach. As we approached the shore we got down as low as possible in the tanks, and as the ramp dropped and we went into the water, our tank was hit with artillery at least four times. One shell hit right by my ear and cracked the side of the tank about a foot long. I still have loss of hearing because of that.

'Captain Warren was calling for someone to help him pull a Jeep from the water, and three sergeants ran to help him. Donald Schlemmer and I got off the tank, ran to the concrete wall, and got into a fox-hole, when we heard a shell coming. When the smoke, sand and water had cleared, the three sergeants lay there dead, and Captain Warren had a piece of shrapnel in his hand. We backed the tank to the edge of the water and pulled the Jeep onshore, and then we did the same thing with a half-track, jamming an opening in the sea wall, pulling it out of the way. Then we went through the wall into an open field, where our tank went into a shell hole and tore off a track. Our tank mechanic and two or three other boys started working on the track, but I felt it was safer in a fox-hole.

'After sitting there for nearly two hours, with shells dropping all around us, I had said every prayer I could think of. I begged the dear Lord not to let the next shell fall in the hole with us.

After running out of prayers I started to think on all the bad things I had ever done and promised not to do them again.

'Believe it or not, I then heard a roaring noise from the west. Coming in were planes, planes and more planes, paratroopers and gliders. Unbelievable! You couldn't see the sky they were so thick. By that time our tank was fixed and we were able to get into a firing position.'

Among the first men ashore that morning was nineteen-year-old Anthony Jele from Albuquerque, New Mexico, then in Company 'C', 1st Battalion, 8th Infantry Regiment. Anthony Jele was carrying his rifle, some grenades, two bandoliers and a case of mortar ammunition for the heavy-weapon crews that would follow him ashore. 'During part of the twelve-hour trip across the English Channel I stood guard and watched the five-pronged invasion. I saw water spouts shooting up next to our landing craft, but didn't know what they were. Somebody else said, "Hey, they're shooting at us."

'The French coast was calm when I got my first glimpse of Normandy just after dawn on June 6, 1944. When I looked at the beach it was all clear and quiet. It looked like a Sunday morning.

'The Germans weren't expecting a landing at "Utah" beach, so the first wave was able to scramble across the sand without many casualties, but Nazi artillery was alerted to the invasion soon after the first Americans waded ashore and the fifth wave nearly got wiped out. Our real baptism by fire came three days later, and on June 9 heavy enemy fire tore our unit apart. All the officers were killed and the rest of us struggled on for about a month with sergeants in command.'

The 8th Infantry should have landed opposite Exit 3, which led to Audouville. Instead they landed over a mile south, opposite Exit 1, leading to Pouppeville. One of the control vessels, which should have led them in, had struck a mine and been lost, and the strong set of the incoming tide sweeping up the Channel then carried their assault craft off course. This initial error could have been disastrous, but luckily landing in the first wave was the Assistant Commander of the 4th Infantry Division, Brigadier-General Theodore Roosevelt Jnr, son of the former American President, Teddy Roosevelt. Although fifty-seven years old at the time, he had persuaded his divisional commander to let him go ashore with the first wave.

This proved providential. General Roosevelt recognized the error, knew what to do, and had the authority to make his decision stick. He signalled out to the following waves of landing craft to ignore their original headings and follow in behind the initial wave. He then walked up and down the foreshore, waving his stick, cheering his men ashore, regardless of the machine-gun and artillery fire now beginning to sweep the beach. The 1st Battalion of the 8th Infantry pressed on towards Audouville, the 2nd Battalion continued towards Pouppeville. General Roosevelt died of a heart attack five weeks after the landings, but his action on D-Day won him the Congressional Medal of Honour.

Many men of the 4th Infantry Division recall seeing General Roosevelt on the beach; men like Jack Capell, then a radio wireman in the 8th Infantry Regiment. 'I spent five months in England before the invasion, and although I saw a lot of the towns in South Devon, I never got to London, which I really regret. One of my buddies did get a twenty-four hour pass to London and while he was there he got caught in an air raid and hit by a piece of shrapnel. He was the first man of the 4th Infantry Division to be wounded in Europe.

'We sailed from Dartmouth in South Devon. The landing craft we boarded was an LST and we were to be carried across on this and transfer to smaller landing craft ten or eleven miles offshore. Once at sea we saw more ships. The sea got rough and it began to rain. We were then told that we were to land in France, fight our way ashore and locate a road inland. Once inland we were to link up with our paratroopers somewhere between the beach and the village of Ste-Mère-Eglise.

'We trans-shipped to small landing craft late on June 5, though the seas were still rough. An LCT came up, the LST opened its doors and I was ordered to drive my Jeep from one to the other; all this while the two ships were rolling in the waves, out of phase with each other. I managed to do this but the transfer damaged our waterproofing.

'To starboard was the island of St Marcouf, and the battle-ship USS *Nevada* was firing on German gun positions and the shore batteries were firing back. Aircraft towing gliders were passing over, and obviously we would be hitting the beach in about an hour. I had a brief vision of being blown to pieces; some men became silent, others became boisterous. We filled in the time by breaking into the ship's stores and loading up with good Navy food.

'We – a sergeant, and Horace Cisk the Company clerk, and I – were ordered off in deeper water than there should have been, and after a few yards my Jeep engine began to misfire and then stopped. We were in deep water and neither of my passengers could swim. I swam for shore, touching bottom in the trough of each wave, left my equipment on the beach and swam back to bring the other two ashore. I got a rope from a DUKW and then towed the Jeep on to the sand. Artillery fire was falling on to the beach and we were strafed by a Messerschmitt. The wounded were already being taken off, many of the men had stepped on anti-personnel schu-mines, which damaged or blew off their feet. We eventually got the Jeep going and drove to the head of the beach. All our food had been lost and for two days we lived on fruit cocktail looted from the Navy; I have never cared for it since.

'By this time most of our rear echelon units had landed, including the artillery and anti-tank companies, military police, and so on. On leaving the beach to find the company we were confused because the terrain did not fit the features given in our briefing. This was because the 8th Infantry Regiment had been landed about a mile south of our intended position. General Theodore Roosevelt Jnr landed in the first wave, and he took charge on the beach where we landed. His words at the time were: "We'll start the war right here." Teddy Roosevelt was the most respected man in the unit and I believe his presence on the beach made the difference between success and failure on "Utah" beach. Unfortunately, he did not stay with us long and was to die in Normandy.'

Another man on the beach that day was a combat medic, Calvin Grose of the 22nd Infantry Regiment. 'When we boarded a transport for the invasion from Plymouth, we were told to stay below decks, but I sneaked top-side to watch the naval bombardment by such ships as USS *Nevada*, plus other cruisers and destroyers.

'We were about the first craft in, and the enemy fire was light until they found out what was going on. We reached the beach with Brigadier-General Theodore Roosevelt Jnr, and he told us not to lay there but to move in off the beach. We had never been under fire before and he walked from soldier to soldier and told us to move. We attacked some pill-boxes and I spent 55 days treating the wounded. I was then hit myself and shipped back to England to recover.'

Corporal Fred Tannery drove ashore in a Jeep. 'We could see the coastline of France as we went in. There was not too much activity, and when the battleships started bombarding the beach I thought this was going to be duck soup. Then the shells started splashing around and wounded soldiers were brought back on board our LST ... so this was it. Our LST hit the beach, the ramp went down and "Pop" my driver, and I, got ashore without even getting our feet wet.

'We drove inland with just a little shell-fire going on, and that didn't bother us. We drove inland until we met a bunch of GIs and settled down with them for a while. My father had fought in France during the First War, and he told me about the red poppies in France, and the field next to the road where we stopped was full of poppies which reminded me of my father.

'Just after dark some German planes came over and every ship in the bay opened up on them – a sheet of red and green tracer; the most beautiful sight I have ever seen. One of the planes was hit and crashed nearby. I'll never forget that. Otherwise it was quiet – and that was my first day in France with the 4th Infantry Division.'

Colonel 'Red' Reeder was there, commanding the 12th Infantry Regiment. 'Before D-Day a conference on the Normandy Landings was held at a theatre in Plymouth, and the Corps Commander, Lt-General Collins, was explaining the missions of the different units in Normandy, indicating their objectives on the map with a long pointer. "Here is the 8th Infantry," he said, "Colonel Van Fleet commanding. I served in the 8th Infantry. It is a fine regiment of great traditions, and it will accomplish its mission. Here is the 22nd Infantry, Colonel

Tribolet. I served in the 22nd Infantry. It is a fine regiment of great traditions, and it will accomplish its mission. Here is the 12th Infantry, Colonel Reeder commanding."

'Then he stopped and talked of the problems of the landing. I felt I could not let the General and his talk end there, for I had ten 12th Infantrymen with me in the room.

'When the General paused I stood up. "Sir," I said. "May I make a statement, sir?" "Certainly, Red. What is it?" "Sir, the 12th Infantry Regiment is a fine regiment, a regiment of great traditions, and it will accomplish its mission," I said. After the applause, Van Fleet howled, "Red, you looked like a West Point pleb correcting a first-classman."

'The four hours from 6.30 a.m. when the first troops landed till we went ashore at 10.30 a.m. were the longest four hours I ever spent. When I climbed down the cargo nets into the bucking LCVP, a young sailor said, "Colonel, sit up here on our perch with the coxswain and me. You can see better." "No thanks," I said. "I read in a book that a leader is supposed to be up front. I'll stand at the front ramp with Colonel Montelbano, battalion commander (Lt-Colonel Montelbano was killed on D+5) so I can be the first one out of this thing." That decision saved my life. When the boat grated on the Normandy shore, I stepped into waist-high water and ran up the beach while light artillery sprayed the sands with iron. A shell hit the LCVP and killed the young sailor, the coxswain, and the last 12th Infantryman leaving the boat.

'All along "Utah" beach 12th Infantrymen were wading ashore and running to the top of the dunes. "Mills," I said, "things don't look right to me. Where the hell are we?" Lieutenant Bill Mills took my map and in a moment justified his grade of 97 per cent on the map-reading exam. He said, "They've landed us about two miles south of where we're supposed to be." "It don't matter," I replied. "We know where to go! Get the word out we're two miles south of where we ought to be."

'At the top of the dunes I passed General Roosevelt, who had landed with Van Fleet's first wave. "Red, the causeways leading inland are all clogged up. Look at it! A procession of Jeeps and not a wheel turning. Something wrong." Roosevelt looked tired and the cane he leaned on heightened the impression. "We are going through the flooded area!" I yelled as loud as I could. Down the dunes I saw Lieutenant-Colonel "Chuck" Jackson of the 1st Battalion, and I gave him an arm signal. I knew the rest of the regiment coming ashore in the next wave would follow us.

'A mile across the flooded meadow lay the village of St-Martin-de-Varreville. Rising above it was a church steeple that looked like a friendly beacon. We waded through water in the German-made lake which varied in depth from waist to arm-pit and in a few spots was over our heads. We had the non-swimmers paired with the swimmers, and even so I was proud of the non-swimmers around me who were holding on to their weapons. The large groups of men in the water made a perfect target, but we waded the water safely.'

Louis Siebel was a Pfc serving in the Quartermaster Company of the 4th Infantry Division. 'I was inducted into the Army in 1942 and had three brothers in the armed services. My younger brother, a bombardier, was shot down over Germany the day I arrived in England. He later died of his injuries. We waited all day on our LST about 3,000 yards off "Utah". We watched a small destroyer go down and an ammunition dump blew up, and at about 5 o'clock in the evening the announcement came that we were about to land. About 170 men in 30 trucks rode on to "Utah" beach, where it was still daylight. We could see shell-holes and bodies covered by blankets, and there was still enemy fire, but we felt relieved because we had landed in France – and that was June 6 as I remember it fifty years afterwards.'

Dominic L. Alfano from Hamden, Connecticut was a member of 'B' Company, 1st Battalion, 8th Infantry. 'Needless to say we were anxious to set foot on land after the gales at sea, but prior to getting ashore we were shelled by the Germans and it seemed questionable whether we would get ashore without becoming casualties. However, we did get on to the beach, where we were strafed by enemy aircraft. Altogether, I spent seven years and four months in the service, being discharged on October 2, 1945, just one year after being wounded in Germany. As you may know, D-Day was not so difficult for us, but that was one of our easiest days. I learned from the accounting that by May 1945 the 4th Infantry Division had sustained a total of 34,000 killed and over 22,000 wounded, the most of any Division.'

Harper Coleman of Tucson, Arizona, was with Company 'H', 2nd Battalion, 8th Infantry Regiment and also recalls seeing General Roosevelt on the beach: 'We went in with the second wave of assault troops. Shortly after the larger ships came to a stop we were to go into the small LCVP. Being with the first waves had some advantage. We were not required to go over the sides of the ship but were put on the LCVP while it was still on the davits of the larger ship and let down in the water with the craft.

'As we started to move towards the beach in lines, we passed Rocket Launcher ships and as we were going past they were releasing many salvos of rockets on the beach. It must have been around 0530 hrs to 0600 hrs, as it was daylight and we were all standing up in the craft watching the show on the beach, which was still some distance ahead. The beach was almost hidden from view by smoke and shell bursts.

'I saw the craft in front of ours going up with some sort of direct hit, which left ours first at this time. Before we reached the shore something came through the side of our craft and tore quite a hole in it, in one side and out the other. It also tore a good sized piece out of my backpack. I don't recall how I replaced it but I did so quickly. Also, while on the way in, I recall seeing some sort of naval ship laying over with many people up on the side.

'The history books say we landed some distance to the left than we were supposed to, and that this was one of the easier landings. I don't know if this was good or bad. It did not seem good at the time. We went in the water somewhat more than waist deep and a good distance from dry land. When we came on shore we were greeted by Brigadier-General Theodore Roosevelt. How he got there, I do not know, other than that he was in one of the first landing craft, but there he was, standing on the beach, waving his cane and giving out instructions as only he could do. If we were afraid of the enemy, we were more afraid of him, and could not have stopped on the beach had we wanted to.

'My squad of six was down to four very early on; we lost one on the beach and another when we came to the higher ridge just over the sandy area. Moving as fast as we could we came to a road that ran down to the beach, and this took us through the swamps that were behind the beach which had been flooded by the Germans. We came up on the small town of Pouppeville. This is where we began to see the results of our work – our first dead enemy. Shortly beyond the town we began to meet some of the airborne people. As I recall, they were rather glad to see us.

'I remember setting up for the first night. It was on a dirt road with a high hedge on either side. We dug in there for the night with a number of enemy dead laying in the roadway close to where we were. One of the remarks of the day was, "These ones won't hurt you." This was more or less the routine for the twenty-one days on the way to Cherbourg. We must have been a dirty and smelly bunch by the time we got there.'

Malcolm Williams was with the 2nd Battalion of the 12th Infantry Regiment and recalls another story of General Roosevelt. 'I once heard General Roosevelt asking Major O'Malley of "H" Company in our Battalion what his secret was for success in always being able to move forward in an attack. Major O'Malley's answer was, "Well, Sir, if my boys get pinned down and can't move, I just crawl a few yards out in front of them and holler for help. When they see and hear me, they think I'm in trouble, so they start moving up towards me. And once I get those boys moving, all hell can't stop them."

'On another day, the day when Colonel Montelbano was killed, I was sent back to regiment to report his death, and Major Burk told me to report to General Roosevelt. Colonel "Red" Reeder, our Regimental Commander, had been wounded that morning. The General asked me to have coffee to calm me. Then he asked what was going on up there. I told him about the Colonel getting killed. I was standing only 20 or 30ft away at the time. The General asked who was left in charge. I told him that Major O'Malley was in command. He said, "You go back and tell all those men that they have the best man in the whole Army." He then said, "Why, that black Irishman, I would trust him anywhere."

'On the day Major O'Malley was killed, we had been receiving a lot of artillery fire. A piece of shrapnel had torn off my gas mask but it didn't hit me. Boy, that was close! When Major O'Malley's body was brought back, I took his gas mask and used it for the rest of the war. All of us admired and respected Major O'Malley. He was a good soldier and I will never forget him. God rest his soul.'

After the infantry had secured the beach, the combat engineers and naval demolition teams came ashore and began to blast and clear away the beach obstacles. Quite apart from avoiding disastrous confusion, Brigadier Roosevelt's action in switching the landing had advantages. The defences to the south of the planned 'Utah' landing area were less strong than those in front of their original landing place, and more easily overcome. The beach obstacles here consisted of three lines of obstructions, mainly steel spikes and wooden posts crowned with fused Teller mines, steel caltrops, tetrahedra and 'hedgehogs', all designed to hole landing craft. All these obstacles were mined. The plan called for the combat engineers to clear a number of fifty-yard gaps in these obstacles to let landing craft in when the tide rose, and they did this quickly and well. By H+3 the beach had been largely cleared and the troops were pouring ashore, though German activity, mostly from artillery, was steadily increasing.

John Ausland, then aged twenty-four, was an intelligence officer with the 29th Field Artillery Regiment. 'The run into the beach was a bizarre experience. Most of us were happy to cower behind the little protection provided by the metal sides of the landing craft. One officer from Regimental Headquarters, however, insisted on sitting on a chair above us, where he was exposed to enemy fire. Arms folded, he announced that he did not want to miss a moment of this spectacular show. A few weeks later, under similar circumstances, he collapsed with a sniper's bullet through his head.

'When the landing craft hit the beach and the front ramp went down, I waded through some shallow water and ran to the shelter of the sea wall that ran along the beach, barely glancing at several soldiers who were lying on the sand as though asleep. I could hear rifle and machine-gun fire beyond the sand dunes, and some mortar shells fell not far away.

'My task, once ashore, was to guide our three artillery batteries to firing positions that we had selected in England from a detailed foam-rubber relief map of the beach. After crossing the sand dunes that lay just beyond the sea wall, I was unable to figure out where I was. When I asked an infantry officer to help me, he laughed and said that the Navy had landed the first wave several thousand yards south of where we were supposed to land. Fortunately, Brigadier-General Theodore Roosevelt Jnr had volunteered to go in with the first wave. He later told some of us how he had gone forward to reconnoitre the beach, and finding that Major-General Maxwell Taylor's Airborne Division, which had dropped during the night, had captured the causeways over the inundated area behind the beach, Roosevelt decided that to try to move the landing northward would only cause confusion.

'When I went back to the beach I told Colonel Thomason that I could find only two firing positions, not three, in the limited area between the sand dunes and the inundated area. He said, "It's all right. We'll only need two. B-Battery hit a mine on the way in and the landing craft sank." Before I could think too long about the sixty men on that boat, Thomason told me to get moving and guide the two other batteries to their firing positions.

'After the batteries were in position, Thomason suggested that we go inland to find the infantry. After crossing a causeway over the inundated area, we found ourselves in the middle of a field. We froze when we heard a soldier on the other side of the field shout, "Don't you fools know that you're in the middle of a minefield?" After discussing our predicament, we agreed to separate, so that if one of us stepped on a mine we would not both be blown up. It was a long way to the other side of that field.

'Late in the afternoon, after our batteries moved inland to support the infantry, the clear, blue sky was filled with coloured parachutes. From these were suspended boxes of supplies for the paratroopers. A colourful sight turned to horror, however, when gliders loaded with soldiers and equipment started to circle and land. Unnerved perhaps by German anti-aircraft fire, some of the pilots crashed their gliders into the hedgerows.

Whenever I recall that scene, I can still hear the terrible screams of pain that filled the air around me. My last memory of that day is watching multicoloured tracer bullets arch through the sky over Ste-Mère-Eglise, which had been captured by our paratroopers but was still surrounded by German forces.

'I fell asleep well after midnight in a ditch by a road – a road that would lead us first north to the capture of Cherbourg and then south to the breakout from the bridgehead at St Lô.'

Girden 'Griff' Griffith came ashore with Company 'I' of the 12th Infantry. 'My battalion landed in the second wave of assault troops on "Utah" beach. Like everyone else, I recall D-Day as a time of saying my prayers and trying to stay alive. On the third day I was wounded by artillery fire near Emondeville and evacuated back to a hospital in England.'

The 4th Infantry Division had the easiest of all the D-Day landings, partly because of the southward shift on the beach, partly because the paratroopers had disrupted the German defences, partly because the landing plan worked. The entire 'Utah' beach area was captured at a cost of just forty-five men killed and injured. Initial opposition on the beach was fortunately light, because during the hour or so it took to clear the beach and the causeways and let the traffic off, the tanks and vehicles began to assemble in a manner that would have provided sitting targets for German artillery. In the main the opposition came in the form of undirected artillery fire from inland batteries and mortars, which were swiftly engaged by the big guns on the warships offshore.

The German infantry manning the coastal positions had first been shocked and dazed by the bombing, shelling and rocket fire, and startled by the sight of the DD tanks rearing out of the waves. Coastal strongpoints were soon reduced, and as more men came ashore, the chief problem on the 'Utah' beachhead was traffic congestion. Owing to the southward swing of the landings, only Exit 2 could be used by vehicles, and this was both mined and defended by pill-boxes. Behind the beachhead the fighting intensified, both along the causeways and across the flooded fields, as 4th Infantry got into its stride and began to force a passage inland.

William Garvin from Epping in New Hampshire was a Pfc in

Company 'K' of the 12th Infantry Regiment. 'Three months after war was declared, I volunteered for Army service, foolishly choosing the infantry because I loved the outdoors and felt I could shoot a rifle well. I thought I could best serve Uncle Sam as a rifleman and foot soldier. After about two and a half years of rugged training at various Army installations in the US, our Division boarded the USS *George Washington* and set sail for Liverpool, England.

'On the night of June 5, we lifted anchor and pointed the ship's bows eastward, headed out into the night and the nervous unknown. It was required that all troops remain below decks for the crossing with the exception of Cpl John Delevan, the company radio operator, and his assistant, yours truly. We were to maintain radio transmission silence but to operate the SCR 300 radio set for message receiving only.

'Guns from some ships were lofting shells inland as the first wave of infantrymen hit the shores. Our turn came much later as we were scheduled for the ninth wave. We had transferred to LCIs (Landing Craft Infantry) and had rendezvous'd in a constant circle before our turn came to break out and head for the shore. The LCI pilot was kind enough to run the boat right up on to dry land before discharging his human cargo. This hardly proved beneficial to us, however, because the "shore" was but a mere sandbar which we quickly crossed before plunging into hip-deep water. Facing us was over two miles of inundated terrain with deep irrigation trenches about every two hundred yards. We had kept our Mae-West life-jackets on since debarking, which proved to be a tremendous aid in staying afloat while floundering across the flooded ditches, weighed down with heavy fighting gear.

'For us, the landing at "Utah" beach was a relatively pleasant adventure. There had been no visible casualties, though there were some light artillery shells exploding on the beachhead some distance away. After sloshing about and hand-paddling for about one and a half hours, we breathed easier on reaching above-water ground. We began to see the results of early-morning skirmishes as, with mixed feelings, we observed the corpses of the enemy. The regiment's mission was to push inland to relieve the paratroopers who earlier that morning had descended on the sleepy Normandy village of Ste-Mère-Eglise. Evidence of savage fighting grew as we neared the village and dead from both sides became commonplace. Torn parachutes hung from trees and buildings and broken branches and shattered buildings indicated fierce fighting had occurred.

'We accomplished our mission with little effort. Perhaps we were lulled into a feeling of complacency from having done little more than observe the countryside and the results of the actions of others. None of us in Company "K", to my knowledge, had fired a shot, but little did we realize how rapidly this scenario would switch to a frightful and costly nightmare. Before it was all over, my left arm received a bullet, my forehead a shell fragment, and my feet frostbite. I considered myself extremely fortunate to have emerged from the war with body and mind intact; many others were far less fortunate.'

By 1000 hrs on 6 June the seaborne forces were pushing inland hard from 'Utah', drawn on by the sound of firing up ahead, where mixed groups of paratroopers from both airborne divisions were striving to keep the landward exits clear. The first formation ashore, the 2nd Battalion of the 8th Infantry Regiment, was now heading fast for Pouppeville, harassed across the marshes by small-arms fire. On the way they found and recruited a DD tank, which then led their advance along the causeway until at the far end they were met with a hail of fire, which forced the tank to halt and the infantry to take cover in the water. The fire sounded familiar and stopped abruptly when yellow recognition flags were displayed by the tank and the infantry. Down the causeway to meet them, with wide grins spreading across their blackened faces, came the men of the 101st Airborne, and the first man they met was Captain George Mabry from South Carolina, the first seaborne soldier across the causeway.

By the evening of D-Day, 4th Infantry Division was well ashore, with the advance elements eight miles inland. Over 23,000 men had been landed on 'Utah', together with tanks and artillery, and they were now linking up with the paratroopers all along their divisional front. The 4th Infantry Division took only 210 casualties during the entire day and this included 60 men lost at sea. Although the 4th Infantry Division was to see much hard fighting in the following days as they pushed north to Cherbourg, their first day in battle had gone well.

Others were not so lucky. Just a few miles away, on the north coast of Calvados, two other American infantry regiments, from the 1st and 29th Divisions of General Gerow's V Corps, were being cut to pieces on 'Omaha' beach.

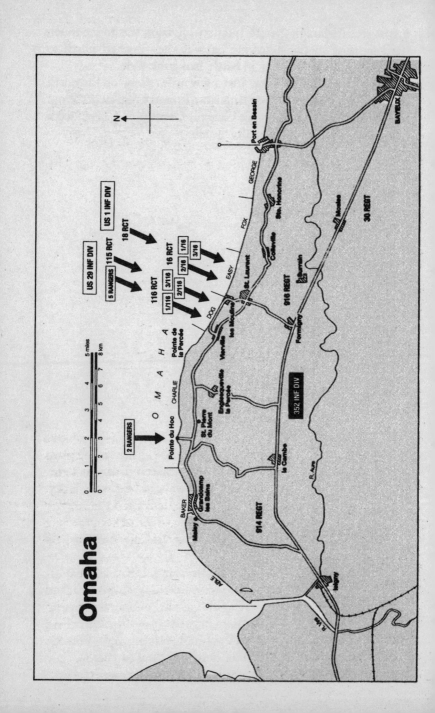

Omaha

CHAPTER EIGHT
'Omaha'

'The only people on this beach are the dead
and those who are going to die – now let's
get the hell out of here.'
Colonel George Taylor
16th Infantry Regiment, 1st Infantry Division

Every campaign ever fought seems to involve at least one pounding match, some point on the battlefield where fine plans and well practised tactics dissolve into sheer murderous fighting. So far the invaders had done very well, or been very lucky. The airborne forces were at work on the flanks and the landing on 'Utah' had been very successful. A major setback somewhere was only to be expected and it came along the Calvados coast, on the beach codenamed 'Omaha'.

The USS *Ancon*, flagship of Admiral Hall, USN, commanding Task Force 'O' headquarters ship for the V Corps, reached the transport area twelve miles off 'Omaha' about 0230 hrs on the morning of 6 June. Out there in the Bay of the Seine there was little shelter from the full fetch of the gales, and the laden men of the two assault divisions were in difficulties before they began to climb down the scrambling nets into their assault craft.

The two divisions of General Gerow's V Corps leading the assault on 'Omaha' were the 1st Infantry Division (the Big Red One) commanded by Major-General Clarence R. Huebner, and the 29th Infantry Division (the Blue and the Grey) commanded by Major-General Charles Gerhardt. These two divisions had different origins. The 'Big Red One' was a regular infantry division, and although it contained many drafted men, the backbone of the division was made up of professional officers, NCOs and private soldiers, drawn from every state of the Union. The 29th Infantry Division (the Blue and the Grey), on the other hand, was a National Guard formation, the equivalent of a British Territorial Army unit.

The 29th Division recruited in the states of Virginia, Maryland and Pennsylvania, and many of the men in its ranks had joined up before the war in order to serve with their neighbours and buddies when the big war came. The 29th was drafted into Federal service in 1942 but had seen no action before D-Day. This local recruitment was to give the losses sustained by the 29th Infantry Division on 'Omaha' beach a particular poignancy when the casualty lists for D-Day arrived in the small towns back home. To give two examples, the town of Roanoke lost 18 men on D-Day and the town of Bedford lost 23 of its sons. Many of these men including three sets of brothers, were serving in 'A' Company of the 116th Infantry Regiment.

The assault formations for 'Omaha' were two Regimental Combat Teams (RCTs), the equivalent of a British brigade, made up from the 16th Infantry Regiment of 1st Infantry Division, landing on the left, or east, on 'Easy Red' and 'Easy Green', and the 116th Infantry Regiment of the 29th Division landing on the right, or west, on 'Dog Green, White and Red'. Both regiments, and their supporting assault engineers, DD tanks and artillery, came under General Huebner's command for the assault phase.

For support these regiments had 2 US battleships, the USS *Texas* and the USS *Arkansas*, the British cruiser HMS *Glasgow*, and 2 French cruisers, the *Montcalm* and the *Georges Leygues*, as well as 11 destroyers and squadrons of LCRs and some LCGs. The infantry were accompanied by special teams of combat engineers who, as at 'Utah', would land immediately after the assault waves to demolish and clear away the beach obstacles for the landing craft bringing in the follow-up waves. In this task they would be assisted by bulldozers as at 'Utah'. Unfortunately, 'Omaha' was not to be like 'Utah' at all.

'Omaha' beach is a wide, gently curving beach, some four miles long, which occupies the only gap in the 100-foot-high cliffs that run from the Pointe du Hoc north of Isigny, east towards Port-en-Bessin. 'Omaha' was an obvious point for a landing and the German defences here were therefore more developed than at many other points along the Calvados coast. In addition they were manned by the trained and resolute 352nd Infantry Division, the only full attack division on the Normandy coast. This division had only arrived in Normandy at the end of May and had moved to the Cotentin coast on an anti-invasion exercise in the first days of June. The presence of the 352nd was completely unknown to Allied Intelligence, and an unpleasant surprise for the assaulting infantry.

The defences at 'Omaha' were formidable and helped by the nature of the terrain. The beach shelves gently but leads up to a high shingle bank, along the top of which now runs a narrow road which rests on the sea wall. Behind the road is a shallow belt of sand, leading to high sand dunes and cliffs which provide visibility over the entire landing area.

There are only four exits through these cliffs and off the beach. In June 1944 these gaps, or 'draws', were protected by 35 pill-boxes full of infantry armed with rifles, machine guns and grenades. There were 8 concrete bunkers equipped with 75mm guns and no less than 85 machine-gun posts equipped with Spandaus. The heavy guns were sited in concrete emplacements to enfilade the beach, with the concrete on the roof and seaward side strong enough to withstand direct hits from bombs and heavy naval guns. Along 'Omaha' the Germans had laid out 18 anti-tank positions, mounting guns of between 37mm and 75mm, 6 Nebelwerfer (multiple-barrelled mortar) pits, 38 rocket batteries and 4 field artillery positions. To link all this together a network of trenches had been prepared, and the whole complex was manned by well trained infantry, including a good number of snipers. This combination of man-made defences and natural obstacles had turned 'Omaha' into a killing ground ... and there was more.

In addition to weaponry, the Germans had prepared a thick belt of beach obstacles. There were three rows of these set below the high-water mark consisting of mined posts and obstructions, the angular steel girders of 'Element C', 'Belgian Gates', and a variety of other obstructions, all mined and creating a complete barrier to any oncoming landing craft. Behind this was a further wide belt of mines and barbed wire laid along the shingle bank and in the strip between the bank and the dunes. All in all 'Omaha' was the most formidable German position along the Normandy coast. The task of overcoming it was committed to the enthusiastic troops of the 29th Infantry Division and their comrades of the Big Red One, the most experienced American division in Europe, veterans of the fighting in North Africa, Sicily and Italy.

During these early campaigns, 1st Infantry Division had established a great reputation in combat with the enemy at the front and – let it be admitted – an even greater one for combat with the military police in the rear areas. General Omar Bradley recalls in his memoirs that the 1st Infantry Division left 'a trail of looted bars and outraged mayors all the way from Arzew to Catania'. The Big Red One was a feisty, hard-fighting division, which needed careful handling in and out of combat.

After the conclusion of the Sicilian campaign, General Bradley decided that the time had come to find a new commander for the Big Red One, and he found just the man he wanted in Major-General Clarence R. Huebner, by repute the fiercest disciplinarian in the US Army. Huebner had enlisted as a private soldier in 1910, and had already served in the 1st Infantry Division, in every rank from private to colonel.

Clarence Huebner was a fighting soldier. During the Great War he had served with 1st Infantry in France and fought in the battles along the Aisne and Marne, at St Mihiel and in the Argonne. He had been wounded twice and received the Distinguished Service Medal, the Distinguished Service Cross and the Silver Star. General Huebner was not a man to mess about. He took firm command of 1st Infantry in North Africa and began to crack the whip, using methods which included the general officers' universal panacea for such situations, large amounts of close-order drill.

Major-General Charles H. Gerhardt of the 29th Infantry Division was another fighting man. Commissioned into the US Cavalry in 1917, he had served in France during the Great War and taken part in the fighting around St Mihiel and in the Argonne offensives. General Gerhardt took command of the 29th Infantry Division in May 1942.

General Huebner was in charge of both RCTs for the landing phase. Each RCT consisted of three battalions of 1,000 men apiece, and these were to be supported by combat engineers, field artillery and DD tanks with further support from aerial bombardment and guns of the fleet.

Each regiment was to put ashore two battalions at H-Hour, 0630 hrs, to clear the beach defences. This done by H+3, the assault battalions would be followed by the reserve battalion, and then by the 18th and 26th Infantry Regiments, who would spread out inland to occupy a bridgehead six miles deep astride the Bayeux to Isigny road, by midnight. The 116th Infantry of 29th Division would also be responsible for capturing the German batteries on the Pointe du Hoc (or Hoe) to the west of the beachhead, for which tasks they had under command elements of the 2nd US Rangers commanded by Lt-Colonel James Rudder.

The most important job of the assault battalions was, as at 'Utah', to clear the exits from the beaches, through the cliffs and dunes to the villages behind – Vierville, St Laurent and Colleville. All these 'draws' were mined and wired, and covered by fire.

The assault began at H-50 minutes (0540 hrs) on 6 June, when 32 DD tanks of the 741 Tank Battalion entered the tossing Channel seas 6,000 yards offshore. Their waterproof screens could not withstand prolonged battering by the waves and soon collapsed. Only 5 tanks made it to the beach, and 3 of these were put ashore 'dry' by an LCT that could not lower its ramp at sea. Most of the DD tank crews drowned, trapped and entombed in their foundering vehicles. Had all the tanks got ashore it might have been very different. As it was, the defences and defenders of 'Bloody Omaha' gave the Allied armies the toughest fight of D-Day.

The defences at 'Omaha' were simply too strong for the forces sent against them, but the trouble began at the assembly point far offshore. The infantry went into their LCAs up to ten miles from the beach, and out there, in the middle of the great Seine bay, there was none of the protection from the weather that the Cotentin Peninsula offered to the landing craft off 'Utah'. The sea was very rough and many craft, especially the DUKWs (always known as 'Ducks'; a form of amphibious truck), carrying field guns, were swamped during the run-in. Most of the infantry were racked with seasickness.

An early account of the situation off 'Omaha' comes from a British midshipman, Austin Prosser. 'I was the First Lieutenant of an LCT No. 1171, one of a flotilla of 12 LCTs allocated to the American Navy. We had long battles with the Americans over the rum ration served to the crews on British ships, because American ships are dry and they thought that as we were now part of their Navy we should be dry also. As there were signs of a Royal Navy mutiny the problem was resolved to our satisfaction.

'We loaded 6 Sherman tanks, 2 half-track ammunition lorries, and 2 half-track ambulances, and when the time came for us to sail we had a last party with the Americans, during which we drank every drop of alcohol on board. When the invasion was delayed for 24 hours there was great consternation, but one of the American officers produced a jar of medical alcohol from one of the ambulances and mixed this with orange juice. The result was not only lethal but revolting.

'After a very traumatic trip to the beaches we arrived at "Omaha" beach on time, at 0800 hrs. We reached the spot where we had to unload, but the beach was littered with wrecked assault craft and wounded and dead Americans. The Beachmaster was desperately looking for engineers to blow a way through the obstacles, and we were caught in a crossfire from the bunkers at either end of the beach, and lay off for a while as a destroyer sailed up and down firing its guns over open sights against the beach emplacements. About 10 o'clock, after pulling some of the broken-down assault craft off the beach, and removing some of the bodies, we put our tanks ashore, but I think very few of them ever got off the beach. We were then told to stand by to evacuate the troops as things were going badly and there were a lot of casualties ashore. I should mention that the skipper of our landing craft was just twenty-two years old.'

With their DDs sunk and all but one of the vital field guns lost at sea, their craft either flooded or destroyed by shell-fire or mines, the American infantry now approaching Omaha beach were without close support. Many of them were put out in the wrong place or on to an offshore sandbar, and had to abandon their equipment to swim across the deep-water channel to the beach. Enemy fire was smacking into the bow doors of the landing craft even before the ramps went down, and the killing began before the craft could beach. The infantrymen landing on 'Omaha' hardly had a chance.

Of nine infantry companies landing in the first wave at H-Hour that morning, three were swiftly decimated by machine-gun fire. Two clustered together under heavy fire near the Les Moulins exit in the 116th Regiment section. Elements of four companies of the 16th Infantry came to ground under fire below the cliffs before Colleville and one company's landing craft was swept so far to the east that they did not actually land for another hour and a half. The same thing was happening all along the beach, where a veteran now takes up the tale.

J. Robert Slaughter of Roanoke, Virginia, was a nineteen-year-old heavy weapons sergeant, serving with 'D' Company, 1st Battalion, 116th Infantry, 29th Division. 'My thinking, as we approached the beach, was that if this boat didn't hurry up and get us in I would die from seasickness. This was my first encounter with this malady. Woosiness became stomach sickness and then vomiting. At this point death is not so dreadful. I used the first thing at hand – my steel helmet. I didn't care what the Germans had to offer, I wanted to get on dry land. Nothing is worse than motion sickness, except maybe 88mm's and MG-42 machine-guns.

'About 200 or 300 yards from shore we encountered the first enemy artillery fire. Near misses sent water skyward, and then it rained back on us. The British coxswain shouted to step back, he was going to lower the ramp and we were to disembark quickly. I was stationed near the front of the boat and heard Sergeant Norfleet counter, "These men have heavy equipment and *you will take them all the way in*." The coxswain begged, "But we'll all be killed!" and Norfleet unholstered his .45 Colt pistol, put it to the sailor's head and ordered, "All the way in!" The craft proceeded ashore, ploughing through the choppy water until the bow scraped the sandy bottom.

'About 150 yards from shore I raised my head despite the warning from someone to "Keep your heads down!" I could see the craft to our right taking a terrific licking from small arms. Tracer bullets were bounding and skipping off the ramp and sides as they zero'd in on the boat, which touched down a few minutes before we did. Had we not delayed a few minutes to pick up the survivors from a sunken craft, we might have taken the concentration of fire that boat took. Great plumes of water from enemy artillery and mortars kept spouting close by.

'We knew then that this was not going to be a walk-in. No one thought that the enemy would give us this kind of opposition on the water's edge. We expected "A" and "B" Companies to have the beach secured by the time we landed. The reality was that no one else had set foot in the sector where we touched down. This turned the boys into men. Some would be very brave men, others would soon be dead men, but all of those who survived would be frightened men. Some wet their breeches, others cried unashamedly, and many just had to find it within themselves to get the job done. This is where the discipline and training took over.

'As we approached the beach the ramp was lowered. Mortar and artillery shells exploded on land and in the water. Unseen snipers concealed in the cliffs were shooting down at individuals, but most havoc was from automatic weapons. The water was turning red from the blood. Explosions from artillery gunfire, the rapid-fire rattle from nearby MG-42s, and naval gunfire firing inland was frightening.

'I was stationed on the left side of the craft and about fifth from the front. Norfleet was leading the right side. The ramp was in the surf and the front of the steel craft was bucking violently up and down. As my turn came to exit, I sat on the edge of the bucking ramp, trying to time my leap on the down cycle. I sat there too long, causing a bottleneck and endangering myself as well as the men who followed. The one-inch steel ramp was going up and down in the surf, rising as much as 6 or 7ft. I was afraid it would slam me in the head. One of our men was crushed by the door, killing him instantly. There were dead men in the water and there were live men as well. The Germans couldn't tell which was which. It was extremely hard to shed the heavy equipment, and if one were a weak swimmer, he could drown before inflating his Mae-West. I had to inflate mine to get in, even though I was a good swimmer. I remember helping Private Ernest McCanless, who was struggling to get closer in, so he wouldn't drown under all the weight. He still had one box of precious 30 cal. One of the dead, Mae-West inflated, had turned a dark colour.

'There were dead men floating in the water and there were live men acting dead, letting the tide take them in. I was crouched down to chin-deep in the water when mortar shells began falling at the water's edge. Sand began to kick up from small-arms fire from the bluffs. It became apparent that it was past time to get the hell away from that killing zone and across the beach. I don't know how long we were in the water before the move was made to go. I tried to take cover behind one of the heavy timbers, and then noticed an innocent-looking mine tied to the top, so I made the decision to go for it. Getting across the beach became an obsession. The decision not to try never entered my mind.

'While lying half in and half out of the water, behind one of the log poles, I noticed a GI running from right to left, trying to get across the beach. He was weighted with equipment and looked as though he was having a difficult time running. He was probably from the craft that touched down about 50 yards to our right. An enemy gunner shot him as he stumbled for cover. He screamed for a medic. One of the aid men moved quickly to help him, and he also was shot. I will never forget seeing that medic lying next to that wounded GI and both of them screaming. They died in minutes.

'The tide was rushing in, and later waves of men were due, so we had to get across. I believe I was the first in my group, telling

Pfc Walfred Williams, my Number One gunner, to follow. He still had his 51-pound machine-gun tripod. I had my rifle ready to fire, safety off, and had also fixed the bayonet before disembarking.

'I gathered my courage and started running as fast as my long legs would carry me. I ran as low as I could to lessen the target, and since I am 6ft 5ins I still presented a good one. I had a long way to run – I would say a good 100 yards or more. We were loaded down with gear and all our clothes were soaking wet. Can you imagine running with shoes full of water and wet wool clothing? As I ran through a tidal pool with about six or eight inches of water, I began to stumble. I finally caught my balance and accidentally fired my rifle, barely missing my foot. I continued on to the sea wall. This is the first time I have admitted the embarrassment of inadvertently almost shooting myself!

'Upon reaching the sea wall I looked back for the first time and got a glimpse of the armada out in the Channel. It was an awesome sight to behold. I also saw that Williams, Private Sal Augeri and Private Ernest McCanless were right behind. I didn't see Norfleet until later. Augeri had lost the machine-gun receiver in the water and I had got sand in my rifle. We still had one box of MG ammo but I don't believe we had a weapon that would fire. The first thing I did was to take off my assault jacket and spread my raincoat so I could clean my rifle. It was then I saw bullet holes in my raincoat. I didn't realize until then that I had been targeted. I lit my first cigarette. They were wrapped in plastic, as were the matches. I had to rest and compose myself because I had become weak in the knees. It was a couple of days before I had enough appetite to eat a K-ration.

'All the squad crossed the beach unscathed except Private Robert Stover and Medic Private Roland Coates, both of whom were killed. I don't know what happened to either of them. Stover was behind me in the boat and I didn't see him in the water or on the beach. (Records show Coates died of wounds on 7 June.) I didn't see Coates's fate, but knew Stover was a poor swimmer. A minor wound or accident could cause drowning in the rough surf.'

Alfred Lang of Linwood, New Jersey, came ashore with the Headquarters Battery of the 110th Field Artillery. 'British sailors manned the landing craft which brought our group ashore. They were good, they brought our landing craft right up on the sand and we didn't even have to wade through the water. We went across the beach in a weapons carrier which became bogged in the embankment on the sand, and the GIs laying about had to give us a hand to get us free. German artillery fire was pounding the area and snipers were holding out and taking pot shots at the invaders. We didn't get much chance to sleep for five days. Everyone was exhausted but we couldn't risk sleeping, and fear would keep you awake.'

Bob L. Sales of Madison Heights, Virginia, was then serving in 'B' Company of 116th Infantry. Like Robert Slaughter, he had previously served in the Ranger Battalion of 116th Infantry, a force trained at Achnacarry in Scotland by British Commandos. 'I really wanted to fight with the Ranger Battalion; they were picked men, all first class, but it was not to be. The Battalion was broken up and I returned to "B" Company, where I became bodyguard and radio man to our Company Commander, Captain Ettore Zappacosta. Anyway, on D-Day we thought we were just going to run up the beach and keep on going, but it wasn't going to be like that at all ...

'How did we feel going in? Difficult to explain. . . . You're so scared. Anyone who says he wasn't scared isn't telling the truth. But we knew what we had to do and we just did our best. On the way in I was standing up and watching, because I knew it was the only time I was ever going to do this. It was now getting light and the French coast was in sight, and we could see smoke where the big guns on the ships had been firing. Guns were going off ... the excitement was unreal ... it was unbelievable. The closer we got we could tell that there was trouble. We didn't see any of "A" Company, couldn't find them, and the coxswain said he couldn't go in any further. He dropped the ramp and when you open up the ramp on a landing craft, that's when the machine guns open up on you.

'Captain Zappacosta was the first man off and he was hit immediately. Machine-gun bullets were rattling off that boat. The next two men off were both hit and fell into the water, and I was the fourth man off. What saved my life was that the boat reared up and I went off the side of the ramp with that 30/40lb radio on my back, and went up to my neck in the water. I knew I couldn't keep the radio. Zappacosta came up and mumbled something – I think he said, "Help me!" and he went back down and we never saw him again. I tried to get in closer and kept looking back at the craft and who was following, and they were being cut down just like you wouldn't believe. No one have I ever met until this day who survived that boat. It was the command boat, with Captain Zappacosta on there, an officer from "C" Company was on there, the Forward Observer for the Artillery was on there, some of the radio operators were on there . . . it was the Headquarters boat for "B" Company.

'This time I was in the water and shells were hitting all around and I could see we had a disaster on our hands. I didn't know how bad it was at that time. I met a fellow in the water I didn't know, and he helped me get rid of the radio, which was full of seawater anyway. A few minutes later a shell hit and knocked me groggy – I was almost out of it. I hung on to a log that had a mine on it and pushed it in front of me, moving as slow as possible because the Germans were sitting right up there and they could see all over the beach, and if you moved, well. . . . I finally made it to the beach and crawled up, and laying there was Dick Wright, Communications Sergeant. Dick raised up on his hands a little bit, and a sniper hit him in the head. He was not only my Sergeant, he was my friend for many years.

'I was really beginning to get uneasy at this point because there really wasn't anybody around to amount to anything, so I made my way along the beach a little at a time to a small wall where I found four or five other men, one of them a friend of mine, Max Smith from West Virginia. Max's eye was laying out on his face. I bandaged it up as best I could until a medic came along and bandaged up some of the other men. Max went on to recover from the war and died a few years ago of cancer in West Virginia.

'We had a little protection behind the wall. All day we dragged the dead and wounded in, slipping out to pull them up the beach as the tide was bringing them in. All day long shells were hitting that beach and tanks and men were landing. Some boats never got in at all but were blown up in the water. "Toad" Paget was one of the men who got his group ashore in pretty good shape. Lieutenant Williams, who later became Company Commander, was storming pill-boxes almost single-handed out there. These men were almost unbelievable.'

The experiences of Bob Sales and Robert Slaughter were endorsed by many other men trapped on the shrinking sands of 'Omaha' that day. The infantry of the 16th and 116th Regiments were trapped between the cliffs and the sea, unable to move forward or back and under heavy fire. Soldiers have a name for such a place; they call it a killing ground.

The 1st Battalion of the 116th Infantry landing on 'Dog Green' section of 'Omaha' beach suffered terrible casualties. Company 'A' landing at 0630 hrs had 91 men killed and almost as many wounded. Less than 20 men got across the beach. 'B' Company suffered a similar fate. Robert Slaughter's Company 'D', landing at 0710 hrs, had 39 men killed and 32 wounded. On D-Day they lost their company commander, 5 officers, the First Sergeant, and 10 other non-commissioned officers killed. Five other non-commissioned officers were wounded. In all, the 116th Regiment lost 800 men on D-Day.

The two right-flank companies, from the 2nd Ranger Battalion and Company 'A' of 116th Infantry, suffered even before they got ashore. One landing craft sank in the surf and another received direct hits by four mortar bombs. Company 'A' then lost about two-thirds of its strength to small-arms fire and half the Rangers were shot down as they waded ashore. Only half the regiment's supporting tanks – 8 out of 16 – made it to the beach, and all these came in on LCTs. There was a 1,000-yard gap between these right-flank companies and the rest of the battalion, and only two of the three rifle companies of the 2nd Battalion landed in the regimental area. One promptly lost 25 per cent of its men to small-arms fire just crossing the beach, which took 45 minutes.

Over on the left, the 16th Infantry of the 1st Infantry Division were not faring any better. Some squads of the 2nd/16th got across the beach below Colleville with the loss of only two men. The rest of the 2nd/16th battalion landed directly in front of the Colleville strongpoint and were immediately swept by enemy fire. Half of Company 'E' were killed there or wounded and later drowned by the incoming tide. Machine guns continued to sweep the beach as the rest of the companies came ashore.

Lawrence Bour of Williamsburg, Virginia, was in the 16th Infantry Regiment. 'Our slice of "Omaha" beach was code-named "Easy Red". Maybe some staff officer's black sense of humour. It was red, but not easy. The run-in from the assembly area was rough. Three of our amphibious trucks went under with their howitzers. Three out of four of the amphibious tanks had their flimsy canvas skirts crumble and went to the bottom with their crews.

'We drove in in our LCVP, me on the left, Major Washington, the battalion exec., in the centre, and my communications sergeant on the right. I never saw the sergeant again, incidentally. I rolled over a body in the surf, thinking it might be he, but there wasn't much left of the face. Suddenly the growl from the engines died, but it wasn't dropping us on sand or shingle. We were fifty yards from the shoreline, just short of the obstacles, and due to touch down in the fourth wave at 0640 hrs, behind the assault waves. The assault waves would have cleared the beach of small-arms fire from the machine guns in the concrete bunkers, and we would take our chances with the shelling – a piece of cake!'

James Watts of San Diego, California, then a lieutenant serving with a mortar unit with the 16th Infantry, came ashore on 'Easy Red'. 'My Company Commander, Captain Thomas P. Moundres, had a meeting with all the company officers, at which he wished us good luck and said goodbye. I think he had a premonition of impending death. He was killed by a mortar shell just as he reached the land, and is now buried in the American cemetery above the beach.

'The view of the beach from the landing craft showed the inferno that lay ahead. It was already a dull overcast morning. The explosions and the resulting smoke and debris laid a blackish pall over the beach. Survival that day was a matter of luck. You made it, the man next to you didn't.

'When the landing craft reaches the shore, the ramp is dropped and you exit the craft on the diagonal to avoid the craft broaching and catching you in the back. I went off the left side of the ramp into waist-deep water. Even so, the ramp swung left, knocked me off my feet and underwater. The sergeant coming off behind me said the water boiled with machine-gun fire just after I went under. I came up near the rear of the landing craft untouched.

'When we left the landing craft the leading elements of the infantry were just a few yards ahead, pinned down by fire from the top of the hill above (where the American cemetery is now). I have no recollection how long we were there before the infantry could clear the area at the top of the hill. We set up a mortar on the beach and tried to fire at the top of the hill. It was a futile effort because the distance to the top of the hill was under our minimum range of 600 yards. When the squads with the mortars landed, they used two hand-pulled carts per squad, one with the mortar, the other with the ammunition. This made them a very attractive target. Part of the squad was pulling by a handle and chains attached to the front of the cart. One man, Pfc Baumgartner, was behind pushing the cart. As I watched I could see his jacket puff from machine-gun rounds. He went to his knees, then got up and pushed for another step or two, then went down dead. The memory is still vivid, a brave, dedicated man trying to do his duty to the very end. The beach was full of such people that day.'

The underwater obstacles off 'Omaha' also took their toll. Craft sank or blew up, sending crews and occupants sky high, while from their vantage points high on shore the Germans flailed the oncoming craft with machine-gun and artillery fire. Within minutes the infantry assault of both RCTs was halted on the water's edge, the troops taking heavy casualties and unable to hit back, but still the infantry came on, adding more wounded, more dead, to the holocaust developing on 'Omaha'.

Other units coming in later did no better; the assault at 'Omaha' was stalled. Anthony J. Di Stephano came ashore about 0830 hrs with the guns of 'C' Battery, the 111th Field Artillery, part of the 116th RCT, and tells what happened to his unit. 'At H-Hour the tide had been low; now it was coming in fast, narrowing the flat expanse of sand, and as it came it swept the dead, the abandoned life-belts and the mess of wrecked equipment before it, tidying up the appalling scene like a huge broom. It also caught and drowned the wounded who were powerless to move. There was not much blood because the water was so cold and the sand acted as a blotter. The dead, looking as young and strong as ever in their brand-new uniforms and web equipment, began to form an irregular dark line at the waves' edge.

'The artillery forward observers and reconnaissance parties came in with the second wave. Lt-Colonel Thornton L. Mullins, our CO, was with them, already wounded. He didn't know that his batteries had lost all but four of his guns, but he saw immediately that the beach was no place for artillery. He began to put some fight back into the little knots of stunned, inert riflemen along the sea wall. Most of them had lost their weapons or dropped them in the sand. Lt-Colonel Mullins crept along, talking to one man after another. While he was urging one small group to clean their guns and start returning the fire from the bluffs, a sniper's bullet drilled through his hand. Mullins ignored this second wound as he had his first one, and started moving a pair of amphibious tanks into decent firing positions. He led one forward and showed its gunner a target. Then he looked for a mine-free site for the second tank. His search led him across a completely open patch of sand where a third bullet hit him in the stomach. Lt-Colonel Mullins fell forward on his face and died.

'Meanwhile, several thousand yards offshore, the "C" Battery DUKW right behind Captain Shuford's had caught a wave broadside and was sinking rapidly. Captain Shuford asked the coxswain of the guide LCVP to take off the gun crew in order to lighten the load and possibly save the howitzer; he left only the chief of section and the DUKW driver to carry on. The transfer was simple enough, but the Navy coxswain then decided to turn back and look for some place to deposit the twelve cannoneers. "Easy Green", he told Shuford, was straight ahead.

'About 1,000 yards from the shore the little procession ran into a bunch of other small craft, including a number of other DUKWs and the last two – "C" Battery's crewless DUKW and the "B" Battery DUKW with Dempsey in command – got separated from Shuford and Wilson. The crewless DUKW wandered in pretty close, its engine stalled.

'At about 9 o'clock, some 600 yards off Easy Green, Captains Shuford and Wilson lashed their boats together with a length of rope so they could talk over the situation. It was a fairly gloomy conversation. It would have been gloomier if they had known what was happening on the beach. Even without specific information, however, they could see mortar and artillery fire bursting on the beach. There was no sign of infantry activity, no movement of traffic towards the beach exit.'

To trace the cause of this state of affairs one must go back to the original assault plan. This left too much to the infantry. Little use was made of the available supporting arms and some planned support was less than fully effective. The aerial bombing, for example, had been moved well up the beach to avoid the risk of bombs falling among the landing craft. As a result, most of the bombs missed the beach entirely and fell up to three miles inland. The naval bombardment was also too light and too short to shatter the beach defences. Offshore obstacles were virtually intact and still a barrier to the assault craft which were held out at sea under German gunfire.

The landings, supposedly at half-tide, were upset by the weather, but as the tide was flooding, it was clearly vital to clear the beach obstacles before the rising tide covered them, so that the big landing ships, the LSTs, could bring in more guns, more tanks and, above all, more men to secure the foothold. This task might have been much easier had the infantry had the support of the specialized armour used by the British and Canadians on the beaches further east.

The task of clearing away the obstacles on fire-swept 'Omaha' was left to the unprotected combat engineers of the US Army's demolition teams and they didn't have a chance. Their casualties were appalling. By nightfall on D-Day over 40 per cent of the assault engineers on 'Omaha' were dead or wounded. Most of their equipment had been lost during the run-in. A shell exploded the demolition charges being brought ashore by one team, blowing every man to pieces. Other engineers, working around the obstacles in the open, were picked off by snipers or cut down by the machine guns. When they could attach charges to obstacles they had to kick away the men hiding under them before they could pull the fuses. The gallantry of these combat engineers is beyond all praise.

John McAllister of Torrington, Connecticut, was a lieutenant with Battery 'C' of 227th Field Artillery. 'We were assigned to "Omaha Dog Green" but I couldn't tell you where we actually landed. The water obstacles were still plentiful, indicating that the engineers assigned to clear the beach must have suffered heavy casualties. After an eternity the ramp was dropped and we jumped into the water, which came up to my waist. We instantly came under machine-gun fire and two of my small party were hit. My radio man and I went back for them and managed to drag them up to the sea wall where I gave them my canteen and a syrette of morphine.

'The radio man and I found some cover along the wall and began to reorganize to carry out our mission, recruiting two infantrymen who had become separated from their units to help carry our radio equipment. My first impression of "Omaha" was one of chaos. Smoke covered the ridge and a good part of the area between the sea wall and the top of the dunes, and the bodies of both German and American infantrymen were everywhere. I will never forget it.'

The Americans had taken bulldozers but only three out of sixteen got ashore. There they did sterling work, though the unprotected drivers were fully exposed to snipers' shells and machine-gun fire. Years after the war, Don Whitehead, an American war correspondent who landed on 'Omaha' that morning, recalled seeing Private Vinton Dove of Washington DC: '... he drove a bulldozer off his landing craft and began clearing the beach, as calmly as though grading his driveway back home ... he sat up there with only a sweatshirt and a helmet to protect him from bullets and shell fragments ... his name has stayed with me to this day.'

Until the obstacles were cleared, the follow-up craft could not get ashore. While waiting they milled about in the tossing seas offshore, still under shell-fire, the coxswains unable to find the gaps they had been promised. Meanwhile, the slaughter ashore went on.

The pitiless hail of fire went on for hours, until 'Omaha' beach was a shambles of dead men, burning tanks and wrecked landing craft. Only fragments of this story were getting back to USS *Ancon*, but more and more men were coming ashore where they could, simply adding to the carnage and confusion on the beach.

Peter Chambers was then a Royal Navy petty officer serving on USS *Ancon* as a 'Headache' operator. 'Our task was to maintain a listening watch in the radio room for German E-Boat transmissions, hoping to pick up any information regarding an E-Boat attack on the ships waiting offshore. When we weren't actually on duty we had no tasks to perform, so we stayed in our bunks or hung about on deck. I certainly had no idea of what was happening on "Omaha" beach. There was a battleship nearby firing salvos, but the atmosphere on board the *Ancon* was quite calm.'

At 0730 hrs the second group of assault troops, the reinforcement battalions of both regiments, came in at five separate points. This wave included more combat engineers and the rest of the assault regiments, including the vital heavy weapons companies. The rest of the 1st/116th were to land behind Company 'A' of the 1st/116th which had already been shattered, but the rest of the battalion did no better, meeting the same destructive fire as their craft came in to beach. The heavy weapons company was scattered at once and took two hours to assemble. Battalion HQ, including the Beachmaster who was charged with sorting out the chaos on shore, was pinned down by small-arms fire for much of the day.

Company 'C' was carried 1,000 yards to the east and landed in comparative safety covered by smoke from burning heather on the clifftops, and was able to cross the beach and re-group by the sea wall. The 5th Rangers followed Company 'C' in and also got ashore without heavy loss, but two companies of the 2nd Rangers, landing on the right, lost between a third and a half of their men just crossing the beach.

Shortly after this, Brigadier-General Norman 'Dutch' Cota, Assistant Divisional Commander of the 29th Infantry Division, came ashore near Les Moulins, but taking command was difficult. Most of the radios had been either lost or drowned and

communication by runner was perilous or impossible. Brigadier
Cota rounded up what men he could find and began to organize
the fightback. All over the beach other men were doing the
same.

Mario Porcellini was then a private in Company 'E' of the
116th. 'I was Captain Madill's runner and radio man and was
with him on D-Day when he was killed. Alongside him was our
BAR man, Alex Bereski, who also got it – a day I can never
forget. I just want to say that I was with one of the greatest
outfits and I'm still proud to have been a member of the fighting
29th.'

At about 0930 hrs General Omar Bradley sent a staff officer,
Colonel Benjamin Tallen, off in a DUKW to examine the
situation and report back. Tallen returned an hour later, soaking wet, to report landing craft milling about in confusion off
the beach, 'like a stampeding herd of cattle', chased by shell-
fire, while the 1st and 29th Infantry RCTs were pinned against
the sea wall. Only in one section, 'Easy Red', had the beach
obstacles been cleared and craft making for this area to unload
were creating a monster traffic jam that provided wonderful
targets for the Germany artillery. 16th Infantry were enduring
heavy losses; all their companies and battalions were mixed up
but fighting back in small groups.

At about 1000 hrs, some men managed to get across the beach
and took shelter in the cover of the shingle bank. Here, in the
few yards hard up against the shingle, they were comparatively
safe from all but mortar- and shell-fire. As the morning wore on,
more men arrived by the sea wall, wet, exhausted, frequently
without equipment or weapons. Many who came in were
wounded and they were the lucky ones. The wounded left out
on the open beach were drowned as the tide came in. Many of
the wounded came crawling up the beach with the tide, only
their heads exposed above the waves, and even these were
sniped at by Germans from their posts above the beachhead.

The American infantry did not just lie there and take it. They
were firing back where they could, scrambling for positions,
digging shell-scrapes, rescuing their comrades and attending to
the wounded. John Pinder Tanon, a radio operator, was to
receive the Medal of Honor for re-crossing the beach three

times to recover the vital radios, and he was just one man among many, doing what he could on 'Omaha' beach. On his third trip into the surf John Tanon was shot and killed.

The losses were not all one-sided, for the German defenders were also taking casualties. The 916th Regiment, which occupied the centre of the beach, reported to the Divisional HQ that while they were holding the Americans on the beach, their own casualties, principally from naval gunfire, were very heavy, and infantry reinforcements were urgently needed. Even so, they held on, flaying 'Omaha' beach with fire.

At noon, with the situation still critical, Bradley contemplated switching his follow-up forces to 'Utah' or the British beaches, and was about to order the evacuation of 'Omaha' when he received a message from V Corps: '*Troops formerly pinned down on beaches now advancing up heights behind.*' Somehow, here and there, the men of the 1st and 29th Infantry Divisions had pulled it off.

Many factors combined to halt the American assault at 'Omaha'. Many others combined to get it started again, but the main ingredient that turned disaster into success on 'Omaha' was simple human courage.

It takes courage to move out into the open, even from behind the elusive safety of a bullet-swept wall or a beach obstacle, but all along that beach, after hours of endurance, men found the courage to move. The advance seems to have begun in several places all around the same time. In one place an officer led a sudden rush over the shingle bank and found that the machine-gunning on the far side was less intense and movement possible. A combat-engineer sergeant moved up and down collecting explosives until he had enough to blow a hole in the sea wall and let other troops through. In some places, men simply decided they had had enough and it was time to move. They stood up and walked quietly across the shingle wall. Those who made it across gapped the minefields, often by hand, digging up the mines with bayonets. Losing men all the way, slowly and painfully, the 1st and 29th Infantry Divisions began to get off the beach.

Urged on by Brigadier Cota, on the west, Company 'C' of the 116th left the sea wall and crossed 150 yards of beach to the base of the cliffs. These they climbed, scrambling up shallow gullies, and found that the crumpled ground on the top gave them good protection. After them came men of the 5th Rangers, and together they began to snuff out the German machine-gun posts. At about the same time, over to the east the 3rd battalion of the 116th, in groups of 20 or 30 men, began to advance up the bluffs around Les Moulins. Company 'G' and Company 'E' of the 2nd/16th – the latter now down to 23 men – fought their way up the cliffs between Colleville and St Laurent. Second Lt John Spalding of Company 'E', 2nd/16th, attacked the maze of enemy positions defending the St Laurent draw, and after a two-hour battle with rifles and grenades, forced the garrison to surrender.

Shortly after 10.00 a.m. there was another welcome reinforcement when two landing craft, LCT 30 and LCT(L) 544, swept in to land and barged the obstacles aside to run hard on to the beach, all their guns firing on the German positions. Two destroyers also came in to 1,000 yards offshore to add the weight of their guns to the supporting fire. Slowly, painfully, the battle was tilting the Americans' way.

As at 'Utah', there were general officers ashore, men like Brigadier-General Cota, to get a grip on the fight and point the way. Most memorable of all was Colonel Taylor of the 16th Infantry, who declared: 'The only people on this beach are the dead and those who are going to die . . . now let's get the hell out of here.'

The 29th Infantry RCT had come ashore opposite Vierville and taken another thrashing there from the enemy guns. Here again, Brigadier-General Cota was around to point the way with his cry, 'They're murdering us here. Let's move inland and get murdered. 29th, Let's Go!' '29th, Let's Go!' remains the motto of the American 29th Infantry Division.

Scores of men were now on their feet and crossing the sea wall. Once the situation onshore became clear, General Huebner had acted fast to help his beleaguered troops. He called for naval help and destroyers were sent in close to shore to engage the German emplacements over open sights. He stopped the rear echelon support troops landing, sending more infantry instead, most notably the 115th Infantry Regiment which came ashore at H+4. He sent in engineers to blow the beach obstacles. Thanks to him, and those like him, and the courage of countless unnamed individuals, the American assault began to move forward again. In little groups and small companies the infantry began to infiltrate the enemy defences, to take them in the rear and, one by one, to eliminate them. There was much bitter fighting on the cliff heights behind 'Omaha', but by mid-afternoon the advance inland had begun.

German resistance at 'Omaha' came as an unpleasant shock to the American command. The Americans had expected to encounter second-rank troops but the battle-trained troops of the 352nd Division contested every step of the landing, even reporting back to Von Rundstedt at one point that they had thrown the invaders back into the sea. However, even as the 352nd were making this report, the battle was moving in the Americans' favour. The point of the American spearhead may have been blunted, but there was a lot of weight behind the shaft, and remorseless pressure, together with the naval gunfire and the constant arrival of fresh troops, gradually wore the Germans down. By 1500 hrs the situation seemed to warrant another close inspection, and General Omar Bradley again sent a staff officer ashore to check on the troops' progress.

He reported back with a story of a beach strewn with bodies and wreckage, but with the men fighting their way inland. The most pressing need now was for artillery and bulldozers. Bulldozers could clear away the beach obstacles and make a path for tanks through the shingle bank and into the dunes. These were sent in, together with men of the 18th Infantry Regiment. By nightfall, elements of this regiment had joined the 2nd Battalion of the 16th south and south-east of Colleville. The Americans had gained a shallow but secure grasp on the 'Omaha' beachhead, and during the night more infantry and seventeen tanks were moved in to reinforce the leading elements now digging in on the heights above 'Omaha'.

While 1st and 29th Infantry were slogging it out on Omaha, another vicious battle was going on a little to the west, on the Pointe du Hoc. The Pointe du Hoc, or Pointe du Hoe as it was called at the time, is a tall cliff or bluff jutting into the sea just west of 'Omaha'. Aerial reconnaissance had revealed that the Pointe du Hoc contained 155mm heavy guns in well protected concrete blockhouses – guns like those of the Merville Battery over to the east, which could wreak havoc among the shipping crowded offshore. These guns had been heavily bombed by the US Ninth Air Force and would be subjected from first light on D-Day to a heavy bombardment by the guns of the fleet, but in case all this failed, this battery, like the Merville Battery, was to be assaulted by infantry.

The men chosen for this venture came from the 2nd Ranger Battalion, three companies under the command of the CO, Lt-Colonel James Rudder. His men were to land at the base of the Pointe du Hoc and scale the 100-ft cliff on ropes fired on to the clifftop by grapnels. This force was to have been supported by the rest of the Ranger battalion and elements of 116th infantry, but in the event the follow-up force became involved at 'Omaha'. Colonal Rudder's 225 men were on their own.

The assault on the Pointe du Hoc was a most desperate venture. The Germans were alerted by the grapnels and quickly harassed the climbing men with grenades and rifle-fire, cutting the ropes and hurling the Rangers back into the sea. Only machine-gun fire from the British assault craft and LCAs kept the cliff edge clear, and only about half Rudder's force – some 150 men – made it to the top of the cliff. Once there they drove off the German infantry and stormed the blockhouses, only to find them empty.

The guns were eventually located 700 yards inland, well prepared and supplied with ammunition but totally deserted. Rudder's men blew them up and held the position for two days before the surviving 90 men of the original 225 marched on to join the battle beyond 'Omaha'.

General Gerow, Commander of V Corps, went ashore at 1930 hrs on the evening of 6 June, and set up his headquarters near Colleville. General Huebner found the atmosphere warmer when he joined the forward elements of his 1st Infantry Division on the evening of D-Day, while on the right flank the 29th Division were pushing hard towards the Pointe du Hoc to relieve the Rangers.

Behind them the tide was going out on 'Omaha' beach,

uncovering the dead and an immense litter of equipment. Reinforcements were coming ashore and would come ashore all night and for days thereafter, the new arrivals awed by the evidence of battle. Guided by tired, wet men from the combat engineers, these reinforcements made their way slowly along the taped gaps in the minefields, up the 'draws' and past the blackened emplacements of the Atlantic Wall, scorched by shell-fire, littered with their dead defenders.

The Americans lost over 3,000 men, killed or wounded, along that three-mile strip of sand. Those who fought there have never forgotten that hard day on 'Omaha' beach.

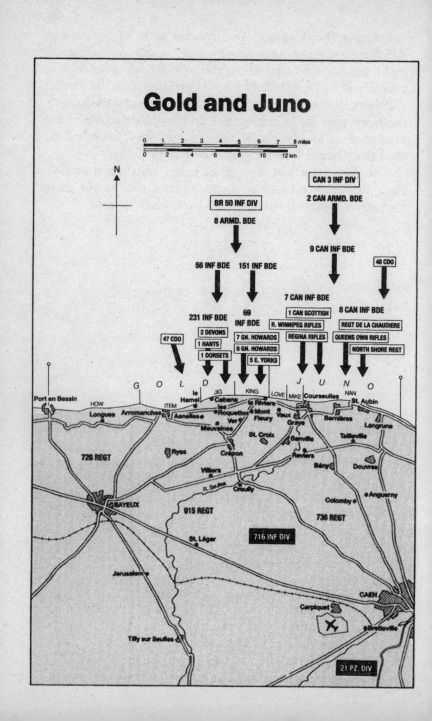

Gold and Juno

0 1 2 3 4 5 6 7 8 miles
0 2 4 6 8 10 12 km

N

CAN 3 INF DIV

2 CAN ARMD. BDE

BR 50 INF DIV

8 ARMD. BDE

9 CAN INF BDE

48 CDO

56 INF BDE   151 INF BDE

7 CAN INF BDE   8 CAN INF BDE

231 INF BDE   69 INF BDE

1 CAN SCOTTISH   REGT DE LA CHAUDIERE
R. WINNIPEG RIFLES   QUEENS OWN RIFLES

47 CDO   2 DEVONS   7 GN. HOWARDS   REGINA RIFLES   NORTH SHORE REGT
1 HANTS   6 GN. HOWARDS
1 DORSETS   5 E. YORKS

G O L D   J U N O

JIG   KING   LOVE   MIKE   NAN
le Hamel   les Cabane   la Riviere   Courseulles   St. Aubin
HOW   ITEM   les Roquettes   Vaux
Port en Bessin   Longues   Arromanches   Asnelles   Ver   Mont Fleury   Graye   Bernières   Langrune
Meuvaines   St. Croix   Banville   Tailleville
Ryes   Crépon   Reviers   Bény   Douvres
726 REGT   Villiers   Colomby   Anguerny
R. Seulles   Creully
BAYEUX   915 REGT   736 REGT
St. Léger   716 INF DIV
Jerusalem   CAEN
Carpiquet   Bretteville
Tilly sur Seulles   21 PZ. DIV

————— CHAPTER NINE —————

'Gold'

'People of Western Europe: A landing was
made this morning on the coast of France
by troops of the Allied Expeditionary
Force...'
Communiqué No. 1
General Dwight D. Eisenhower
6 June 1944

To the east of 'Omaha', beyond the little harbour of Port-en-
Bessin, lay the first of the British beaches. This was codenamed
'Gold', and the troops of the 50th Northumbrian Division
began to come ashore here about 0730 hrs. Their task was to
penetrate the German defences on 'Gold' beach between the
resorts of La Rivière and Le Hamel, and press on inland to take
the town of Bayeux. They also had to take the small port and spa
of Arromanches as a step towards establishing the British
'Mulberry' harbour offshore. The Germans defending this
sector came from the 352nd Infantry Division, which was now
hammering the Americans at 'Omaha', and the 716th Division,
which was deployed along the coast from here to the east. The
716th was another second-rank formation, but as the Americans

had already discovered to their cost, the 352nd was an extremely formidable division.

The 352nd Infantry Division had been raised in the winter of 1943. It consisted of three Grenadier Regiments, Nos 914, 915 and 916, and supporting arms including an artillery regiment, an anti-tank regiment and an engineer battalion. The 352nd occupied the defences of Le Hamel, which proved a particularly hard nut to crack.

General Montgomery had anticipated that there might be problems along 'Gold' beach. This part of the coast was studded with strongpoints and well supplied with infantry, but the defenders also enjoyed cover in the small resort towns and scattered villas, which run east from Port-en-Bessin all the way to the mouth of the Orne at Ouistreham. These towns, and many of the villas, had been converted into strongpoints, the houses reinforced with concrete and transformed into machine-gun, light artillery and anti-tank positions. Minefields lay behind all the beaches and many of the streets had been blocked with barbed wire and anti-tank obstacles.

The Atlantic Wall here was strong and stoutly defended. The naval bombardment therefore began at 0510 hrs and continued until H-Hour, 0730 hrs, though this did not knock out as many strongpoints as the assault plan required. Most of the strong-points were sited to fire along the beach rather than directly out to sea, their roofs and seaward walls reinforced against bombing and naval gunfire. The German strongpoint on the beach at Le Hamel, for one, remained in action until noon and took a heavy toll of the infantry crossing the beach. The success of the landing on 'Gold' was largely due to the specialized armour of the 79th Armoured Division, which was able to breach the defences in various places and let the infantry and follow-up forces through.

It has to be remembered that the D-Day assault was made on a *flooding* tide. As time wore on, so the beaches got narrower and narrower, yet the invasion, once started, could not be stopped. More and more troops, tanks, guns, and vehicles kept pouring ashore on to an ever-smaller strip of beach, and without breaches in the Atlantic Wall these forces would have piled up on the foreshore, an easy target for the German guns. The troops landing on the D-Day beaches always had the tide pressing at their backs.

The plan for the British landings on 'Gold' beach was for the 50th Division to land with two brigades forward and one in reserve. The assault brigades were the 231st (Malta) Brigade on the left and 69th Brigade on the right. These brigades were to storm 'Jig' and 'King' beaches respectively and push inland as quickly as possible towards Bayeux. The beaches chosen for the landings consisted of low-lying sand dunes interspersed with patches of clay that could seriously hamper the movement of both the tracked and wheeled vehicles. 'Jig' beach was also dominated by heavily fortified strongpoints within the coastal villages of Le Hamel, Asnelles-sur-Mer and Les Roquettes. These positions were garrisoned by infantry companies amply supplied with machine guns and mortars, each company supported by at least two anti-tank guns.

H-Hour for the assault brigades was 0730 hrs. The 231st Brigade had two battalions in the first wave, the 1st Hampshires and the 1st Dorsets, who were met with heavy fire from a battalion of the 716th Division dug in around Le Hamel. Also landing with this brigade was 47 (Royal Marine) Commando, of whom we shall hear more later.

For support they had a squadron from the 6th Assault Regiment, Royal Engineers, and a squadron from the Westminster Dragoons, both equipped with specialist armoured vehicles, such as flail tanks, one of the many detachments of the 79th Armoured Division in action that day. Further support was given by the DD tanks of the Nottinghamshire Yeomanry and Centaur tanks of the First Royal Marine Armoured Support Regiment. Artillery support would be provided by 90 and 147 Field Regiments, RA, who opened fire on to the beaches from their landing craft during the run-in.

Corporal Lewis Richards was Signaller to the Commander of 231 Brigade, Sir Alexander Stanier. 'Wireless sets were to open at H−60 and wireless silence was not to be broken until H−30 unless any emergency arose. I was awakened at 0445 hrs and went on deck to see if anything was happening. Our ship was moving very slowly so I concluded that we were not far from our allotted position. The coast was now receiving the attentions of the Royal Navy and squadrons of planes and was soon covered by a pall of smoke. The cruiser HMS *Orion* was firing broadsides not far from us ... my brother was serving on that ship. The Brigadier came on deck and together we watched a rocket-firing LCT run in to the shore and discharge her salvo.

'H-hour was now rapidly approaching and the Navy was giving the coast all it had. Rocket-firing planes swept in towards the coast while the planes constituting our umbrella continued to weave and turn, but the enemy planes did not come to give battle.'

Reginald Rham was with the 9th Battalion, Royal Fusiliers. On 6 June he was his colonel's driver and batman. 'I wondered what hell was awaiting us when we reached the beaches, and I was soon to find out. Such were the sea conditions that I don't think anybody cared about what lay in front of them, it could not be worse than what they were suffering from seasickness. For the moment the firing had quietened down, and I could see the coastline of Normandy. We were now coming under fire from German big guns and it was getting extremely uncomfortable. I saw that the infantry assault craft had dropped their ramps and the infantry were running ashore.'

The most westerly beach, 'Jig Green', was the target for the 1st Hampshires. The battalion's plan was in five phases with the object of capturing the eastern half of Le Hamel, with 'B' Company capturing Asnelles-sur-Mer. Companies landing twenty minutes later at around 0745 hrs would take the western half of Le Hamel, while 'D' Company was directed on to a gun position near Cabane. Once all these initial objectives had been carried out, the next phase was the capture of a radar station just along the coast to the west.

This task was given to 'B' and 'C' companies with the support of a tank squadron. The battalion also had to secure the cliffs above Arromanches. Finally, Arromanches itself must be cleared and occupied. Those last two phases were very important, as Arromanches overlooked the area chosen by the planners for the British 'Mulberry' harbour.

To the left of the 1st Hampshires, the 1st Dorsets were also to land on 'Jig Green' east of Les Roquettes, subduing a machine-gun nest at Meuvaines, before advancing on Puits d'Harcot. This position covered Arromanches and its approaches.

Once the two lead battalions were ashore and secure, the 2nd Devons would land at H+40. They were to deploy south, around Asnelles, then press on to Ryes, several miles south of Arromanches, to deepen the assault area.

The success of the brigade plan clearly depended on the reduction of Le Hamel. Typhoons of the 2nd Tactical Air Force (2nd TAF) were to attack the German defences with rockets, and prior to this American Flying Fortresses – B17s – would bomb the beach defences. Unfortunately, the bombs fell inland and the strafing Typhoons failed to subdue the defenders. The rough seas prevented the DD tanks from being launched and they came ashore from landing craft arriving behind the infantry. The rough seas also took a toll of the RM Armoured Support Regiment tanks, whose landing craft had great difficulty in beaching. Of the 10 Centaurs that should have landed, only 5 made it, and those were knocked out almost immediately.

More specialist troops and vehicles came from 'B' Squadron, Westminster Dragoons and 82 Assault Squadron, Royal Engineers, who were detailed to clear six gaps in the beach defences. Due to the rough seas they landed late so, like the Americans on 'Omaha', the British assault infantry landing on 'Gold' went ashore without their close support.

Frank Wiltshire was a twenty-two-year-old mortarman with the 1st Dorsets. 'I jumped from the LCA straight into about 7 ft of water. I was the No. 1 of the mortar team and I had to jettison the base plate of my mortar as it weighed over 50 lbs and it would have kept me under. After wading ashore I made a dash across the sand to reach the bank before Le Hamel. Eventually we managed to assemble one mortar out of the six; the other five were lost. I got the mortar in a firing position but the barrel was full of sand and water because somebody had dragged it along the beach.

'After seeing my friends killed and injured around me, I thought it would be my turn soon, but I got off the beach after about two hours. The bloodshed was terrible and the Germans were tough fighters.'

The 1st Dorsets managed to get off the beach once the

specialist armour, the mine-clearing flail tanks and the rest, had cleared suitable lanes through the minefields. Working through these man-made obstacles the engineers were further hampered by boggy patches of heavy clay and a salt marsh directly behind the beach road.

Edgar Lawrenson was in one of the flail tanks, or 'Crabs', from 'B' Squadron, the Westminster Dragoons. 'At dawn on 6 June we brewed up and the few who felt like eating had breakfast while the landing craft sailed for the beach. It was deathly quiet and my driver and co-driver were sealed in with a reminder that if we were hit the turret had to be traversed to enable them to undo their hatches and escape.

'During the final run-in I sat on top of our tank, giving a commentary to the three crew members inside. Captain Taylor was on the bridge checking landmarks for the lane we had to sweep through the minefields. Hostile shelling and small-arms fire had started and 16 LC(R)s opened fire over our heads.

'Our tank beached safely with the other flail tank. We blew off our water-proofing and, dodging between the beach obstacles, headed for the thick wire and sand-hills with the other flail tank slightly in front. We flogged through the heavy barbed wire into the minefield, while the other flail tank turned right and headed for Le Hamel and its second objective.

'My tank hit a mine which blew off the front bogey assembly and later we found the front driving sprocket had been hit by an AP round. Over 40 per cent of our chains had been blown off. The explosion had damaged the radio so I was sent back through the minefield to find Major Elfinston, who commanded our beaching party. He had been killed and the beach was now under heavy fire from strongpoints in Le Hamel.'

With gaps flailed through the minefields, the 1st Dorsets were able to get off the beach, and they found one of their initial objectives, Les Roquettes, in the hands of the 1st Hampshires. They left a company and battalion headquarters here and pressed on towards Puits d'Harcot.

Landing just behind the assault companies were the DD tanks of the Nottinghamshire Sherwood Rangers Yeomanry, officially known as the 'Notts Yeo' but more often called the Sherwood Rangers. One of the troop commanders was Lieutenant Stuart Hills. 'The original intention was to launch us 7,000 yards offshore for our swim to the beach. The problem that faced us was a difficult one – should we launch and risk sinking in the heavy seas, or take the landing craft inshore? The decision lay with our squadron leader, Major Stephen Mitchell, MC.'

The decision was made to bring the LCTs in as close as possible to the shore and not trust the tanks to the rough seas. Lieutenant Hills continues: 'There seemed to be very little opposition coming back from the shore at that time, except for a few odd shells which raised columns of water high in the air. "B" Squadron, over on our right were up in line with us, and I saw them drop their ramps to launch their DDs. Major Stephen Mitchell's craft, which Bill Enderby and I were watching, never did, and later we learned that during the night their craft had collided with another, damaging its bows and ramp, so that they eventually had to beach. All I could hear over the air was some other station netting in, and Stephen's furious cries of, "Get off the air, I'm trying to fight a battle."

'Bill Enderby gave the order to move and we prepared to launch. We were now about 700 yards from the shore and as the ramp was lowered I could see two of the flails brewing up just to my front, and I could not help wondering what had caused them to catch fire, and whether our tanks would meet the same fate.

'Sure enough the shots soon came, one on the side of the ramp and the other on our starboard beam, the latter wounding Sergeant Sidaway. Without more ado I gave my driver the order to go, and down the ramp we went. As soon as we hit the water I knew something was very wrong. The screen was very flimsy in the rough sea and water poured in everywhere. I gave a few technical orders to try and save the day, but when I saw that things were hopeless I gave the order to bale out. I can only imagine that the first shell which landed was our undoing and that it must have holed one of the bottom plates.

'Corporal Footitt pressed the button on our rubber dinghy, which inflated automatically, and Trooper Kirman, the only non-swimmer, put it over the side. I scrambled inside the turret to get my map-case out, but we were going down so fast that I didn't have time to retrieve it, and in my haste to get out again I tore the headphones out of the set altogether. I followed

Troopers Reddish and Storey over the side and a few seconds later our tank disappeared into the murky depths.'

The 1st Hampshires came ashore alongside the 1st Dorsets. The stormy conditions and rising tides caused them to drift eastwards on their final run-in, which brought them ashore opposite Les Roquettes, a 1st Dorsets' objective, which they quickly stormed and occupied.

1st Hampshires landed in the face of heavy machine-gun, mortar and artillery fire, with some of the heaviest concentrations coming from Le Hamel. Had they landed at the intended point, they would have had to contend with even more problems, as the main German position at Le Hamel, based in an old sanatorium, would have been directly in front of them.

'A' and 'C' Companies of the Hampshires were pinned down on the beach, while 'B' Company took Les Roquettes, the 1st Dorsets' objective, and pressed on towards Asnelles. Meanwhile 'D' Company came ashore and moved inland, again under heavy fire, to attack the gun position at Cabane.

It was fast becoming obvious that the immediate problem on 'Gold' beach was the village of Le Hamel, especially the seafront fortifications set in the sanatorium. The 1st Hampshires could not deal with it without tanks, and to compound their problems they lost their commanding officer, Lieutenant-Colonel Nelson Smith, who was wounded twice shortly after coming ashore.

Rescue came from the 'Funnies', the specialized armour of the 79th Division. One of their devices was the 'Petard' tank which mounted a huge mortar designed to shatter concrete pill-boxes, and it was one of these that came to the help of 1st Hampshires.

Trooper Joe Minogue was a twenty-year-old gunner in a flail tank of 'B' Squadron, the Westminster Dragoons. 'The scene on the beach is etched so deeply in my mind that I can hear it, feel it, smell it in fine focus so many years after the events of that summer day. We rolled off the tank landing craft into 4ft of water and hit "Jig Green" at 0725 hrs. Within seconds of landing, Major Elfinston was killed and Major Stanyon's tank was knocked out and set on fire, and some of his crew burned and wounded.

'It was a sobering sight as the Hampshires left their smaller infantry landing craft. German machine guns must have been firing along fixed lines, for men were dropping while still in the shallow water, to be dragged forward by their mates and left on the sand, while their comrades ran on in a purposeful steady jog trot, which betrayed no sign of panic.'

The flail tanks swept a path through the beach minefields and allowed an AVRE 'Petard' tank to get up to the Le Hamel strongpoint and deploy its weapon against the walls, firing two rounds into the enemy position. The 'Petard' then went on to engage and silence a large anti-tank gun emplacement. Once the strongpoint had been breached the infantry swarmed forward with grenades. This finally did the trick and the concussed German garrison surrendered about noon after five hours of stiff fighting, although the battle continued around Le Hamel throughout the day.

While the two assault battalions were battering their way off the beaches, the brigade's third battalion, the 2nd Devons, started landing just after 0800 hrs, closely followed by 47 (RM) Commando, which had to make a flanking march behind the German lines and attack Port-en-Bessin from the rear.

Private George Laity was a PIAT gunner with the 2nd Devons. 'I wondered what we were in for when we hit the beach. As we got nearer, shells began to burst around the landing craft and we hit the beach at half-tide, with the iron obstacles showing. The barrage, the noise, the infantry, the little LCAs . . . it was all confusion and bewilderment. German 88s started pounding the beach. My company was pinned down for some time and it seemed endless.'

During the afternoon, with the main threat to the beaches now gone, traffic which had jammed up on the beaches was able to flow more smoothly to its allotted points inland. Among the units now advancing inland was 47 (R M) Commando, whose task was to capture Port-en-Bessin. Port-en-Bessin was defended by at least one company of German infantry, entrenched in pill-boxes overlooking the town and in strongpoints within the town itself. It was decided to take Port-en-Bessin from inland, which meant that 47 Commando had a march of ten miles through enemy territory to reach their assault positions.

Their troubles began as the Commando approached the beaches. Three LCAs were sunk on the way in, and on landing at Le Hamel, which should by then have been quiet, the Commando found the 1st Hampshires still fighting for a foothold. They found their intended assembly area held by a company of Germans and suffered 40 casualties before they cleared them out of it. They did, however, take 60 prisoners, whose weapons served to re-equip those men from the sunk LCAs who had had to abandon their own equipment and swim ashore. 47 Commando reached Port-en-Bessin at nightfall and attacked at dawn the next day, losing over 50 per cent of their strength before they took the town.

With the beaches taken and the Wall breached, the field artillery and more tanks could come ashore. Gunner Frank Topping was a driver and radio operator of a Sherman tank in 147 Field Regiment, Essex Yeomanry. 'A few yards from the beach the ramp flopped down with a crash. I thought we had hit one of the submerged mines we had been warned about, so I ducked, caught my waterproof trousers on a tank projection and ripped the suit. This meant that when I jumped into the sea – only about 3ft deep at that point – I touched bottom as my suit filled with water. The others had difficulty standing up as their suits were filled with air! We managed to get the obstacle out of the way, and the tanks landed without mishap.

'Soaked to the skin I ran up the beach to my tank, intent on climbing into the turret to get out of the way of mortar shells and snipers' bullets. Just as I reached it a shell exploded in a ditch alongside and I felt a blow between the shoulder blades. I was sure I had bought it, but the co-driver leaned down and picked a lump of dried mud off my back. Apart from subsequent bruises I wasn't even scratched.

'Once aboard we moved on towards the small hamlet of Le Hamel, and I was beginning to feel I had had enough excitement for one morning. It was not to be. We had not travelled many yards from the beach when an anti-tank gun opened up at one side and we received an armour-piercing shell in the engine. We all baled out and lay with the infantry at the side of the road. After hitting two other tanks, the German gun was knocked out by one of our SPs firing over open sights.'

Reginald Rham came ashore early, driving his commanding officer's Jeep. 'As I drove off the ramp into the sea, which was about 3ft deep, I saw one of these obstacles in front and I steered away from it but the wheel of the trailer caught it. I knew that some of these obstacles had mines attached to them and I yelled to the two radio operators to free the trailer from the towing socket. They were concerned about the rations that were on the trailer and I quickly replied, "Sod the rations … if we don't move we won't be alive to eat them anyway!" Having released the trailer I was able to make the beach.

'There I lit a cigarette and surveyed the scene. My instructions were to meet up with the CO. He was on one of the landing craft controlling the run-in and had given me a map reference to rendezvous along with the Command Centre tank. While I was waiting for the tank to come ashore there was machine-gun and rifle fire coming from behind the dunes and we quickly dug some shallow trenches alongside the Jeep. I then saw the tank come ashore and drove along the beach to join up with it. The Second-in-Command was standing in the turret, and suddenly there was a sharp crack of a bullet and the officer disappeared. Sadly he had been hit by a sniper and died a few minutes later.'

Attention now turns to the 69th Brigade landing on 'King' beach, just to the west of La Rivière. Like 231 Brigade, 69 Brigade landed with two battalions in the first wave. The most easterly was the 5th Battalion, the East Yorkshire Regiment, while to their right was the 6th Battalion, the Green Howards. Armoured support for the first wave was provided by the DD tanks of the 4/7th Royal Dragoon Guards with the beach obstacles and mines being tackled by squadrons of 6 Assault Squadron, Royal Engineers and the Westminster Dragoons. The main German positions were in fortified strongpoints in La Rivière and around the high ground near Mont Fleury and its lighthouse. From La Rivière, after the third battalion of the brigade, the 7th Green Howards, had come ashore, they were to push inland towards Crépon and St Léger, enlarging the beach-head to allow the follow-up brigade, 151st Brigade, to land and deploy south. To complete this task, 69 Brigade were given just two hours.

5th East Yorks landed on the outskirts of La Rivière, and although initially pinned down by very heavy fire, managed to take their primary objectives with the judicial use of naval gun fire. The seas were too rough to swim the 4/7 Dragoon Guards' DD tanks ashore, so the Navy beached their LCTs, exposing themselves to direct fire from those batteries that had not succumbed to the bombardment.

Two 88mm guns and machine guns enfiladed the beach and these opened up on the LCAs as they beached and the infantry waded ashore. More fire came from houses in the village, and some LCAs were spiked or blown up on the beach obstacles, killing or maiming passengers and crew. Two 'Petard' tanks were hit immediately they came ashore and blew up, covering the infantry with a shower of debris. The survivors of the assault companies of the East Yorks had to crouch for shelter under the sea wall. Here they were joined by the reserve company, also harassed on landing by machine-gun and mortar fire.

Help, however, was at hand. A DD tank came along the beach to engage the machine guns, and under cover of the tank's guns two platoons crossed the wall and began to wipe out the machine-gun nests. Another tank of the Westminster Dragoons fired two shots which penetrated the slit covering the western 88mm gun, which then fell silent, while the one to the east was also knocked out. AVREs and DDs then forced a passage through the sea wall and La Rivière was captured by 0900 hrs after more than an hour of stiff, expensive fighting on the beach. This action on 'King' beach at La Rivière fully justified the specialized armour of the 79th Division. Tanks of the division were now in action all along the British and Canadian beaches, punching holes in Hitler's Atlantic Wall.

One of those who landed with 5th East Yorks was Frederick Ayliffe, a REME craftsman attached to 'S' Company's Mortar Platoon. Landing one hour after the initial assault troops, he recalls what it was like on the beach. 'Our carrier followed the rest down into the water, levelled out, and half submerged began to make our way to dry land. We had to avoid knocked-out vehicles and blackened bodies floating face downwards in the water.

'The beach in front of us was crowded and we came to rest in about two feet of water awaiting our turn to get into the taped-off lanes. The exit was over to our left near some houses down the beach. We slowly made our way in that direction, having to avoid a lot of wheeled vehicles that were stuck in the soft sand. The RAMC were attending to the wounded who were sheltering under the sea wall, where there were also groups of German prisoners. We had just reached the exit, which was between two houses, when enemy shells started coming in. A single-track lane led us off the beach, which was quite steep with a high wall on each side. When we reached level ground the column came to a standstill owing to a vehicle in front having a track blown off by a mine. We were stuck here for quite a while and most of us climbed out to put our feet on firm ground.

'I was standing with our driver, Corporal Johnson, Nobby Clark the batman, and Private Morrikin, the driver of the carrier in front, when there was a blinding flash followed by a terrific explosion and we were blown off our feet. I remember hitting the ground with the others falling on top of me. Nobby Clark was screaming for help with a gash in his thigh, Corporal Johnson was wounded in the chest and appeared to be unconscious, and I could not get up until some help came and moved Private Morrikin, who had been killed instantly, with one side of his face blown away. On getting to my feet I was thankful to find that my only injuries were temporary deafness and concussion.'

The 5th East Yorks made good progress once they got off the beach, capturing the Mont Fleury position and advancing towards Ver-sur-Mer, further south.

Another regiment from Yorkshire, the 6th Battalion, the Green Howards, also came ashore on 'King' beach. This battalion had studied the German defences in great detail and knew they had to face a series of six pill-boxes, containing machine guns with interlocking fields of fire. One of these pill-boxes mounted a 105mm gun. These pill-boxes were situated on the battalion's right flank, in front of a series of five trenches straddling the Meuvaines ridge. On the left flank was a formidable coastal battery containing four 150mm guns, protected by its own entrenched defence force.

The battalion landed on their allotted beach at 0737 hrs. There they encountered heavy mortar and machine-gun fire. 'A' Company lost several men drowned in the surf, but ran up the beach, led by their company commander and supported by a solitary DD tank, until they reached the sea wall. Here they paused, with the Germans throwing grenades on to them over the top of the wall. The Company Commander, Captain Honeyman, though wounded, then led an assault over the wall and drove the enemy back, an action for which he was awarded the Military Cross.

'D' Company also ran into trouble. Many men, including four of the NCOs were cut down by heavy fire as the company waded ashore, but the advance continued in the face of stiff opposition. Evidence of the hard fighting comes from the award of the Victoria Cross to Company Sergeant-Major Stan Hollis of the Green Howards. The official citation tells his story:

In Normandy, on June 6th, 1944, during the assault on the beaches and the Mont Fleury battery, C.S.M. Hollis's Company Commander noticed that two of the pill-boxes had been by-passed, and went with C.S.M. Hollis to see that they were clear. When they were twenty yards from the pill-box a machine-gun opened fire from the slit, and C.S.M. Hollis instantly rushed straight at the pill-box, recharged his magazine, threw a grenade in through the door, and fired his Sten gun into it, killing two Germans and making the remainder prisoner. He then cleared several Germans from a neighbouring trench. By his action he undoubtedly saved his Company from being fired on heavily from the rear, and enabled them to open the main beach exit.

Later the same day, in the village of Crépon, the Company encountered a field gun and crew, armed with spandaus, at a hundred yards range. C.S.M. Hollis was put in command of a party to cover an attack on the gun, but the movement was held up. Seeing this, C.S.M. Hollis pushed right forward to engage the gun with a PIAT from a house at fifty yards range. He was observed by a sniper who fired and grazed his right cheek, and at the same moment the gun swung round and fired at point blank range into the house. To avoid the falling masonry C.S.M. Hollis moved his party to an alternative position. Two of the enemy gun crew had by this time been killed, and the gun was destroyed shortly afterwards. He later found that two of his men had stayed behind in the house, and immediately volunteered to get them out. In full view of the enemy, who were continually firing at him, he went forward alone using a Bren gun to distract their attention from the other men. Under cover of his diversion, the two men were able to get back.

Wherever fighting was heaviest C.S.M. Hollis appeared, and in the course of a magnificent day's work he displayed the utmost gallantry, and on two separate occasions his courage and initiative prevented the enemy from holding up the advance at critical stages. It was largely through his heroism and resource that the Company's objectives were gained and casualties were not heavier, and by his own bravery he saved the lives of many of his men.

Archibald Cairns was a member of the Royal Signals. 'Battalion HQ was to land at H-Hour plus 20 minutes on "King Green" sector of "Gold" beach. I don't suppose many people have ever tried pushing or pulling a 22 set through 3 or 4 feet of water on top of sand laden with other equipment, but we were pretty fit in those days and we managed it, though I couldn't push my youngest grandchild up a 1 in 20 gradient nowadays.

'I could see spurts of sand on the beach where mortar bombs were landing and the road at the top seemed a long way away. I was not destined to get further than the road for about half way up some Germans dropped a mortar bomb which wounded me in the right leg. It also damaged the set. It was only a flesh wound, though nasty enough, and I made it to the top where my friend managed to summon the MO who dressed my leg. I think that excitement turned to apprehension as the mortar bombs kept falling. I lay there for a long time among other wounded and some German prisoners, before being carted back in an American LST.'

Lt-Colonel Richardson, commanding the 7th Green Howards, realized on reaching the beach that he was some 400 yards to the west of his planned landing point. He led his battalion along the beach and then south towards Ver-sur-Mer. Their initial objective, a coastal battery, had already been knocked out by naval gun fire, and they pressed on to Crépon supported by the 4/7th Dragoon Guards and their field battery.

Ken Calver was a command post assistant with the 86th

Field Regiment, Royal Artillery. 'One clear recollection, which gave light relief to the lads, involved me conveying a message – a simple thing. I was instructed to take a map to an officer of one of the gun troops, and feeling that here was an opportunity of bringing an early end to the war, I hared off across a field which was bisected by a small river. I made a bee-line for a wooden bridge but as I was about to cross I had a flash of inspiration – the Germans would have mined all bridges! I moved a few yards down-stream, deciding to jump across. Half-way across, in mid-air, I had another flash of inspiration – that's just what the Germans would expect me to do and they will have mined the bank! I tried to stay airborne but gravity won and I landed in mid-stream, to the raucous cheers of the onlookers.'

The support battalions were now coming ashore behind the assault waves. Among the men landing was Lieutenant Frank Pearson, commanding the Assault Pioneer Platoon of the 2nd Devons. 'The 2nd Devons had already served in Sicily and Italy, where I had been wounded twice and contracted malaria. I was only twenty years old and still recovering from an attack of malaria but I would not have missed D-Day for anything. We were the support battalion to the 1st Hants and the 1st Dorsets in 231 Brigade, with the job of passing through these battalions and heading for the Longues Battery.

'My experiences had made me a realist and I thought our chances of surviving D-Day were small. The noise was tremendous near the beach with everything banging away, but I don't think much of it was coming from the Germans. Our LCA grounded on a sandbank, but it came off again and drifted ashore and we were able to wade ashore and reach the high-water mark without any casualties. One or two of the tanks were knocked out and beside one lay a Tommy without a head. It is strange to remember such details after all this time but they stay at the back of the mind like old photographs.

'There was a lot of fire coming from Le Hamel in the 1st Hampshires area, but only stray bullets and shrapnel were landing near us. We assembled our Bangalore torpedoes and pushed them through the wire and lit the fuses, but nothing happened. Everything was soaking wet and all we could do was lay the pieces on the sand and hope they would dry out. Our rifle companies had now landed and were joining us by the sea wall and trying to figure out what to do. I suggested that if we had any buckets, which we hadn't, we could make sand-castles.

'Meanwhile the tide was coming in as well as more and more troops, so the beach got smaller as the numbers on it grew. It seemed to me that the whole of 50th Division was pinned down on this beach and likely to remain so, and then the break-through came. A flail tank, one of the "Funnies", climbed the sea wall and began to flail a path across the minefield. We peered over the wall, holding our breaths, and watched it flail across. Then, to the best of my knowledge, and against all that the history books say, most of the 231 Brigade and the forward elements of 50th Division followed in the wake of that one flail tank. Perhaps it wasn't like that, but that's how it seemed to me.

'On the other side of the minefield it was very quiet, with no sign of friend or foe. There were some of our tanks around and we hurried to catch up with our rifle companies, coming to a French hamlet which I suppose was Asnelles. There was still nobody about, no Germans, no French, no 2nd Devons. Acting in the well tried Eighth Army tradition, "When in doubt, brew up", we halted in a back garden and made tea.

'Surprisingly I didn't feel too bad, but I remember thinking how I missed my friend Corporal Jewell. He had served with me in Sicily before being wounded and had always been a tower of strength. Most of my men were completely untried, and although they turned out to be absolutely splendid, I did not know that then. Then, suddenly, Corporal Jewell arrived. It seems he had landed separately as a reinforcement, and without his equipment, but the important thing was that he was back with me again.

'While we were brewing up, the rifle companies began to arrive and we pushed on towards our objective at the battery. Just before dark we halted with orders to dig in and attack the battery at first light. I remember there was quite a lot of optimism about – some felt that the Germans wouldn't make a fight of it but just let us walk in. What a pity they didn't.'

With the assault brigades ashore, more and more men and equipment began to pile up behind them. All over the beaches,

teams of men were unloading much-needed supplies and vehicles. The task of controlling traffic on the beaches, bringing
the follow-up landing craft ashore, and directing their passengers and contents to the right destination was entrusted to a
number of Beach Groups. These were usually commanded by a
naval officer, who had a group of Navy Commandos and sometimes a battalion of infantry under command, to provide local
protection.

Able Seaman Norman Harris was a member of 10 Beach
Group, landing just below the cliffs at Le Hamel. 'Our job as
Naval Beach Commandos lay solely on the beach and its surrounding area, and had nothing to do with advancing inland.
We had to secure the beach and defend it and get the rest of the
invading force in with the least number of casualties as possible.
We all had different jobs to do; Taffy Williams and I had to get
radio equipment ashore to a certain part of the beach. This was
carried in a box with two handles back and front, just like a
sedan chair without the top. We jumped out of the craft up to
our waists in water and ran for the back of the beach, passing a
pair of legs without a body on the way.

'Our next job was to erect a great big beach sign about 20 feet
high and 8 feet wide. It consisted of two poles with a canvas
sheet secured to them, painted bright green with a large letter 'J'
on it denoting 'Jig Green Beach', and craft allocated to that
beach could see it when out at sea, giving them a point to land
on. Within minutes of erecting this sign the Germans started to
concentrate their mortar and machine-guns on it, and we
started exchanging fire with them. While this was going on the
Germans had an 88mm gun dug in at Le Hamel, and this was
knocking seven bells out of everything that beached. Something
had to be done about it. LCT D28 beached about 30 yards away
and within minutes it had more holes in it than a sieve. We saw
one man staggering about on the stern of the craft, so Geordie
Farrow and I waded out and got him ashore. He was a young
Sub-Lieutenant from Manchester, and although he was
covered in blood he wasn't seriously wounded, so we advised
him to get down to the water's edge and jump on one of the
landing craft which were disembarking, as we had no medical
services with us.'

Sapper Ralph Rayner was one of the crew in an armoured bulldozer of the 149th Assault Squadron, Royal Engineers. 'We landed with our waterproof bulldozer on the left flank of "Gold" beach, just west of La Rivière. It was a frightening experience, because just as we came out of the water two AVRE tanks (Assault Vehicle Royal Engineers) exploded and disintegrated. They had been hit by an 88mm further up the beach, and this enemy gun was put out of action by Petard fire from another AVRE commanded by Captain King RE, who was awarded the Military Cross.

'Our task was to clear the beach of all obstacles and we worked with the Royal Navy Commandos. Their divers made safe the explosive charges attached to underwater obstacles and secured the bulldozer winch rope so that we could tow the obstacles ashore. It took five days to clear the beach of all obstacles, but we carried out a number of other duties. On D+1 a padre requested our assistance in recovering a number of bodies which were floating just offshore, and we recovered about 20 or 30, mostly from 47 (Royal Marine) Commando, whose landing craft had overturned during the approach to the beach.

'The highlight of our time was when we recovered two crates floating ashore from one of the sunken ships. One contained five-and-a-half gallons of 100 per cent proof Navy rum and the other contained two-and-a-half thousand Players cigarettes. I think I had better leave the consequences of this find to your imagination.'

Gunner Frank Davies came ashore with the 73rd Anti-Tank Regiment. 'Our Battery consisted of four Sherman M10s mounting 3-inch American naval guns, which, according to our BSM Silver, fired effectively round corners. Our officer, Lieutenant Brown, had a Bren gun carrier. I was his Gunner Signaller, and there was a driver and one other man who kept repeating at intervals, "We'll all get killed!"

'Following us were our four M10 Shermans plus a 3-tonner and a water cart, and so on. The "Rhino" raft we were on was driven by two outboard motors mounted on the rear corners, steered by switching the motors on or off as required. Progress to the beach was slow and we had time to study the amazing scene. To the left, to the right, and behind, were hundreds of ships, many of them sporting a barrage balloon which shimmered in the bright sun. There were multi-rocket firing-ships on the right and left of us. We couldn't see the one protecting us from behind but it put the fear of hell up us at intervals. To our right, supporting the Americans on "Omaha" beach and firing shells on to gun emplacements, was a British warship, the cruiser HMS *Ajax*.

'On the beach we made out carriers, mine-flailing tanks, bridging tanks, and so on. Infantry were dotted all over the place and occasionally an enemy shell landed on the beach. Suddenly we were looking to our "Rhino"'s left-hand outboard motor area which seemed to be out of commission, and we realized we were out of control and had become a lethal threat to the ships around us. The remaining outboard motor operator was soon doing a magnificent job, using the cross tide as the missing engine. Our hearts were in our mouths as our pilot, with great skill, weaved in and out and around the ships. I remember noticing open-mouthed faces looking down at us as we missed ships by yards. We grounded on the correct "Gold" beach, which I recall was divided into four colours, and I think we were only a few yards from the correct colour. A splendid effort, worth a VC we thought.'

Able Seaman Norman Harris and the 10th Beach Group were still having problems. 'To get back to that 88mm gun that was doing all the damage; Petty Officer Taffy Williams and Petty Officer Paddy Hodgetts took on the job of having a go at it, and ran along the beach under heavy fire and knocked it out with grenades. Taffy Williams was wounded in the legs in the process but Paddy Hodgetts got away without injury, a very courageous act that received no recognition, although the incident was reported.'

The beaches now had to be cleared of both obstacles and wreckage. Norman Harris again: 'One of the first jobs was to remove the steel girders and the mines on them. A few tanks had survived the landing, which we used to drag the girders out of the sand and pile them up, away from the water's edge.

'Between the beach and that road was a minefield full of Teller mines, so they had to be cleared before the beach became cluttered with the expected traffic. This was our next job. We didn't have mine detectors but used our daggers to feel for them. When we found one, we cleared the top away and felt underneath and around it for booby traps. All being well, we unscrewed the detonator which was in the centre of the mine, got hold of the handle and lifted it out. Eventually we had a pile of mines and detonators which needless to say we kept well apart.'

By mid-afternoon, with 'Gold' beach now in British hands, the follow-up brigades came ashore. These consisted of the 56th Infantry Brigade (the 2nd South Wales Borderers and the 2nd Battalions of the Gloucester Regiment and the Essex Regiment); and the 151st Infantry Brigade (the 6th, 8th and 9th Battalions of the Durham Light Infantry); for support they had the 8th Armoured Brigade, formed from the 4/7th Dragoon Guards and the Nottinghamshire Yeomanry. Their tasks now were to expand the bridgehead, take Bayeux, and occupy all the land up to and beyond the N13 road between Bayeux and Caen, and occupy the coast to the west as far as Port-en-Bessin, linking up with the Americans coming from 'Omaha'.

The 56th Brigade should have come ashore at 1000 hrs, but did not land until after midday, when their planned landing area, Le Hamel, was still in German hands. They therefore landed 1,500 yards to the east and were quickly ashore and heading down the La Rivière–Bayeux road.

Les 'Titch' Holden was a private in the Pioneer Platoon of the 2nd Essex. He was one of a party of four chosen to act as an advance party and lead the battalion through the lanes cleared in the minefields. 'We had to liaise between the RE sappers clearing openings through the minefields, mark the routes as they were cleared, then convey the information by wireless to the incoming ships. Regimental banners were to be erected for quick recognition by the incoming troops and indicator signs fixed to assist in the rapid movement of troops off the beaches and through the minefields.

'Captain Chell told me to extend my area of watch while he went towards Le Hamel to find alternative exits for the battalion transport. It was almost midday when I saw what I had been waiting for, LCIs spilling out men of the 2nd Battalion, the

Essex Regiment. They waded ashore and marched up the beach in single file led by their Colonel.

'It was my duty and honour to welcome my Colonel and fellow "Pompadours" and relay to them their marching orders which, if my memory serves me right were, "Black route is open, Sir." Colonel Higson slapped me on the back and said, "Well done – stay on the beach, recover your Jeep and rejoin us in due course."'

Lieutenant Bert Jalland was a platoon commander in 'B' Company, the 8th Durham Light Infantry. 'My recollection of the countryside that day is that it was pleasantly rolling, with numerous hedgerows and trees, scattered farmhouses and other buildings, and fields golden with ripening crops. There were plenty of cattle and other farm animals, but few people because most of the inhabitants had fled the bombardment or were in hiding where they hoped to be safe. It must have been a ghastly day for them.

'Our first major objective was the town of Bayeux, and we set off along the road leading towards it in single file and widely spaced, in order to limit possible casualties – a tactic that we had successfully adopted during the advance on Messina in Sicily. There was occasional enemy artillery and small-arms fire, but nothing that affected us directly.

'In the main, we did not know what was happening. Information was not getting down to the companies and certainly not to the platoons. We had to rely upon "news" given to us in passing by despatch riders and members of other units, gunners or tank crews, with whom we came in contact. The lack of any clear idea of what was going on is a very lasting impression of D-Day, but the absence of communication to the lower ranks was to be a feature of the whole of the Normandy campaign. Many of us had little idea of where we were, what action was taking place, or what we were supposed to do about it.

'We met few of the enemy on that first day, but those we did capture were infantry and gunners wearing German uniforms who claimed that they were Russians and were keen to surrender. They were obviously shocked by the ferocity of the bombing and the bombardment, but they received very little sympathy from our troops, who regarded them as traitors to the Allied cause.'

With the whole of 50th Division ashore, steady progress was made southwards. Joe Minogue of the Westminster Dragoons was now off the beaches with his flail tank, and his services were in great demand. 'Sergeant Poole was involved in a fierce argument between an irate major in the Royal Artillery and a subaltern in the Hampshires. For our next move, Sergeant Poole wanted to get into Le Hamel, as did the infantry officer, but the artillery major wanted us to flail a nearby field. The Major won, by virtue of his superior rank, and we began to clear mines for his guns, while Sergeant Poole went off on foot to try to get some new orders.

'There were few mines in that field but each time we struck one of them, the 75mm in the turret went off of its own volition. Neville Duell slammed another shell in the breech while at the same time trying to raise some of the squadron's other tanks. Eventually I had to bash him on the head to point out that the firing mechanism had gone wrong, probably knocked out of sequence by the mines as we came off the beach. By then it was time to change the flail chains, replacing them with the grease-covered spares kept in bins at the side of the tank.

'Although we had done it many times before, the crew never really became accustomed to the awkward moment when the chain, bolted to the flail drum, falls free, invariably to swing against one's shinbone to send a crew member hopping and cursing and wishing the 5-foot-long flail chain to the far depths of hell. We were sitting by the track, smoking and looking out to sea, where a stream of vehicles were using the lane we had cleared of mines. At that moment we felt proud that all the training we had undergone had been worthwhile and that the faith of the Commander of the 79th Armoured Division, Major-General Sir Percy Hobart, in his beloved "Funnies", had been justified.

'While we were having our smoke, Neville Duell was scrabbling about idly in the loose flailed earth. "What's this then?" he asked in alarm. It was a German box mine which the flail had missed. It was armed, with the wooden wedge that drove into a trip wire showing red side up. We shouted a warning, got back

into the tank, and Sam Hardy turned the flail round and we
went back to detonate the mine, resuming our interrupted
smoke and watching in horror as the driver of a Bren gun carrier
got down to pick up some object in his path, which turned out to
be an anti-personnel mine that blew up in his hands. His
screams as his hands were blown off put all the other noise in the
shade.'

To George Laity, the PIAT man with 2nd Devons, 6 June
was a mass of conflicting recollections. 'We moved off inland
eventually, with no idea of time. I remember it being a very long
day. I saw my first dead German laying in the road and also
remember seeing dead cows in the fields, blown up like barrage
balloons, on their sides with their legs sticking out.

'We advanced through Normandy, avoiding minefields and
looking out for snipers. I assisted in knocking out a gun emplacement near Port-en-Bessin, after which we came under fire
again in a cornfield and had to cross a large gap in a hedgerow. I
ran like hell and the PIAT weighed a ton. A few of my mates
didn't make it. By the end of the day, tired and hungry, having
not eaten all day, the company consolidated and as it was getting
dark we dug in. The presence of one of our tanks made us feel
somewhat safer. We heard on the radio that the beachhead was
secured and the invasion was successful, and I thought the
worst was over – or was it? A week later I was a POW.' George
Laity was captured at Tilly-sur-Seulles and remained a prisoner until April 1945.

Gunner Edwin Bartholemew was a despatch rider in the
102nd Anti-Tank Regiment, the Northumberland Hussars.
'Moving inland, a big French woman tugged at us and pointed
to a burning barn, crying. We broke down the door thinking
children were in there, and the biggest pig I have ever seen ran
out. We seemed to come together as a regiment. Some were
telling tales of meeting Germans but I hadn't seen any, only two
Italians shouting that they were on our side – "German, son of a
bitch." I remember thinking that war gives up strange
bedfellows.'

Frank Davies of the 73rd Anti-Tank Regiment found little
German tank action to the front of the division, and for the
moment there was not very much for them to do. 'It was a great

relief to be safely on *terra firma*. After exchanging greetings with Engineers and Pioneer Corps chaps and thanking them, we scurried off into the well worn tracks of the tanks, which had gone ahead of us. We saw a British Tommy flattened out in the right-hand track and this sight made us feel very hard towards the Germans, which was probably a good thing at the time.

'As we went through a village we passed German prisoners who had been told to make for the beach for transport to POW camps. A number of them had French girls still hanging on to their arms. Our Lieutenant, "Topper" Brown, was excellent and kept all his men up-to-date with the changing situation. We carried on and noted the various signs of battle, including hastily evacuated German camouflaged tents, cooking and eating utensils, and in a hedge a mobile anti-tank gun mounted on a tripod with straps for carrying it on the shoulders. This was new to me.

'Light was fading and we leaguered in a large pit. The sergeant removed the firing pins and placed rags into an ammo box lightly dug into the hedgeside. The officer and all the other men went off on a local recce, leaving me alone with four M10s, one Bren gun carrier and, of course, my own Sten gun. When they had left, a lone aircraft passed overhead, which I could only just make out. An eerie silence followed, which seemed a very long time, and I was relieved when they all arrived back. I asked Lieutenant Brown how long they had been and he said 20 minutes, but it was the longest 20 minutes I have ever known.'

Frederick Ayliffe, of the 5th East Yorks, had been in the thick of it all day. 'There was some hard fighting during the day and gaining ground was very slow. Knocked-out vehicles littered the roads, forcing us to take to the fields. Our objective was to capture Bayeux, but the enemy resistance hardened and it did not fall until midday on 7 June.

'It was early evening before we reached a road that was not under shell-fire and we were able to move forward about four miles. We passed farms on fire and scores of German prisoners who were being escorted to the rear. As night fell the gunfire lessened and we moved across a field to take cover in an area surrounded by trees. With darkness falling, tree roots every-where, and everyone wanting to get their heads down, most of us gave up the digging, took a blanket and crawled under the vehicles. So ended a very long day.'

Enemy prisoners caused problems for the 10th Beach Group. Apart from Germans and Austrians, the prisoners also included conscripted soldiers from many East European nations. Norman Harris recalls them: 'During this time, German prisoners were being brought in and had to be contained. Some were very arrogant, some glad to be out of it. I remember one prisoner, a bomber pilot, very arrogantly saying that the German Air Force would blow us off the beaches and back into the sea, so I reminded him that very shortly he would be behind barbed wire in England and wouldn't be playing any part in it. The prisoners were a mixed bunch; Romanians, Poles, Czechs, and so on, but they gave us no problems except where to keep them as priority was given to our own wounded. As the landing craft emptied, the wounded were loaded aboard and taken back to the hospital ships moored off the beaches.'

Joe Minogue had an eventful evening. 'Our Colonel, Blair-Oliphant, came striding along, wearing white overalls and looking like an itinerant house-painter who had stumbled into the act by mistake. He had hitched a ride in one of the regiment's recovery vehicles and now he was asking us what had happened to our tank commander. Then, with a brief word of praise to the crew, he strode off again.

'Soon after this, our tank commander returned to tell us we were to join another of our flails on the road leading into Le Hamel, where we spent most of the afternoon, being cursed roundly by other drivers trying to squeeze past our 8-ft-wide jib. I reported the loss of my pistol to Sergeant Poole, who said he had seen a German rifle on the roadside and some ammunition. I recovered this, with his words following me: "You're going on about a lost pistol ... just think of the poor bastards who have lost their lives."

'That night we moved to the small hamlet of Meuvaines, little realizing what a slender toe-hold we had in Normandy, and because we were only two scratch crews the Colonel joined me on our first night's guard in France.

'He thought he saw a German moving in the bedroom of a shell-shattered house. "Run and get me a Mills bomb from one of the flails, Trooper," he ordered. I did so and he threw it towards the bedroom window. Unfortunately, it hit the window sill and began to roll off. Although Colonel Blair-Oliphant was a tall man, we both made even time in diving for cover behind the low garden wall, which was destroyed, covering us both in stones and fragments of mortar.

'It turned into a lively night when two German fighters began to strafe the many ships still lying off the invasion beaches, which put up such a barrage of anti-aircraft fire that the night sky was lit by tracers, providing only a half-dark at the end of an exceptionally long day. After we were relieved we slept like dead men, realizing just how much we had yet to learn but satisfied that we had somehow survived a truly memorable day. Just glad, in fact, to be alive.'

For some men there was still no rest. Bert Jalland, with 8th Durham Light Infantry, having dug himself in for the night, was summoned to Battalion Headquarters. 'When I got there I found some confusion. Apparently Brigadier Senior had disappeared and our Commanding Officer had gone to HQ 151 Brigade to command the Brigade. Our Senior Company Commander, Major George Chambers, was temporarily commanding the Battalion. I was told that the Brigadier's Jeep had been ambushed, his jeep driver and signaller had been killed, and the Brigadier was missing. I was instructed to take out a patrol and endeavour to find him. I was to concentrate upon searching woods and copses. We were to use bicycles so that we could cover a wider area.

'I collected three volunteers from my platoon and we set off, having no map and no real idea of our location. The pass-words that day were "Bread and Cheese". If we came across anyone in the woods during our search, I was supposed to whisper "Bread" and the reply "Cheese" would be given to me. In the event the whole expedition became farcical. I challenged a number of people in the dark with the word "Bread" only to be met with profuse apologies, usually in broad Geordie dialect. It was clear that the people we were addressing had not been given the pass-word.

'We approached many woods during the night but they were all occupied by our own troops and we never found Brigadier

Senior. We were told later that he had been taken prisoner but had escaped. Anyway, we arrived back with the battalion at "stand-to" (about 0400 hrs). I was utterly exhausted but even at that time I realized that it was highly unlikely that I would ever have to live through a more varied and adventurous day.'

During that night, many had time to reflect. Lewis Richards, signaller to the Commander of 231 Brigade, recalls: 'I arrived back from the last visit of the day in time to do "stand-to". It was getting dark and for the first time I saw German planes. They were attacking our shipping but the flak did not give them a very pleasant welcome and I saw two shot down in flames. After "stand-to" I ate the remainder of my box of rations and borrowed a box ready for breakfast. I borrowed some blankets as I had lost my own and all my kit had been in the Jeep which we had lost in the LCM.

'My clothes had dried on me during the day and I slept with them on. Before going to sleep the events of the day passed through my mind and I could not help thinking that at last we could say that the war was entering its final phase.'

Reginald Rham recalls his thoughts at the end of that day. 'My personal reflections at the time were that here I was, sitting in a slit trench, enjoying a cigarette in the fields of Normandy, and not all that long ago I had been enjoying a hot meal in the New Forest. Today, when I read the histories of D-Day and look at the photographs which have been published, I think to myself, "Christ, I was lucky."'

Norman Harris's 10th Beach Group recorded the final positions on D-Day in a news-sheet issued to the troops.

10 Beach Group Intelligence Summary
and News No. 1 dated 7 June 1944

50 Div. Situation a.m. 7 June

231 Bde occupying Longues.
56 Bde north of Bayeux, and moving into town, against slight opposition.
151 Bde across railway Bayeux–Caen, from Point 788078 – Nonant 8275.
69 Bde across road Bayeux–Caen as far as Port-en-Bessin 9072.

Prisoners: Total captured is not known, but some 500 have passed through 10 Beach Group area.

Casualties: Unknown on either side.

Booty: (Apart from what has inserted itself into pockets.)
Stocks of reserve ammo., grenades, rifles, LMGs, etc. are being counted. It is estimated that there are sufficient supplies for the whole Beach Group to blow itself up, if they go the right way about it.

General:
After very hard fighting in the early stages, the operation has gone well and we are now firmly established. German retaliation after the opening phase has been slight, and it is likely that they are planning a large-scale armoured counter-attack. Tanks and A/Tk guns are coming ashore and getting forward in large enough numbers to deal with anything of this kind.

The fighting on 'Gold' beach cost the 50th Division about 1,000 casualties, killed, wounded and missing. This total would have been much higher had it not been for the gallant and resourceful men of the 79th Armoured Division – the 'Funnies'. Many of them were going into action for the first time in these strange and specialized machines, but thanks to their efforts in breaching the Atlantic Wall, the infantry were able to get through and advance towards Bayeux before the Germans had time to occupy it. Bayeux is one Norman town which survived the fighting virtually intact, an enduring tribute to the men who came ashore on 'Gold' beach.

CHAPTER TEN

'Juno'

'I don't care if there are 50 million
Germans on the beach; just let me off this
goddam boat!'
Corporal Hughie Rocks
The Queen's Own Rifles of Canada
off 'Juno', 6 June 1944

Three miles east of 'Gold' beach lay 'Juno', the landing area for
the 3rd Canadian Division. This division was to assault the
coast through a line of small resort towns, from Graye-sur-Mer
just west of Bernières-sur-Mer along to St Aubin-sur-Mer
further east. The Canadian beaches lay on either side of the
oyster port of Courseulles, at the mouth of the River Seulles.
This was the 'Mike' and 'Nan' section of the invasion coast and,
from the west, the Canadian landing areas were codenamed
'Mike Green' and 'Mike Red', followed by 'Nan Green', 'Nan
White', and at St Aubin, 'Nan Red'.

This entire coastline was, and still is, lined with houses and
villas which virtually link the small resort towns together. The
Germans had turned many of the towns into strongpoints,

using reinforced concrete to fortify the cellars of the houses and villas, laying plenty of mines along the roads and in the gardens, while mazes of barbed wire covered by anti-tank and machine guns lay behind the beaches. The Canadians would be involved in street fighting from the moment they stepped ashore, and street fighting is both notoriously difficult to control and a great consumer of infantry. The German troops in this section came from the 716th Infantry Division, commanded by Lt-General Wilhelm Richter, and they were more than willing to make a fight of it.

The assault troops came from the 3rd Canadian Division of General Crerar's Canadian Army, under the command of Major-General R. F. Keller. General Keller's division had been attached to the British Third Army for the assault phase in Normandy and would return to the Canadian Army when sufficient Canadian divisions had come ashore.

General Keller decided to put his infantry ashore astride Courseulles, with close support from DD tanks of two Canadian tank regiments, the 6th Armoured Regiment (the 1st Hussars) at Courseulles, and the 10th Armoured Regiment, better known as the Fort Gary Horse, at St Aubin. The assault infantry would come from the Royal Winnipeg Rifles, the Regina Rifle Regiment, the Queen's Own Rifles of Canada (QORC) and the North Shore Regiment.

Follow-up waves in the assault brigades would consist of French Canadians from a famous Quebec regiment, the Regiment de la Chaudière, and the 1st Battalion of the Canadian Scottish Regiment. The third brigade of the Division, the 9th Canadian Infantry Brigade, which contained the Highland Light Infantry of Canada (HLIC), the Stormont, Dundas and Glengarry Highlanders, and the North Nova Scotia Highlanders would come ashore later.

The Canadians would have the support of British units, the 8th Battalion of the King's Liverpool Regiment acting as the Beach Group and, landing at St Aubin, 48 (Royal Marine) Commando. This was the latest and last of the Royal Marine Commandos to form, and after landing at St Aubin had the task of taking a German strongpoint at Langrune-sur-Mer to the east and so linking up with 41 (RM) Commando coming west from 'Sword'. There would also be armoured support from 'C' Squadron of the Inns of Court Regiment and the 2nd Royal Marine Armoured Support Regiment in Centaur tanks.

The 3rd Canadian Division on D-Day actually consisted of 15,000 Canadian and 9,000 British troops. The main force would land at 0745 hrs while 48 Commando would come ashore at St Aubin at around 0830 hrs, after the beach had been taken by the North Shore Regiment and the tanks of the Fort Gary Horse. That, at least, was the plan; as usual on D-Day, it was not to work out like that.

Air cover would be provided by the 2nd Tactical Air Force and gunfire support would come from 2 British cruisers, HMS *Belfast* and HMS *Diadem*, and 11 destroyers, including the French *Combattant*, and 2 Canadian Tribal-class destroyers, HMCS's *Algonquin* and *Sioux*, as well as the DD tanks and the 107mm mortars from the Cameron Highlanders of Ottawa. The Canadians were to capture all the coastal towns from Graye-sur-Mer to St Aubin and then advance inland as far as a defence line, codenamed 'Oak', which lay along the railway line running from Caen to Bayeux, some seven miles inland.

The accounts in this book all describe how most of the landings got off to a bad start, and the Canadian assault was no different. Bad weather delayed the landing craft and many of the obstacles were already covered by the tide before the craft reached the beach. Many craft were blown up on these obstacles. Others capsized in the surf or were driven onshore. At high tide the beach was far too narrow to let the men and their tanks and vehicles get organized, and an immense traffic jam soon built up on the narrow sand strip above the waterline, under German artillery and machine-gun fire.

Robert Pullin was a coxswain on an LCA and gives a vivid account of the 'Juno' landing. 'On the evening of 4 June we took on board six platoons of French Canadians (Regiment de la Chaudière) and proceeded into Cowes Road and anchored. We did not up-anchor till late evening on 5 June, and met up with the rest of the convoy to France, dropping anchor again eleven miles off the coast. We were then mustered and given our orders. The six LCAs, of which I was coxswain, were to head straight for the gun emplacements holding 88s, and were to land one platoon directly in front of them. We were given a course to follow on leaving the ship; I was given the spire of the church at Courseulles-sur-Mer. My oppo. was to land a mile up the coast at another pill-box – he had a water tower to aim for. Each craft had an LCR behind, blasting at the emplacement and any obstacles. Fortunately, there were none to be seen on arrival, as I had to go in on one engine. To make sure that we could get off the beach, I had to drop a kedge-anchor so that we could pull ourselves off.

'The 88mm was out of action and there were no casualties; the Canadian lads were lying in front of the pill-box. We were not so lucky. My seaman and signalman were in the water pulling on the kedge rope to get us off. They managed it, but on clambering on to the stern the enemy opened up with machine-gun fire and my seaman was shot through the knees. My signalman was hit in the shoulder. They were given morphia injections after we got back to the ship through mountainous seas. The next day my seaman was transferred to the hospital ship. Of the other five LCAs, four returned; the other had blown up on a mine, killing the seaman and wounding one CO and the coxswain.'

Royal Marine Corporal Lionel Long put his Canadians ashore at Bernières. 'We transferred our commandos and picked up 35 Canadian troops and put them ashore safely. On leaving the beach we were holed by an obstacle and started to sink. We were then picked up by a Canadian LCI and she was then hit by three bottle mines and began to sink. We were ordered by the crew to throw everything movable over the side to lighten her. We then went with the crew to the engine room with two pumps working and a chain of buckets. We were waist-high in water, but we managed to save her by applying large mats to stop the water coming in the holes in the engine room.

'We were then taken to our mother ship, which was anchored ten miles off the beaches. An LCA was sent across for us and a wounded Canadian seaman, who had been shot in the chest by a sniper. Our doctor operated on him and saved his life. I'm sad to say we lost 17 LCAs out of 20. Seven other ranks were killed and 6 wounded.'

The naval and air bombardment had clearly failed to knock out the beach defences, for the landing craft suffered severe losses getting ashore and the Canadian infantry suffered heavy casualties just getting off the beach. At Bernières the Queen's Own Rifles of Canada had a very bad time on landing, and only got off the beach with the help of DD tanks and flails of the 1st Hussars. When the reserve battalion, the Regiment de la Chaudière, came ashore half an hour later, they found 'Mike Green' and 'Mike Red' beach still under fire, strewn with dead and wounded and littered with the wreckage of landing craft and vehicles.

Major Max Morrison, MC was then commanding 'A' Company of the 8th Battalion the King's Regiment, which landed at Graye-sur-Mer on the west flank of the Canadians. 'The sea was very rough with troughs so deep that our assault craft appeared to be the only one around although there were hundreds about. Thirty-five close combat soldiers and a crew of three Royal Marines were packed together aboard. We were trying to avoid seasickness but there was nothing to look at except the sea and all around seasick soldiers. Just on H-Hour (0730 hrs) the line of landing craft stormed the beaches. Underwater obstacles, mined angle irons slanted in close ranks, great pointed logs called "Belgian Gates", caused havoc.

'A craft to my left was blown sky high. We manoeuvred through the gap which had been created. Under heavy fire from the beach we landed head-on. I was first off and disappeared under the waves in 9ft of water. Needless to say no one followed. When I surfaced I told the commander to bring the craft further in while I made for the shore. I was the first to feel the dry sand of "Mike Green" beach; there was a feeling of tremendous elation and the seasickness vanished.

'Mortar and artillery fire saturated the beach area, a burst of machine-gun fire swathed through our small group, leaving six or more men killed or wounded. We reached the limited shelter of the sand dunes and established a command post. We moved back to help casualties and strangely we were not fired on. A formidable concrete German command post dominated our beach. Orders were quickly issued and grenades were hurled through the gun ports. Germans emerged with their hands up. I like to think that having witnessed the complete destruction of the machine-gun position they decided that enough was enough, but there was no time to linger. Germans appeared from everywhere, surrendering in droves, but we were still harassed by mortar fire from beyond the beach.

'The Canadians pushed on to deal with the artillery and I took a strong patrol to clear a large group of buildings just off the beach. It was another furious and hectic assault but we cleared the buildings with grenades and took many more prisoners.' For storming the command post and other actions on D-Day, Major Morrison was awarded the MC.

Lt John (Dinty) Moore was also in the 8th Battalion of the King's Regiment. 'Our task was to act as a Beach Group for the 3rd Canadian Division on the western part of the "Juno" landing, to disembark at the same time as the Royal Winnipeg Rifles west of Courseulles, to clear up any opposition on or near the beach and to protect the flanks while the Canadians moved forward.

'As we neared the Normandy coast, well before daylight, after a rough crossing, the shattering barrage on the coast started, first with bombers, then with a terrific bombardment from the Navy. The six Canadian self-propelled 105mm guns on the LCT opened up, blasting the beach area. Slowly the darkness gave way to light. Gradually the dim silhouettes of our landing area at Graye-sur-Mer, to the west of Courseulles, became discernible, with the dull green countryside rising slightly beyond. There were hundreds of landing craft firing at the coast, and behind them the cruisers HMS *Belfast*, *Diadem* and others. There were ships as far as the eye could see.

'Three Allied planes raced over towards the coast just at that moment, and the second one, hit by one of our own rockets, simply blew up in thousands of pieces. The coast, its forts, its obstacles, were now very close and clear. A German reinforced concrete pill-box fired a hail of 20mm shells at the landing craft just to our right, but the landing craft was a Landing Craft Gun (LCG) with two 4.7 inch guns, and having turned slowly around, it fired a salvo which blasted the pill-box to pieces.

'The small assault craft, the LCAs, were now slowly overtaking us, having been lowered from the troop-carrying ships well to our rear, the *Langibby Castle*, the HMCS *Prince Henry*, the *Mecklenburg* and others. These LCAs had been tossed about cruelly in the still rough sea and most of the troops packed in them were terribly seasick.

'We watched as the LCAs carrying the assault troops of the Royal Winnipegs and the Liverpool Irish tried to manoeuvre through the gaps in the obstacles. Some had the bottom of the landing craft torn off by the jagged obstacles, others were sunk or blown up by the exploding mines and shells. Almost a third of the assaulting landing craft were sunk or badly damaged.

'For the Germans to have survived the monstrous barrage was quite surprising, but several of their reinforced concrete gun-posts, buried in the sand dunes, were virtually intact, and the first troops ashore, two companies of the Royal Winnipegs, one company of the Regina Rifle Regiment together with "A" and "B" Companies of the Liverpool Irish, were met with machine-gun fire. German gun and mortar fire now started to rain down on the beach, the machine-gun fire sweeping the length of the narrow shore and catching the debarking troops in enfilade. Several men were killed or wounded while still in the water; others staggered limp, wet and seasick to the shore where bullets were kicking up spurts of sand.'

The Royal Winnipeg Rifles and Regina Rifles made good progress at Courseulles, and by mid-afternoon the Canadian armour had cut the Caen–Bayeux road, after a speedy advance inland of more than seven miles, but before this could be exploited the Germans counter-attacked.

The War Diary of the Queen's Own Rifles spells out their D-Day situation in detail:

0750 hrs
H-Hour postponed 30 minutes. DD tanks and AVREs behind schedule. Up to 0745 hrs no sign of action on beach but now anti-tank shells begin to drop around LCAs which makes heads go down in fast order.

Unfortunately postponement has definitely messed up support fire and all that is firing now is an LCF which cruised right in close to shore and let loose with a lot of tracers.

0805 hrs
Assault companies go in. As yet no DDs or AVREs can be seen which looks ominous.

0815 hrs
A & B Coys touch down. 'B' immediately catches a packet of trouble as they are landed in front of a heavily defended position. Several of the LCAs of both companies are blown up by mines but only the front two or three men are injured. 'A' Company are a little better off than 'B', able to get off the beach. As soon as they hit the railway they come under heavy mortar fire and are pinned down. Casualties mount; Lt Rea wounded, Sgt Charles Smith extricates platoon. Balance of 'A' Company get through. 'B' Company finally outflanks position.

0830 hrs
'C' and 'D' Coys and alternate Bn HQ touch down. Casualties among LCAs heavy. Almost one-half blown up by underwater mines. Personnel get ashore and pass through assault companies.

0900 hrs
The support all around has been very disappointing – none of the beach defences has been touched and this caused very high casualties among the assault companies.

0940 hrs
Bn HQ arrives. At this time it is noted that a café just 100 yards off the beach is opened up and selling wine to all and sundry.

Considerable delay as companies assemble. 'B' Coy casualties so heavy they gather first off the beach and try to sort themselves out. 'A' Coy moves to the forming-up place. Regiment de la Chaudière has now landed but are prevented from passing through us by the very accurate fire of a Battery of 88mm guns located just south of Bernières.

W. T. Jones of Peterborough, Ontario was with an artillery unit supporting the 7th Canadian Infantry Brigade. 'This is an honest account, years and memory permitting, of six Canadians who landed on D-Day. "G", "H" and "K" were three Troops of the 3rd Regt RCA, and had loaded on their LCT, Queen's Docks, Southampton. "G" was to support Regina Rifles, "H" Winnipeg Rifles, and "K" Canadian Scottish.

'Our Gun HI was to be the first towed gun of the regiment to land. We were to land on "Mike" sector of "Juno". This was the plan, but what action goes to plan? On our run-in to the

beaches, about three miles from the shore we were ordered out
of the landing order and fell back about five miles. Here we
circled for hours, which seemed like days as the seas were rough
and we weren't sailors. We had been told our beach exit was
plugged and closed to vehicles.

'Finally, our turn came and in we went. The tide, however,
was now not suitable for a direct landing, i.e., ramp down, drive
off, as we had rehearsed for many months. Major Scott
informed the Gun Sergeants we would be loading on a small
"Rhino" raft. This was the first time we had heard about
"Rhino" rafts and we sure weren't crazy about the word "raft".
There were the usual derogatory remarks about the Canadian
Brass. We were assured that four Bren gun carriers and guns
could fit on these rafts "if properly handled". Out from the
beach puttered our raft, a low-slung affair with steel decking
and no railings, powered by two outboard motors and crewed by
two REs who looked about forty years old. How they did it
without loss of life or limb I'll never know, but they did.

'The Troop Commander had landed earlier, as planned, and
had dropped off the Bombardier from H2, who was to guide us
to Troop HQ. As we were hours behind schedule, we attempted to de-waterproof on the run. Splash shields were
knocked off, life belts and waterproof covers removed from
small arms, all tossed over the side. Bombardier Tom Grant
(killed 8 June by 12 SS Panzer) was sitting by a wall, and when
we halted, his first words to me were, "Where the hell have you
been?" So much for rank respect in the Canadian Army this
day.

'H Troop caught up to the Winnipegs and assumed our
support role. A Captain in the "Pegs" wanted a house "taken
out". Up went H1, unlimbered, put one up the spout and fired.
What a commotion! In our eagerness and nervousness we forgot
to remove the muzzle cover which sailed about 40ft down the
road. The gun and road was enveloped in a huge cloud of blue
smoke (grease not cleaned off breach and barrel). When the
smoke cleared the gun sat alone and the crew had taken cover in
a ditch. This was the first shot of H Troop, 14th Bty, 3rd Regt
RCA. The rest of the day was spent performing the 3Ds of an
Infantry division: Digging, Ducking, Dodging. At Creully,

with the Royal Winnipeg Rifles, we dug in for the night. Our Troop Commander, Lt Reg Barker (killed 8 June by 12 SS Panzer) and Troop HQ and Major Scott caught up with us about 2300 hrs.'

The Canadians advanced further inland than any other troops on D-Day, threatening Caen. The Canadian 7th Brigade on their right flank linked up later that day with the 50th (Northumbrian) Division to give the Allies a beachhead 15 miles long and up to 7 miles deep on the east flank. So far, so good but as some of the above accounts indicate the 3rd Canadian Division was soon involved with heavy and extremely bitter fighting with the 12th (SS) Panzer Division, and these two divisions continued to slog it out for much of the subsequent Normandy fighting.

Courseulles was the main landing area for the Canadian 7th Infantry Brigade. The port was classified as a strongpoint, and apart from entrenched infantry and concrete blockhouses, contained three 75mm mortar positions and twelve machine-gun posts. Courseulles was the most heavily defended point along the Anglo-Canadian beaches and took a severe toll of the attacking force.

The 7th Infantry Brigade decided on a frontal assault by a mixed force of tanks and infantry, made up of two companies of the Regina Rifle Regiment which would land east of the mouth of the Seulles on 'Nan Green', supported by 'B' Squadron of the 1st Hussars in DD Shermans. The DDs were launched 4,000 yards offshore, in very heavy seas, but fourteen of them made it ashore and went straight into action against the beach defences.

'A' Company of the Reginas attacked the centre of Courseulles. They found it virtually untouched by bombs or shells and none of their tank support turned up, so 'A' Company took heavy casualties before the enemy was subdued. 'B' Company, with AVRE 'Petard' tanks and DDs, cleared the pill-boxes along the promenade east of the River Seulles and opened beach exits, freeing more DDs to enter Courseulles and assist 'A' Company. The follow-up Regina Rifles companies, 'C' and 'D', had a mixed reception. 'C' got ashore virtually intact and went to the support of 'A', but 'D' Company's craft ran into mined

obstacles, and only 49 of the Company got ashore. Still full of
fight, they picked up some tanks and marched on their objective, the village of Reviers, three kilometres inland.

West of the Seulles was the province of the Royal Winnipeg
Rifles, a regiment known in Canada as 'The Little Black Devils'.
The Winnipeg battalion was commanded by Lt-Colonel John
Meldrum, who had no tank or AVRE support on landing and
had to take the enemy positions by infantry assault, with rifles,
Bren guns and grenades. Fortunately, the DDs then arrived
and began firing into the strongpoints and blockhouses, while
the 6th Field Company, Royal Canadian Engineers, began the
work of clearing away the mines and beach obstacles. This field
company of 100 men was down to just 26 by the end of the day,
sustaining one of the highest casualty rates on D-Day.

Fortunes could vary, even along a few yards of beach. 'A', 'C'
and 'D' Companies of the Winnipegs got ashore without heavy
loss and moved on Banville, west of Reviers, but 'A' Company
then took losses at Ste Croix-sur-Mer, which was stoutly defended by a company of infantry from the 716th Division. The
eastern part of this beachhead was the task of 'C' Company of
the Canadian Scottish, which the Winnipegs had under command for the operation. This company had a successful day,
taking their initial objective and the Château-Vaux, just outside
Courseulles, where the three reserve companies of the Canadian
Scottish came to join them. The Winnipegs' War Diary briefly
covers these events:

0749 hrs
In spite of air bombardment failing to materialize, RN bombardment
spotty, the rockets falling short and the AVREs and D.Ds being late,
'C' Company Canadian Scottish Rifles and Royal Winnipeg Rifles
land.

0900 hrs
The bombardment having failed to kill a single German or silence one
weapon, these companies had to storm their positions 'cold' and did so
without hesitation.

1800 hrs
'D' Company had by this time gapped a minefield at La Valette and
cleared Graye-sur-Mer. 'B' Company crossed the Seulles, cleared out

four positions on the island. ... 'A' Coy started inland 0805 towards
Ste Croix pinned by six to eight MGs. 'C' Coy approached Banville,
pinned down by three MGs on commanding ground.

The Battalion Diary carries a special note:

It is desired to make a special note of the services rendered to the Bn
during the first day of Ops by our MO (Capt Robert M. Caldwell) and
the Bn RAP Staff – and the assault sec. of 14 Canadian Field Ambulance u/c Capt. Harry Dixon. Not only were the wounded cared for
with skill and despatch but confidence was developed and morale
increased accordingly. A very special note, too, should be made about
the general tone of the Bn during this day, called D-6 Jun. 44. Not one
man flinched from his task, no matter how tough it was – not one officer
failed to display courage and energy and a degree of gallantry. It is
thought that the Little Black Devils, by this day's success, has managed
to maintain the tradition set by former members. Casualties for the day
exceeded 130.

The 'C' Squadron, Inns of Court Regiment, in armoured
cars, landed in support of the Winnipegs at Graye-sur-Mer.
David Swynne, then aged twenty-four, recalls the Graye beach
area. 'The landings on the beach proved to be more difficult
than had been expected, and on our arrival at first light at
"Juno" beach (Graye-sur-Mer) the beach had not, in fact, been
cleared and many of the Canadian infantry were still trying to
negotiate the minefields at either side of the beach exit.

'Steel posts with mines on top could clearly be seen at the
water's edge. At the time of our arrival the water was deeper
than had been anticipated. We had been prepared for wading in
about four-and-a-half feet of water; the car exhausts allowed
only a few inches more than that. Our craft was the first to land
but hit a mine which badly damaged the ramp, and by the time
this had been dealt with the water was too deep for wading and
we had to wait for the tide to recede. Our sister craft was able to
unload and all that we could do was to watch.

'The Canadian infantrymen (the Winnipeg Rifles) 3rd Canadian Division, were finding the opposition more than had been
anticipated and were having considerable problems with anti-
personnel mines, which were profusely scattered in the sand
hills either side of the beach exit. The mined areas were well
marked with tapes and signs, but not the 88mm gun, which

scored a direct hit on the first of our Daimler armoured cars to attempt to leave the beach. I could only sit and watch the driver, Trooper Dixon, a very good personal friend, burn to death.

'By the time the tide had receded, the beach exit had still not been fully cleared, and I and my car commander, Ewart Simms, were instructed to reconnoitre along the beach away from the exit, and to ascertain whether or not the next exit was clear. After about half a mile we were fired upon, and almost at the same time ran over a mine which caused no personal injury but completely destroyed the rear suspension. We were under small-arms fire at the time and so Ewart Simms and I hastily abandoned the car, lay on the ground and fired off a couple of magazines in the direction of the enemy.

'We then ran back to the beachhead, taking our Bren gun and personal arms with us. At the beachhead we joined the rest of the survivors. I think there were about a dozen of us. Some hours later we returned to our car to find that it had been completely burned out. We could find no trace of the remains of our personal kit or the ample supply of tinned food, etc., which we thought must have been removed prior to the car being fired upon.

'All the beach survivors of my own unit remained on the beach for the next three or four days. During this time our REME Sgt, Sgt Pratt, together with myself and one or two other members of the squadron, stripped down the engine of a "drowned" half-track which was then rebuilt; after which we all somehow managed to squeeze into it and so return to our unit. Sadly, in retrospect, we were the lucky ones. Many of those who managed to leave the beach early had been killed or badly wounded. Four of our armoured cars and one half-track vehicle were destroyed in an attack by American Thunderbolt aircraft.

'Because it was expected that some of us may have to operate at night, which indeed we did, all our armoured cars were painted jet black, with no corps signs or other means of identification, other than a yellow sheet which could be draped over the turret as a sign of recognition when required. Sadly, in practice, the Americans did not appear to understand this and many lives were lost, and particularly so at the Jerusalem crossroads when American Thunderbolts dropped a stick of bombs from rooftop level, which left four of our armoured cars and one half-track vehicle blazing furiously. It was thought that the entire population of the village had been killed, together with Lt Lofts RE, Lt Gwynne Jones and five other ranks. Lt Reeves and five ORs were wounded. In the event, a few civilians survived. I understand that a few of our veterans visited the rebuilt village some years later and were made very welcome.'

One of the German soldiers in action this day was Herbert Muschallik. 'I was on guard early in the morning and I remember an officer came running down the field, shouting, "They've landed! They've landed!" We moved all day towards the coast and ended up in a forest. We were all scared stiff and there were bullets ricocheting off the trees. I was on the crew of a Pak-38 anti-tank gun and we saw a tank, maybe British or Canadian. I don't know where we were but we were going to engage it and I was bringing up the ammunition when the tank fired and the explosion threw me into the ditch. We fled into a village and there was a lot of firing going on. About 10 o'clock I was hit by shrapnel in the right shoulder. I remember taking my helmet off and putting my face in it. I tried to get up but I couldn't and I stayed in the ditch all day long, getting hit again in the side.

'The next thing is a British or Canadian soldier prodding me with his bayonet. I remember he had a little spiked bayonet. They took me out of the ditch and made me put my hands up, and then a man came with a Red Cross and bandaged my shoulder and took me to a medical point, where I was given an injection and a cup of tea. Then I was put in a tent with four or five British soldiers, all wounded. They were talking to me but I didn't understand. They wanted to know how old I was, and I signalled "eighteen" with my hands, and suddenly cigarettes and biscuits were thrown on to my bed . . . that was something. I wish I could meet those men some time if they are still alive, and thank them.

'That night there was bombing, and next day I was put on a ship and ended up in a hospital at Epsom in England. I stayed there for five weeks before being shipped on a US transport, the USS *West Point* to Boston. I ended up picking peaches in South Carolina. I was sent back to England in 1947, a very hard winter shovelling snow, and one day I was given tea by a girl in the

Land Army, who is now my wife. In 1952 an X-ray found a bullet in my back which was taken out in Maidenhead hospital, and I still have it.'

The Allied forces now coming ashore were meeting the men and women of the French Resistance, emerging to play their part in the battle. Henri Lamperière, the policeman from Bretteville, near Caen, had been out all night. 'As you know, the Germans were executing Maquis prisoners in Caen on the night of 5/6 June. Three of my comrades, Chef Caulet, Gendarme Ménochet de Vassy and Gendarme Guilbert, were shot by the Gestapo that night in the prison at Caen. We had already suffered a lot of arrests, deportations and executions before 6 June, but we had been able to inform the Allies about enemy positions and especially about the V1 and V2 rocket sites, which had then come under attack by the RAF.

'On 5 June, our group, which then belonged to the "F" Section of SOE, received the invasion message from the BBC: "*Le champ du laboureur dans le matin brumeux.*" Later on, even 30 kms from the coast we could hear the sound of the bombardment, and I returned at once to Bretteville. Monsieur Le Nevez, who was responsible for our sector as far as Thury-Harcourt, alerted all the men available and launched an attack on the railway line between Caen and Flers at the Grimbosq halt, making the line unusable. They also attacked a German column of 40 trucks full of soldiers at Meslay. Five officers and many Germans were killed before the Maquis had to withdraw. The Maquis Surcouf attacked the German *feldgendarmerie* post at Pont-Audemer.

'There were now many German troops and SS coming into the area and it was difficult to get news of all the attacks. Capitaine Danby of the SOE organized a system of communications with his radio officer, Maurice Larcher, but our main task was to hold up movement of German troops towards the invasion front. We multiplied our efforts to fell trees across roads and scatter tyre-piercing nails – *crève-pneus* – on all the roads. This last method was very effective. By these methods we created a number of road blocks and the German transport was attacked next day by British rocket-firing fighters.'

*

The second assault brigade, the 8th Canadian Infantry Brigade, were to land on the 'Nan' beaches to the east, running from Bernières to St Aubin. The weight of this assault was carried by two infantry battalions, the Queen's Own Rifles of Canada, landing in the centre at 'Nan White', and the North Shore Regiment on 'Nan Red'. These battalions were supported by the reserve companies of the QORC and the Regiment de la Chaudière.

Don Doner of Alliston, Ontario, was in the first wave ashore. 'We were 8 Section of 9 Platoon, "A" Company of the Queen's Own Rifles of Canada, and we were elected to be assault section for the platoon, which meant that we would be first to leap off the assault craft, carrying Bangalores, steel ladders, wire mesh and any other material that would assist us in scaling the sea wall and blowing holes in the barbed wire if necessary. We didn't particularly like the thought of being assault section, but not one of us ever thought that we couldn't do it, and we prepared ourselves accordingly.

'We lined up down the centre of the assault craft as follows: our little Corporal Hughie "Rockie" Rocks, a diminutive fellow of 5ft 3in, full of get-up-and-go and more fun than a picnic, aged thirty-eight and married to a girl he affectionally called Big Elsie. Next myself, then Ernie Cunningham of Toronto, a groaner like myself, who didn't like the army, and didn't mind telling everybody about it. Gill "Gabby" May sat in the next slot, and as his name implies, he was never lost for something to say. Then came the only guy in the section to admit that he was scared to death, and that was old John "Dinty" Moore.' (This was not the same John 'Dinty' Moore whose account is given earlier. 'Dinty' Moore was a cartoon character of the day and a popular nickname, but it is curious that two John 'Dinty' Moores, from two different regiments, landed on the same beach on D-Day.)

'"Dinty" had tried to evade all this, but now that he was into it he was readily admitting that he was scared out of his pants. Some of the guys teased him about it; as for me, I kept my mouth shut. After all, how did I know how I would react? As a matter of fact, how did any one of these guys know how they would act when they were staring death in the face?

'When the guys would start in ragging "Dinty", old Buck Hawkins, our Bren gunner, used to drawl out, "I wouldn't get too mouthy, you guys, 'cause you're not kiddin' anybody. Every one of ya is just as scared as Dinty there, but ya haven't got the guts he has to admit it." Jackie "The Kid" Bland was next in line, and here was a kid who was liked by everybody. Jack had joined the army when he was fifteen and that was the reason why everybody called him "Kid". But he was no kid and had one of the levellest heads in the platoon, if not the whole company. Then there was big Harry "Buck" Hawkins, and he was the pride of the section. Buck was our Bren gunner and the greatest single factor in the success of the section. He was the guy everybody respected and looked up to. He was the guy you took advice from, the guy who slugged the Bren gun on twenty-mile route marches, and he was the guy we all had confidence in.

'For me to think that I would never see a lot of those guys again seemed impossible, and I looked forward to seeing them all at Hill 80, our consolidating point, after we had swept the beach clean and the Regiment de la Chaudière had passed through us.

'Well, the bombardment had started and it grew in intensity as we lurched and tossed the eight miles in to the beach. The big guns from the battleships and cruisers, Mosquitos and Spitfires all added to the roar of the rockets that crushed the sound of our own voices like matchsticks. Most of the guys were sick. The spray kept flying over the front into the craft, dowsing us to the skin and, standing up in the front, I cursed and swore until our officer, Lieutenant Raey, asked me if I would stop my groaning as it might affect the morale of some of the other boys whose morale was low enough as it was, being seasick and all. I was standing up in the front of the craft, not by choice, but because I knew if I sat down it would make me sick, and also because I have always had a desire to see where I'm going and what I'm heading into.

'We were right in close now and the Bren on our craft opened fire straight ahead and we weaved in and out between the ugly tripods standing in the water, with big black bottles full of explosive on the end. To hit one of those meant death or injury to most of the men on board. The last thing I saw before I ducked my head was one of the craft about a hundred yards down to our left blown sky-high from a direct hit. Just then two sharp cracks overhead sent all those still with heads scrambling for the bottom of the boat. A few seconds later we felt the scrape as the craft struck the sandy beach, and in no time the door was down and we were leaping into the foam.'

Les Wagar was a rifleman in 'C' Company, the QORC. 'H-Hour at Bernières was 0730 hrs. "A" and "B" Companies would take the beach and the wall. "C" and "D" would land twenty minutes later to take the town. Now we began to pick out the features of Bernières ahead. Support started up. Shells from battleships we couldn't see began hissing high overhead, exploding somewhere inland on targets we couldn't see. A line of four Spitfires swept low along the line of the coast, blazing away at God knows what. To our left, someone pushed the firing button on a long, converted LCT, bristling with bank after bank of heavy mortars. We watched nests of mortar shells lobbing up and over and down, and the town blowing up in slow motion. Someone – it had to be the CO, Major Nickson, cursed, "Damn! They're supposed to be hitting the beach."

'Now the Spitfires were coming back along the coast, higher up, and swinging out over us, heading home. The last one in line was on a collision course with the last nest of mortar shells lobbing up from the LCR. I watched their trajectories closing, and wondered if the guy would know what hit him. The plane exploded and fell into the water just offshore. The CO was trying to pick things out with his binoculars and suddenly blurted, "My God! There's a Frenchman in a boat out there, pulling the pilot out of the water."

'The unreality of things was creeping in. With our heads down as ordered, tucked safely behind the shelter of steel plates, and all hell breaking loose around us, here was a mere civilian who didn't know he was in a war – just knew that somebody had to get a man out of the water.

'Now we were maybe a quarter-mile off the beach, flanked by our other two LCAs, revved up on our final run-in, when the orders were changed. Our LCA turned, the CO waving the other two after us, and headed back to sea. I don't know where the message came from, or how it got to us, but now we were told that "A" and "B" hadn't landed. Our tank support had been slowed down by the heavy seas and hadn't arrived yet. "A" and "B" had been turned around about half an hour ago. H-Hour was now tentatively one hour later, and someone had forgotten to tell us. Forgot to tell the mortar ships, too, I was thinking. More cursing. About 1,000 yards offshore we turned again, and began doing slow circles, waiting. The odd shell began throwing up waterspouts nearby. Any help the earlier support fire had given us was rapidly disappearing.

'Now the order came to go; all the tanks hadn't arrived but we were going to have to go with what we had. The tide was coming in, and the higher the tide moved up the beach, the bigger the problem for the assault craft to keep clear of the mines. This time, over to the left, there were craft going in ahead of us. Our LCA revved up and we started in again.

'Some of the mines were in three or four feet of water. The coxswain was fighting surf to keep clear of them, trying to run a path that he'd also be able to back out of. The ramp dropped and we poured off in single file into waves up to our waists, running. Idiot orders were being shouted: "Off the beach! Off the beach! Get to the wall!" Relieved somebody's tension, I suppose, but I don't know anybody who had to be told what to do on that beach. As I hit the sand I was thinking, "Thank God for solid ground!" The world wasn't going up, down and sideways any more. In fact, that's all I was thinking. For the first minutes nothing else registered but relief.

'Company HQ set up beside the wall, near a jagged split where one man at a time could climb up to the waterfront road. Most of the company were already in the town when some sniper filtered back into the near houses and lined up on the road. There was a little panic in the rear until the sniper was taken out. Wounded were coming back with stories of snipers holding things up in town. I was thinking I didn't know most of these guys. I'd been in training away from the company for four months. For that matter, I'd never worked in Company HQ, so I hardly knew Major Nickson either – and he'd only known me as an out-of-place kid in a rifle platoon. Word passed down that "A" and "B" Companies had a lot of casualties. "B" Company had landed in front of the main bunker. Compared to that, our beach was a cinch.

'Now a flail tank clanked ashore, rotary chains flailing the sand in front of it to explode the mines, clearing a path up the beach for another vehicle exit into town. A "step mine" blew its left track off and the crew baled out, minus the driver. Some engineers turned up from somewhere with their mine detectors, and started clearing a path the hard way.'

Rolph Jackson of Toronto was in 10 Platoon, 'A' company the QORC, landed on 'Nan White' beach at Bernières-sur-Mer. 'If you are familiar with the area, the half-timbered hotel which gets in all the D-Day photographs was to our right, and the sharp bend in the wall, with the pill-box, on our right front. My section was first from the LCA, and we were slaughtered.

'For some peculiar reason, as we approached the beach, our craft did an about turn, making a large loop, then came in for the landing. How long? Who can say, but the defences were manned as our craft grounded. Our Support Craft was knocked out so we had no heavy weapons. The DD tanks had not come ashore. My platoon, approximately 36 strong, went through what we believe was enfilade fire from 5 machine-guns.

'The official battalion killed in action figures on 6 June 1944 numbered 63, "B" Company, 34. I don't have figures for the platoon but I do know that only 9 men moved inland, 3 of whom were walking wounded. Of the 10 men in my section, 7 were killed and 2 wounded. Of these 10 men, 6 had been in the unit since June 1940. The one survivor, the latest replacement, had never done a "landing" in training.

'We landed in our proper area, but no specialized gear reached the wall. All our Assault Engineers were killed in action. We were still in the water when the section was cut down. Most of us had deflated the Mae-Wests we were wearing, and possibly those that died had drowned. I was a Lance-Jack, Bren crew, loaded with around a total of 300 rounds, plus 36s. The sea was red. One lad was hit in the smoke bomb he was carrying. Another, a human torch, had the presence of mind to head back into the water. Our flame-thrower man was hit and exploded, and we couldn't even find his body.

'I was asked by the Sergeant, acting CSM, to go back to the

beach for Bren mags and grenades. 10 Platoon moved off the beach later, passing three burned-out self-propelled (SP) 25-pounders. 10 Platoon was under the command of an acting Sergeant – me – as one Bren and one other Junior NCO who had been hit in the legs, fell out earlier. The QORC did dig in at Hill 80, their objective. I was sent to the RAP by the A/CSM. The MO had also been hit but he stayed until replaced.

'I had smashed bones in my left hand, grenade fragments from a "potato masher" in one shoulder and minor flesh wounds to one leg. The platoon now consisted of one A/Sgt and five riflemen. The first Dressing Station had no room. The second took us in and we were into three groups: those who were OK to leave, those who could be treated, and the last sad group – "Don't waste time." Late the next day (7th) I went by DUKW out to an American LST with 300 stretcher cases plus the walking.

'A group of us, each 6 June, gather at Toronto's War Memorial to lay a wreath, and remember. We've been doing this since 1946. I belong to what was once a Regimental Legion and still see guys I knew so long ago. We have an annual dinner, and each year fewer stand for "Those who were on the Beach". In one section of Bernières-sur-Mer Canadian cemetery, I know half the graves by first name.'

Peter Rea was a lieutenant commanding 9 Platoon, 1st Battalion QORC. 'I saw a Spitfire shot down by the rockets just offshore, but I am sure many men will tell you about that. I had the advantage of standing up, unlike my men who had to stay under cover and were very sick. As we approached the beach at Bernières, tracer bullets could be seen heading in our general direction from a supposedly empty pill-box about 200 yards on our right. We landed in 3ft of water, and I recall thinking that no matter what lay ahead, it was a great relief to be on dry land again.

'We reached shore safely and raced over the beach to the dunes. Sand had piled up against the sea wall, making it easily passable, but it was soon apparent that the pill-box on our right housed an 88mm gun which was firing on the landing craft and causing extreme damage. We were now coming under heavy mortar fire from inland. I moved to establish contact with No. 2

Section, and ordered the Section Leader to assault the pill-box. By this time I had been wounded twice, once by a mortar and once by a shell fragment which pierced my arm, rendering it useless. I then encountered the No. 2 Section Commander, who later died, and most of his men had already been wounded. I then went to a tank which had its turret closed, and tried banging on the armament with my Sten gun, without success, and it was at this time that, probably in shock and weakened by loss of blood, I collapsed to the ground.

'After the beach had been cleared, the remnants of my platoon, consisting of a sergeant and ten men, passed by, taking the maps from my pack and pressing on to join the company. I rejoined the regiment in October, and we were nearing Emden in Germany when hostilities ceased in May 1945. We returned to Canada in December 1945 and received a tremendous welcome from the City of Toronto.'

According to the Canadian Official History, the QORCs landing on 'Nan White' at Bernières had the toughest task of all the Canadian battalions. The DD tanks and AVREs arrived too late to help the initial assault waves, and one team of AVREs was put ashore a quarter of a mile from their intended position. 'B' Company of the QORC was landed directly in front of a strongly defended position they had intended to outflank, and took heavy casualties before the position was overcome.

Similar problems and the inevitable delays brought trouble to the Regiment de la Chaudière, which came ashore at 0930 hrs, when most of the beach obstacles were still intact and covered by the tide. Four of the five LCAs carrying 'A' Company of the 'Chauds' were damaged by mines on the way in, forcing most of the infantry to abandon their kit and swim ashore through the surf. Even so, by 1030 hrs all the QORCs and the Regiment de la Chaudière were ashore, where the local people, emerging from shelter, were amazed and delighted to meet French-speaking troops. Then the DDs and the self-propelled guns came up and the Regiment de la Chaudière led the 8th Brigade out of the landing area and south into Normandy.

The other Canadian battalion of the 8th Infantry Brigade was the North Shore Regiment landing on 'Nan Red' where, with support from the Fort Gary Horse, it was to take and clear the beach and take St Aubin before the Royal Marines of 48 Commando came ashore and swung east to capture Langrune.

Because of the heavy seas, the DDs of the Fort Gary Horse were not launched at their designated point 7,000 yards offshore but brought in by the LCTs to within a mile of the beach, which reduced their landing to what the Fort Gary War Diary calls 'a wet wade', though the screws had to be raised and the propeller engaged. At first they found 'Nan Red' 'fairly quiet except for sniping', but after 'A' Company of the North Shores left the beach for the town, German resistance began to stiffen.

Lt McCann, who commanded No. 6 Platoon of 'A' Company of the North Shores, recalls the situation on 'Nan Red': 'Our run-in was not bad and apart from small-arms fire and shelling we landed as per schedule and intact, but some of my fellow officers were not so fortunate. Lt Gerry Moran of 5 Platoon had been seriously wounded on the beach and I was left in charge of two platoons instead of one. I could have used six, for after cutting our way with Bangalore torpedos and wire cutters into the village, our communications broke down. During this period we found that the guns and emplacement that should have been put out of business by the Air Force were intact and very much in use.

'The Germans had a beautiful underground system of communicating with their pill-boxes. Perhaps it was as well we didn't know everything, for working on the assumption that we had a pushover, we went into the village in nothing flat. Now came the test. Things weren't going as planned and unless we captured those heavy guns the Germans were potting landing craft with, things were going to get worse – and worse they got. We had nothing heavier than Brens with which to attack heavily fortified enemy posts.'

Lt G. V. Moran of 5 Platoon has also left an account of the landing: 'Frank Ryan was the first man ashore from our craft, followed by his section of six men, then myself with Platoon Headquarters, and the other two sections. We were not too interested in looking around to see whether anyone else had landed but reached the doubtful shelter of the sea wall. It would be hard to estimate the width of the beach, but since the tide was well out I would hazard a guess of 300 feet at the time of our landing. Every square inch was under small-arms fire. The sea wall offered some protection from straight ahead but not from enfilade fire from the houses up and down the beach, and since there were no troops landing on our immediate left to keep the enemy occupied, they threw everything at us.

'Too many of us had bunched behind the sea wall and the second wave was now coming ashore. In order to get the men moving to their objective, I stood in the open and shouted at the top of my voice and, making vigorous motions with my arms, urged the sections around the wall and forward, standing with my back towards the upper beach and "A" Company's position. Apparently a sniper in the upper part of a house in "A" Company's area was watching for just such an indication of authority and laid a sight in the middle of my back. At the instant he squeezed the trigger fate invited me to turn, facing the water, so that I met the bullet with my left arm instead of my back. It passed through my arm, entered my chest under my armpit and ploughed on, coming out through the middle of my back. I didn't know that at the time because a mortar shell landed by at the same instant and I spun around and fell flat on my face. Rising again, I discovered my left arm was useless. Someone pulled me down and I didn't stand again for a month.'

The houses of St Aubin had been turned into fortresses and the streets were blocked with thick meshes of barbed wire. The North Shore Regiment and the Fort Gary Horse were still fighting for a foothold when 48 (Royal Marine) Commando came ashore.

48 Commando were to land at St Aubin from LSIs at 0930 hrs, two hours after the Canadians' first assault, and presumably over quiet beaches. After landing they would assemble, sort themselves out and proceed with their appointed task, taking the strongpoint at Langrune to the east. However, when the Commando's craft arrived off the 'Nan Red' beaches at St Aubin, they noticed that a considerable amount of firing seemed to be going on. Tanks were milling about on the beach and there seemed to be a lot of wreckage onshore. Orders were orders,

though, and at the appointed time, 48 Commando went in to land.

The Commando Adjutant, Captain Dan Flunder, MC, gives his account of this time. 'As Adjutant, I was OC troops and spent the night with them in a cramped little mess-deck; almost everyone was sick. I had the men up on the superstructure early, because I thought the fresh air would restore them, and because men are always happier when they can see what is going on. Soon we were running into the beach, and I walked up and down the bows keeping an eye on the Navy people responsible for lowering the ramps. The sea was covered with craft as far as the eye could see. The shore was under bombardment, craft were sinking, and from where I stood, it certainly didn't look as if the Canadians had secured the beach – things didn't look good at all.

'I didn't realize we were under fire until I saw two men collapse and fall over the starboard side. By then it was too late to beat a retreat, and I later found three bullet holes in my map case ... they must have passed between my arm and body during that period. The tide was high and we had craft hitting the beach obstacles. The CO had our 2-inch mortars firing smoke from the bows, so at least we were not getting aimed fire. When we grounded, we got the starboard ramp down, which wasn't easy with the waves thrashing the stern about. I was halfway down when a big wave lifted the bow and somersaulted the ramp, with me on it, into the sea. I saw the great bows coming over me, and the next thing I remember is walking up the beach, soaking wet, with some of my equipment torn off, including my pistol. I was still clutching my stout ash walking stick. When I got to the top of the beach I was violently sick.

'The beach was covered with casualties, some Canadian, some British. The surf was incredible, with beached and half-sunken craft wallowing about in it. Offshore, other craft came steadily on. Some tanks struggled ashore and some bogged in the shingle. Those that were advancing had their turret lids shut and were heading for a large group of wounded. I was sickened to see one run over two of our wounded, and it was heading for our good padre, John Armstrong, who had been badly wounded in the thigh. I had spoken to him on the way up to the beach;

typically, he had been vehement that I should not stop by him, exposed to enemy fire. I ran back down the beach and hammered on the turret, to try and get someone to put his head out. When this failed I stuck a Hawkins anti-tank grenade in the sprocket and blew the track off – that stopped it.'

Lt-Colonel Moulton, the Commanding Officer of 48 Commando, reached the assembly area, which was found to be under mortar fire, to discover that 48 Commando had already lost all its machine guns, all but one mortar, and 50 per cent of the troops. They had not yet fired a shot against the enemy. 'I began to realize', said Colonel Moulton later, 'that something very like disaster had overtaken 48 Commando. We were not aware that the Germans had built strongpoints right in the water here, and the naval and air support was inadequate and inaccurate. Look at that coast today – it is still lined with pre-war houses, virtually intact in 1944. You have to realize that if a shambles develops on the beach, there is no way of stopping the assault – craft keep coming in, men still push ashore. You have to sort yourself out and get on with the job.'

Like so many other units on D-Day, 48 (Royal Marine) Commando made the best of it and set out to accomplish their allotted task with what they had. After much fierce fighting and further casualties they took the strongpoint at Langrune and linked up with troops coming from 'Sword'.

By noon on D-Day, the 3rd Canadian Division was well ashore and they continued their advance until nightfall. 'C' Company of the North Shore's, with a troop of the Fort Gary Horse, fought their way out of St Aubin and took Tailleville, which contained a battalion headquarters and a full company of the German 716th Grenadier Regiment, finding that the naval bombardment which had missed St Aubin had totally wrecked Tailleville.

Brigadier Blackadder, commanding the Canadian 8th Brigade, had to hold back his troops because an 88mm gun and German infantry were still holding up the Regiment de la Chaudière in Bernières and the 9th Canadian Infantry Brigade, the last of the assault brigades, which had been supposed to land at St Aubin and advance swiftly on the airfield at Carpiquet, was held up by the turmoil ashore and afloat.

The continued fighting and congestion on the beach at St Aubin during the morning had forced the Navy to divert the 9th Brigade and the follow-up forces for 8th Infantry Brigade to the beach at Bernières. This proved of limited benefit as Bernières was still occupied by snipers and a massive traffic jam developed between the beach and the town centre.

At 1215 hrs, 8th Brigade radio'd to 'J' Force Headquarters on HMS *Hilary* and told General Keller that they were held up on their initial line, codenamed 'Yew', and needed naval gunfire support plus more infantry as soon as possible. It proved quite impossible to move anything or anyone through St Aubin or Bernières, which were now totally congested with troops and vehicles. The Official History recalls that in the centre of Bernières 'the entire 9th Canadian Infantry Brigade, complete with bicycles, were waiting, crowded in the streets.'

General Keller went ashore at 1245 hrs to sort out the situation, and by early afternoon the North Nova Scotias of the 9th Canadian Infantry Brigade were on the march for the aerodrome at Carpiquet, and the Canadian D-Day beaches were secure. The QORC were at Anguerny, the 'Chauds' at Colomby-sur-Thaon, and the North Shores were around Tailleville.

Two years previously, at Dieppe, the Canadians had been the first to test the strength of the Atlantic Wall and taken heavy casualties in doing so. The sacrifices of Dieppe, tragic though they were, had provided the blueprint for the landings in Normandy. Although the Wall was stronger and the defenders tenacious, this time the Canadians won through. As D-Day ended, German counter-attacks were developing and the German Panzer divisions, 21st Panzer, Panzer Lehr, and the 12th (SS) Panzer were moving forward to stem the Allied advance.

Over the next few weeks the Canadian infantry and the younger Panzer Grenadiers of the 12th SS were to take a bloody toll of each other's strength, but for the moment all was going well. Canadian casualties exceeded 1,000 men on the beaches of 'Juno', but their follow-up brigades were now ashore and pushing inland. When night fell on D-Day, the Canadian bridgehead was secure.

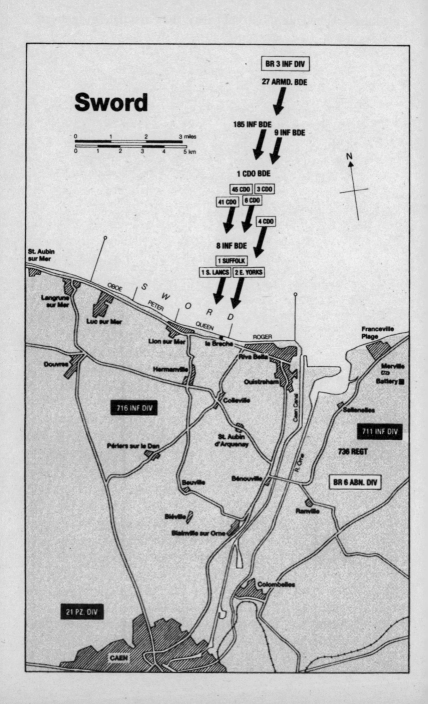

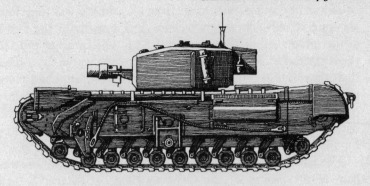

—————— CHAPTER ELEVEN ——————

'Sword'

'Fire? Of course there was fire. The
Germans didn't want us there, you know.
We lost a lot of men crossing the beach at
La Brèche.'
Lt-Colonel Peter Young, DSO, MC
No. 3 Commando

At 0725 hrs, while 6th Airborne continued to consolidate their
gains on the left flank around Ranville, the British 3rd Infantry
Division started to come ashore on 'Sword' beach, west of
Ouistreham. The 3rd Infantry Division was no stranger to
France. It had fought there in 1940 and taken part in the painful
retreat to Dunkirk. Now, four years later, the 3rd Infantry
Division was back on the coast of France.

Although the British and Canadian divisions were supposed
to land at half-tide, they found that the Channel gale, combined
with the prevailing westerly wind, had caused the sea to pile up
over the beach obstacles and run high on the beach itself. This
caused many difficulties, but the British landing on 'Sword' got
off to a good start. The bombardment by Admiral Vian's

squadron of warships was made from close in and was therefore accurate. The beaches were well marked, notably by the crews of the midget submarines X20 and X23, who came gasping to the surface after a submersion that had lasted a whole day longer than they had expected. The DD tanks were launched from close inshore and most of the landing craft hit the right beach at the right time. For all that, 'Sword' beach saw hard fighting, and stiff resistance from the men of the German 716th Infantry Division.

The landing areas of 'Sword' beach ran west from Ouistre-ham at the mouth of the Orne to Lion-sur-Mer. The 3rd Infantry Division, commanded by Major-General Rennie DSO, MBE, had the tasks of capturing Caen, nine miles inland, and forging a link with 6th Airborne astride the Orne, thereby bolstering the left flank of the bridgehead. For the assault the division would be supported by 2 battleships, HMS *Warspite* and HMS *Ramilles*, the monitor HMS *Roberts*, 5 cruisers, including the Polish *Dragon* and 13 destroyers in-cluding the Norwegian *Svenner*. Apart from the USS *Corry* off 'Utah', the *Svenner* was the only Allied warship to be sunk on D-Day.

Their German opponents, from the 716th Infantry Division, were dug-in on the beaches and in a series of defended strong-points on the way to Caen. One of these strongpoints, code-named 'Hillman', was to give the Suffolk Regiment a particularly stiff fight, but pegging out territory well inland was essential, for behind Caen, edging forward into the fight, was the most formidable German unit close to the Normandy coast, the 21st Panzer Division, which had been training and re-equipping on the plain south of Caen. Other German Panzer units were also alert and, although without orders from higher command, were beginning to make their way forward and engage the invading forces. Enemy shell-fire in particular in-creased throughout the day and resistance stiffened as the bridgeheads expanded inland.

The German defences were particularly intricate along 'Sword', and lay among a built-up area. All the houses in the resorts of Riva Bella, La Brèche and Lion-sur-Mer had been turned into fortresses, while the low country behind had been mined. The casino at Riva Bella proved a particularly hard nut to crack, but the open beaches further west were also mined, heavily wired, studded with concrete emplacements and pillboxes, and protected with the usual array of underwater obstacles offshore. No. 3 Commando lost 10 per cent of its men crossing the beach at La Brèche.

The 3rd (British) Division comprised three infantry brigades, the 8th, the 185th and 9th, supported by 1st Special Service (Commando) Brigade (Nos 3, 4 and 6 Commandos and 45 (Royal Marine) Commando) under Brigadier Lord Lovat. No. 4 Commando had two troops of French Commandos and No. 41 (Royal Marine) Commandos attached for the landing phase.

The initial assault on the beach was made by the 8th Infantry Brigade Group, landing on the 'White' and 'Red' sectors of 'Queen' beach, with the task of securing the landing area. 4 Commando, with two French troops of No. 10 (Inter-Allied) Commando attached, were to take Ouistreham, while 41 (Royal Marine) Commando were to advance to the west towards Lion-sur-Mer and link up with the Canadians. Lord Lovat's Commando Brigade, less 4 Commando, would make the six-mile dash to link up with the Airborne at Bénouville and while all this was going on, the 185th Infantry Brigade would advance through the secured beach area and take Caen. The taking of the city of Caen on the first day was an ambitious task for a single division.

The 8th Infantry Brigade consisted of three battalions: the 1st Battalion, South Lancashire Regiment, the 2nd Battalion, East Yorkshire Regiment, and the 1st Battalion, the Suffolk Regiment, with the Suffolks being charged with the reduction of two enemy strongpoints codenamed 'Hillman' and 'Morris'.

8 Brigade was to be preceded by the DD tanks of the 13th/18th Royal Hussars and AVREs of 5 Assault Regiment, Royal Engineers. The latter was to clear the beaches of obstacles and construct vehicle exits. 13th/18th Hussars, normally part of 27 Armoured Brigade, was attached to the division and would land two squadrons on 'Sword' seven minutes before the assaulting battalions. Their tasks were to dominate the beaches, thus covering both the sappers clearing beach obstacles and the

arrival of the assault infantry. Once the beaches were secure they were to provide armoured support for the infantry as they pushed south for Caen.

Emlyn 'Taffy' Jones was an Army Commando serving in the Signal Troop of 45 (Royal Marine) Commando. 'We set sail for France about 9 o'clock on the evening of 5 June. Sailing down the Solent through an array of ships and craft that were at anchor was very impressive. As we passed by the crews stood on deck and gave us a remarkable send-off with their cheering and waving. It made one feel so proud, and above all this glorious noise we could hear the pipes, the bagpipes of Bill Millin, our Commando piper. It certainly made the heart beat that much faster.'

As dawn broke next morning, Naval Force 'S', conveying and supporting 3 Division, lay off the 'Queen' beaches. The medium bombers of the 2nd Tactical Air Force droned overhead on their way to targets just south of the beaches. Rear Admiral Sir Philip Vian, Commander of Force 'S', was flying his flag on HMS *Scylla*. The American 8th Air Force were also giving support along the British beaches.

Marshall J. Rahn of Fort Lauderdale, Florida, was then with the 306th Bomb Group. 'I was a pilot on a B-17 Flying Fortress. Our crew chiefs, or mechanics, were mostly older men, peacetime auto mechanics, who kept aloof from the twenty-year-old flight crews who were flying and (they thought) damaging their aircraft. They took great pride that their airplane was mechanically perfect and always sweated out the return of their baby. Our mission that day was a milk run, just across the French coast into Caen, and we went out to our aircraft about dawn.

'On one of the neighbouring B-17s the pilot shut the engines down and told his crew that one of his magnetos was running rough and he would not fly it. I saw the crew chief leaning over the stabilizer and crying like a baby because his aircraft was not making the most important raid of the war. Ninety-nine per cent of us would have flown with one magneto out. Each engine had two anyway and a mission to Caen counted as much as one to the Fatherland.'

Robin Fowler was a petty officer aboard LCI(L) No. 387.

They had embarked 250 infantrymen from the King's Own Scottish Borderers (KOSB). 'I remember coming up on deck and marvelling at the number of ships which had joined us. Security on board was still maintained and even after we had sailed, we were told nothing other than that this was the Great Day and we were heading for France, but as the soldiers had maps of their landing sectors and we knew our compass course, we had a shrewd idea of our destination.'

Corporal Albert Smith, an anti-tank gunner in the 1st Norfolks, recalls lying off Sword beach. 'By 0530 hrs we were just off the Normandy coast, which was receiving a pounding from the RAF bombers. Then suddenly the guns of our own ships opened up to cover our approach to the beaches, and as the bombers wheeled away towards England, the German artillery opened up. The air cover supplied by the RAF fighters was superb. They ruled the sky, and not a German plane was to be seen . . . a far and different cry from the dark days of Dunkirk.'

Trooper Bob Knight was a Sherman tank driver in 'A' Squadron, the 1st East Riding Yeomanry, part of the 27th Armoured Brigade. 'I knew we were off during the early evening of 5 June, when I saw green-beret'd Commandos heading out in their LCIs. Maps were issued and at last we knew our destination. I remember a small cabin cruiser, maybe 30ft long, keeping station on our port side all the way across. I don't know if they felt as we did, but our ship was rolling with the high waves, and we all felt very seasick. As dawn arrived we were called over the Tannoy to collect our breakfast from the ship's galley – fried bacon floating in fat – and that really got things moving! However, at that precise moment we came under shell-fire from the shore, and that was the quickest cure for seasickness.'

Victor Kontzle was a signaller with 3rd Division Headquarters. 'Our prime function was to mark the route from our particular stretch of beach and establish where 3rd Divisional Signals HQ would be on D-Day. We also carried the spare wireless set for 3rd Division Signals in our "perambulator" contraption, for use in case of emergency. This meant that we would be landing at H-Hour plus 30 minutes, hard on the heels of the 8th Brigade.

'I awoke at just after midnight. The vessel was pitching and rolling, and most of the military personnel were suffering from seasickness. The moon had broken through the clouds and for a moment I had a strange feeling of quietness and tense expectancy. My comrades, Jimmy and Henry, were still asleep by our "perambulator", and making my way forward, I lay down on the deck and the beat of the LCT's engines sent me off to sleep again. It was already D-Day.'

While the ships were nearing the beaches just before dawn, the Allied air forces streamed over on the way to their targets. Victor Jones was a Royal Army Service Corps (RASC) corporal attached to 9 Field Ambulance. 'I remember a most gallant action by the RAF pilot of a stricken bomber. The plane dropped down between our ship and the one next to us, obviously avoiding us, to crash into the sea behind. I can still see the face of the rear gunner looking at us, but no one survived the crash ... that is still my most poignant memory of D-Day.'

After the aerial bombardment and heavy shelling from Admiral Vian's ships, the soldiers embarked in their landing craft and prepared to go ashore. Following Montgomery's plan, DD tanks of the 13th/18th Royal Hussars and assault engineers in bridging tanks and flails were to precede the assault brigade and clear a path for the infantry.

Sergeant Buck was a DD tank commander with 2 Troop, 'B' Squadron, 13th/18th Hussars. 'The code word to launch was "Floater". We launched successfully at 0615 hrs, despite a rough sea and heavy swell. The first one to one-and-a-half miles was uneventful, apart from the noise of shells from our warship and planes passing overhead, but as we approached closer to "Sword" beach, the shells from the German guns and machine-guns started to come closer. The rockets from our own rocket ships also started dropping among us and these caused many casualties among our DD tanks. Then the beach obstacles used by the Germans appeared. These consisted of Teller mines stuck on top of poles, together with triangular steel obstacles; fortunately the tide was still on the flood so these could be seen more clearly and enabled us to take avoiding action. We landed at 0720 hrs.'

Not far away from Sergeant Buck was nineteen-year-old Lance-Corporal Patrick Hennessey, who also went ashore in a DD tank. 'The ramp at the bows of the LCT was lowered and one by one we drove down it. A strong wind was blowing and we shipped quite a lot of water over the top of the screen, so we had to work hard on the bilge pumps. Other DD tanks were launching all around us, and glancing to my right I saw one enter the water and start to make way. Behind it I could see the bulk of its LCT, and to my horror I realized that it was moving forward. Very soon it hit the DD tank, forcing it under the water. The tank commander escaped and was rescued, but the rest of his crew were lost.

'We battled on against the waves for about an hour until we felt the tracks meet the sand of the beach. We rose up out of the surf, dropped the screen, and there in front of us was the line of houses which was our target. By now we were under fire from several positions, so we brought our gun into action and fired our first shots. The infantry were now beginning to arrive, and we were able to provide the support and covering fire which they so badly needed.

'Once ashore we had to decide whether to move up the beach which we knew to be mined, or wait until the mines had been cleared. Suddenly, the problem was solved for us – we had landed on a fast in-coming tide, so the longer we stood still, the deeper the water became. One large wave hit the back of our tank, swamped the engine compartment, and the engine spluttered to a halt. With power gone, we could not move, so we stayed there, firing the guns until the tank was flooded and we had to give up. We took to the rubber dinghy and began to paddle for the shore through the water, which was by now quite deep.

'We had not gone far when we were hit by a burst of machine-gun bullets which capsized our little craft and wounded the co-driver in the ankle. Somehow, we swam and splashed our way to the beach and managed to drag our wounded comrade with us. The beach was a very noisy place with shells, mortars and bullets flying in all directions. Landing craft were coming in, depositing their troops, and backing out to sea again.

'Eventually we made our way inland, to the village of Hermanville, where we met up with other unhorsed tank crews and came together with what was left of our squadron and the five remaining serviceable tanks.'

In all, 31 DD tanks and AVREs reached 'Sword' beach with the assault waves. With the surviving DD tanks ashore and tackling the beach defences, the specialized armour of the Royal Engineers started to land and clear away the obstacles. Their Assault Sapper squadrons were divided into two groups, one to push lanes through the beach defences, the other to clear the beach of underwater obstacles. One of those who came ashore was Driver Beeton of 79 Assault Engineer Squadron, landing on 'Queen Red'.

'I was the driver of a Churchill AVRE tank in the first wave of the assault. Our tanks were fitted with special mortars called "Petards", which were used for destroying pill-boxes. There was a considerable amount of shell-fire offshore and two of our ships were hit and went up in smoke. We watched as our own rocket-firing landing craft discharged their rockets at the enemy, but this was cut short by the order to crew the tanks. I was soon in position with my engine running, ready to leave for the beach. The first two tanks down the ramp were flails, but these were hit by gun-fire and burst into flames. It was not very pleasant seeing your own friends trying to leave their burning tanks. As I came down the ramp I could see German mines everywhere, fixed to cross-pieces on the obstacles about two feet above ground level. Further up the beach I could see the German pill-boxes.

'I was instructed by my officer to pick my way up the beach as best I could. My luck held and I was almost off the beach when we hit a mine which blew the bogey off. Fortunately the tank track held, but the officer and sergeant in our crew were killed. Over half the squadron was wiped out before we cleared the beaches.'

Closely behind the tanks and assault engineers came the infantry. The 1st South Lancs landed with two companies leading, the right-hand company to destroy the German defences on the beach and then move west, or right, for about a mile, clearing the enemy as it went. The left-hand company, having cleared the beach, was to move on and attack a strong-point at La Brèche, codenamed 'Cod', in conjunction with 2nd Battalion East Yorks. Once captured, the battalion was to re-group and hold Hermanville on the right flank of the brigade beachhead.

The 2nd East Yorks, landing on the left of the 1st South Lancs, had similar tasks. The right assault company was to help capture 'Cod', while the left-hand company was to move east and move towards the outskirts of Ouistreham–Riva Bella. When the reserve companies came up it was then to assault two German strongpoints to the south-west of Ouistreham, code-named 'Sole' and 'Daimler'. The latter was a heavily defended coastal battery, mounting four 155mm guns. The Commanding Officer of the East Yorks was further instructed to despatch one of his companies with a squadron of 13/18 Hussars tanks towards the Ranville area, now held by 5 Para Brigade. The battalion was also to secure St Aubin d'Arquenay and be pre-pared to assist 4 Commando in Ouistreham or 6 Commando as it moved forward to the Orne bridges.

The last battalion, the 1st Suffolks, were to land at H+60 minutes and move directly to La Brèche. From here they were to move south and secure the village of Colleville and a four-gun battery on its western outskirts known as 'Morris'. That secured, they were to move a further half-mile forward and capture a defended locality, known as 'Hillman'. From aerial photographs this appeared to be a major task. The position contained at least two 105mm and two 75mm guns, as well as numerous machine-gun positions. All these were linked by trenches and pill-boxes and surrounded by thick wire and minefield defences.

Lieutenant Edward Jones with the 1st South Lancs was suffering from seasickness as he boarded his landing craft. 'It was bad enough aboard a large vessel, but on board the smaller ships the conditions were intolerable. As far as we were con-cerned when the flat-bottomed, shallow-draft LCAs were launched, we bucked up and down unmercifully. Everyone was suffering from violent seasickness after a very short while. Yet this stormy weather was probably one of the causes of our salvation. I am sure the Germans looked out to sea and said, "They'll never land in that lot!"

'As we progressed towards the shore and the light increased, I was distinctly surprised to find ourselves moving towards a holiday resort, Luc-sur-Mer, which looked astonishingly like Blackpool. Instead of the promenade there was a low sea wall, but the gently shelving golden sands were there and the line of boarding houses, though the sands were covered with tripods with mines on top. The boarding houses were somewhat of a surprise, as we had gained the distinct impression that our aerial bombings and softening-up preliminary barrage would have flattened everything.'

'As I jumped out into about 3ft of water, the LCA lifted on a wave and lurched forward on top of me, crushing me into the sand. The Royal Marine coxswain swung the craft to one side and I emerged. We hastened ashore and got down on the beach above the tide to collect our bearings. DD tanks were supposed to land along with us, but there was no sign of these on our section of the beach. Directly ahead of us was a road leading from the beach, the exit choked with coils of barbed wire. While I was debating how to cope with this problem, an AVRE (Churchill) tank fitted with special equipment came waddling up the beach, ploughed through most of this wire and then lost a track on a mine.

'Shells were falling on the roofs of the boarding houses, and I directed my platoon towards a large house to the left of the beach exit. It was then I learned in action one of my first lessons of practical man-management. One of my section leaders, whom I had regarded highly, was a bright lad, a policeman in civilian life. I explained to him what I wanted his section to do, but got no reaction. I had just realized that he was too upset by the situation to comprehend what I was telling him, when another of my section commanders came over, an alert man, a regular soldier, whom I had previously believed to be rather slow, as at "O" Groups he always asked for a detailed repeat of orders. I realize now that he was only making quite certain what my instructions were. He said, "What are you asking him to do, Sir?" I explained that I wanted him to take his section into this house, while the other sections gave covering fire. He turned to his section, said, "Follow me!" and took them into the house. There was no opposition and the rest of the platoon followed – to find the Germans still in the cellars, waiting for the barrage to lift.

'This presented us with another problem. We had received no instructions on how to deal with prisoners at this early stage, so we disarmed them and locked them in the cellar, and moved on down the road.'

The defenders on 'Sword' appeared stunned by the Allied onslaught, but soon started to fight back. Return fire, coupled with a fast-moving tide and the myriad of beach obstacles made life very difficult, especially for the naval and Royal Marine crews of the landing craft. Dennis Osborne was the coxswain of LCT 1068, landing on 'Queen' beach. 'We beached between two mined tank obstacles, our troops disembarked and we made ready to move off. No such luck! We were stuck hard and fast, so there was nothing we could do but wait for the turn of the tide. We were about 200 yards from the road at the top of the beach with beached coasters and freighters all over the place. Amidst the confusion two soldiers were sheltering from enemy fire up against a coaster loaded with ammunition. Three DUKWs approached the beach in spearhead formation; the leading one hit a mine, injuring the driver who was covered with blood. I think he must have been fatally wounded. His passenger must have been blown out on to the beach for he was reeling about. Two stretcher bearers dashed across the beach with complete disregard for their own safety to rescue one of their comrades. They took him to the field hospital at the top of the beach which was shelled soon after. We saw our first POWs, who were set to clearing debris from the beach.

'We only saw one enemy aircraft, a fighter bomber who dropped his bomb further along the beach and hastily departed. A sniper was causing problems on the beach until a destroyer closed as near to the beach as possible and demolished the tower he was situated in.'

Corporal Rayson, of 9 Platoon, 'A' Company, the 1st Suffolks, recalls the landing. 'Have you ever got up in the morning and nothing goes right? Well, this was one of those days. As we approached the shore we were standing up. It was impossible to sit down because of the gear we were carrying. Morale was good but as we got nearer a few machine-gun bullets and some shells went over and we got down as far as we could. Then we ran on to one of those metal obstructions placed in the water by the Germans to tear the bottom out of the boat. The boat stopped, tilted slightly and the Royal Marine coxswain managed to get the ramp down. It didn't look very far to the beach so out went a naval officer, another officer and a corporal.

'Owing to the very heavy swell they disappeared but popped up after a while and swam ashore. No one else moved as a lot of fellows could not swim. I said to the Marine, "Pull back and go in again," and this he did. Still nobody moved, so I thought that if I went, they would follow. So off I went, but no one followed. I thought I was never going to touch the bottom, but I did and shot up again. On reaching the surface the LCA ramp was against my back and before I could move, the boat moved forward and I went under. I came up with the boat three yards in front of me. Eventually I got rid of all my stuff, including the Sten gun. I made a little progress but had to get rid of my steel helmet as it kept going over my face.

'At last I reached the shore, sat down and recovered. The beach seemed to be utter chaos. I took a steel helmet off a dead South Lancs soldier and picked up a Sten-gun magazine and a couple of grenades and put them in my pockets. On reaching the promenade I saw Harry Filby, one of "A" Company stretcher bearers, who said, "Can I do you up?" I replied, "What for?" and he pointed to my battle dress which was covered with blood. I had cut and broken my nose, and it was still bleeding heavily and, being wet through, I looked a sorry sight.'

Corporal Edwin Byatt of 'B' Company, 1st Suffolks, had been in the retreat from France in 1940; now, four years later, he was back. 'I could see a plane in the distance laying a smoke screen along the beach, and further back, HMS *Warspite* was busy firing. A lot of other ships were in action and shells were going over sounding like express trains. The "Success" signal went up from the South Lancashires on the beach and we were going in.

'LCAs were getting sunk and being hit from the shelling. Our LCA managed to get through and the doors went down and we were in the water up to our chests, but we were used to this anyway. I remember seeing bodies floating about, mostly South Lancs lads. Shells and small-arms fire were hindering us and the smell of cordite and smoke was everywhere.

'A Beachmaster was there with a towel round his head covered in blood; his job was to try and keep things moving, so we didn't hang about. I remember having to jump a very wide anti-tank ditch full of water. I just made the bank and was glad I was only carrying a Sten gun. I found I had lost one man in my section and later I found he had been wounded leaving the LCA and taken back to England. We got going fast inland, leaving snipers firing and pockets to be cleared up by follow-up troops. There was no stopping now.'

Eric Rowland, a private with 'A' Company, 1st Suffolks remembers the chaos on the beaches. 'I remember bodies in the surf, and as I ran up the beach I passed a headless body. It was then I realized it was not an exercise and I was in the thick of it.

'We paused on the promenade to re-group, and as I looked out to sea, the sight that met my eyes was something I will never forget. There was an enormous mass of craft of all sizes, some on fire. More and more landing craft were beaching and discharging men.'

The beach obstacles were not the only problems the landing craft had to deal with. Bill 'Mac' Helas was aboard LCT 2433, transporting Royal Marines Centaur tanks. 'We did our landing as instructed, but while on the beach one of our own shells dropped short and almost blew our ramp off. Fortunately the crew had just moved aft, so we did not have any casualties, but a Landing Craft (Rocket) was alongside and had fired one salvo when it was hit. The LCR exploded and we did not see any survivors.'

Having managed to swim ashore, Lt Edward Jones and his platoon of the South Lancs joined the remnants of his company. Their task was to clear the German defences to the west, in the village of Lion-sur-Mer. 'One of those occurrences which were to become so frequent now took place. Up to now the German shelling had been spasmodic and haphazard, but it began to increase and one of the places selected was obviously our crossroad. A shell exploded on the road close by and a fragment of shrapnel ploughed through the torch clipped on my webbing belt. I doubled up with pain and Bob Pearce rushed across and tore open my battledress blouse to reveal the piece of shrapnel which had only just broken the surface of the skin, having been slowed down by the torch. It was hot enough to burn my stomach, hence the pain.

'We now moved rapidly down the road towards Lion. There were no German soldiers about, only a number of French civilians, most of whom seemed too stunned to comprehend what was happening, though despite the bombardment some were still tilling the fields on the south of the road.

'Lion had been cleared of civilians and was occupied by German troops. Buildings had been converted into blockhouses and some streets had been completely blocked with coil upon coil of barbed wire, practically to roof level and 20–30ft in depth. As I reconnoitred cautiously down one of the few streets left open, two of my men, one on each side of me, were expertly picked off by hidden riflemen.

'We therefore moved round to the south of the village and entered farm buildings, which gave us a view across open country to the east. Here we made contact with 41 (RM) Commando and were able both to beat off a German counter-attack from the south and to give covering fire to the Royal Marines' advance to the west. We began to move further inland to the group of buildings from which the Germans had launched their attack. We lost one or two more men in this attempt, but as we reached the safety of a sunken lane with a stone wall on one side and a bank and hedge on the other, disaster struck. Without warning, a cluster of mortar-bombs landed in the middle of us, killing and wounding many of our men. Among the wounded was Lieutenant Pearce, who already held the MC and gained a bar for his D-Day actions. We took the wounded to the shelter of the stone wall and dressed their wounds. I remember we were joined here by a young French girl aged around ten or eleven, who kept repeating, "*J'ai peur*," – "I'm frightened", as well she might be!'

Lieutenant Jones lost many of his platoon in this attack, including his platoon sergeant, Sergeant West. While they were re-organizing, he realized that he was the only remaining 'A'

Company officer on his feet. Re-grouping for another attack, a runner arrived with orders for the company to rejoin the rest of the battalion in Hermanville. 'We made our way back along the lateral road, which the Germans were now shelling constantly, and one of my platoon, a tall, thin young lad with sandy hair, was badly wounded by a piece of shrapnel in the neck. An Artillery captain emerged from a fox-hole alongside the road, expertly applied digital pressure to the wound and said, "You go on! I'll look after him." We heard the officer calling for stretcher bearers as we left. Some weeks later one of my platoon showed me a photograph in a local newspaper depicting this lad, accompanied by a brief account of how he had been wounded on D-Day, and saying he was well on the way to recovery.'

While the 8th Infantry Brigade were advancing inland, 41 (Royal Marine) Commando were battling their way to the west. Marine Raymond Mitchell was a despatch rider with the Headquarters Troop and went ashore on 'Sword' with a 'para-scooter', a small collapsible motorbike. 'There was time for no more than a glance at the beach, a shambles of burning tanks, shattered landing craft and bodies floating in the shallows, as we queued to use the one usable ramp. It was bucking about like a cake-walk, so I had no option but to sit down, cradling the bike in my arms to stop it ending up in the drink. I needn't have worried about it because in trying to keep up with my troop, I found the machine too heavy to carry for very long, and its small wheels simply gouged a furrow in the soft sand when I tried to push it. Some tank men were crouching against their knocked-out Churchill tank. "Here mate!" I gasped to one of them. "Want a motorbike?" Then I abandoned it and ran on.'

Having got rid of the bike, Marine Mitchell soon caught up with his troop. 'We doubled into Lion-sur-Mer, making very little noise in our rubber-soled "brothel creepers". Curious faces peered at us from the windows as we passed, until we stopped on the pavement in front of a small newsagent's shop, where I spent what was probably the very first "Invasion Money" used in France. I was persuaded to go inside to buy some matches for one of our number who had his soaked in the landing. We were left there while the Fighting (Rifle) Troops of the Commando went about their business, and my smattering of

French enabled me to understand some French ladies who came to tell us that they had wounded men in their homes; I sent two of our Sick Berth attendants back with them. Later, when mortar fire became intense, we moved into the church grounds to dig in. I was given a pushbike and did a few local trips, then was sent back on it to the beach to find some of our Jeeps. There was also a "Famous James" 125cc motorbike on the LCT, so I rode it back to HQ, leading the Jeeps, which were put to immediate use, evacuating wounded.'

To the east, Lord Lovat's 1st Special Services (Commando) Brigade was marching to link up with the paratroopers of 6th Airborne. 45 (RM) Commando was part of the brigade with Lieutenant John Day serving in 'E' Troop of 45 Commando. 'I had a specific task for the initial part of our operation; to get ten inflatable dinghies to the River Orne. These would be required to get the brigade over the water if the bridges over the Orne or the canal at Bénouville had been destroyed. I had twenty men from "E" Troop allocated to me for this task and because of our heavy, awkward loads, dinghies, paddles, air pumps and ropes, in addition to our normal equipment, we would be the last to disembark from the LCIs.

'We were due to touch down at 0910 hours and we seemed to be just about on time. I did not even get my feet wet as I went ashore, and the rest of my group landed slowly but safely. Sadly, LCI(S) 517 sank as she withdrew from the beach, but the crew was saved.

'After a slight pause at the check-point while 6 Commando, which was leading the brigade's advance, dealt with some opposition, we moved off, my dinghy group moving slowly some distance behind the main body of the Commando. On arrival at Bénouville we dumped the dinghies by the Café Gondrée and were warned by an airborne soldier that the bridges were still under enemy fire. I sent my party off across the bridges in twos and threes and having seen them reach the far bank safely, I set off at a trot accompanied by Sergeant Hepper and my orderly. I was not conscious of being fired at, but Bob Hepper was hit in the neck as we were crossing the river bridge. Private Dunlop, RAMC, "E" Troop's medical orderly, came back to attend to him and he was then left with the

Airborne. Bob Hepper survived his wound, though I did not meet him again until December 1991, at 45 (RM) Commando's first-ever reunion.'

The Commandos were supported by some of the special Royal Engineer tanks. One of these was driven by Driver Beeton. Having lost a bogey wheel from his AVRE on a mine but luckily not his track, he joined the Commandos in their dash for the Caen Canal. 'I managed to drive the tank behind some sand dunes where we unsealed the hatches and were joined by some Commandos. Our Major arrived and took charge of my tank as his had been knocked out, and I was instructed to drive off along a road. Here we immediately came under small-arms fire which my co-driver returned. We came to a bridge spanning a canal where we saw a pill-box and a number of Germans on the other side, but our mortar had only a short range and we were unable to hit the pill-box with it, so the Major decided to try and cross.

'I was then told to drive the tank on to an open space well clear of the houses and to remain there as the Major had to leave. By this time the engine was running hot, so I got on to the rear of the tank to unseal the engine covers and had just started my task when I heard the sound of an aircraft engine. When the plane first appeared, I thought it was a Mustang, but soon changed my mind when I saw it release a bomb which was coming straight at the tank. There was nothing I could do except to lay down flat on the engine covers and hope for the best. All my strength seemed to ebb away and it was utter relief when the bomb cleared the tank and exploded just in front.'

Major James Cuthbertson, commanding 90 Company RASC, attached to the 27th Armoured Brigade, had a special task on D-Day. His thirty-three trucks were to land at H+6 and move directly to the Orne bridges, taking up vital supplies of food, fuel and ammunition to the airborne soldiers. Major Cuthbertson and a despatch rider were to land on 'Sword' beach at H+2, reconnoitre a route to Ranville on motorbikes and make the initial contact with the Airborne.

Major James Cuthbertson recalls his day: 'The beach was complete chaos. Eventually we moved inland through Herman-ville and made straight for the Orne, so off we went, out into open lanes, no hedges – an open, bare landscape. There was no one in sight. We just followed our maps and pressed on for five miles. It was very eerie – where were the enemy, or our own troops? We went along on our bikes and saw no one.

'At about 1130 hrs, having passed through two silent villages, we went down a steep little slope and around a sharp turn to the Orne bridges, at what is now Pegasus Bridge. We pulled up under some tall trees by a thick hedge and heard someone shout, "Get down, you're under enemy observation!" Looking more closely we saw half-a-dozen paratroopers in defensive positions about the bridge, but no liaison officers. We stayed "doggo" with the occasional recce to the bridge to see if the seaborne troops had arrived, and at about 1330 hrs, Lord Lovat and his Commandos arrived at the bridge, down the same road we had used. Apart from ourselves, these were the first seaborne troops to reach the bridge.'

By 1400 hrs, with no one arriving from the Airborne HQ, James Cuthbertson decided to ride back to the beaches to see if his vehicles had landed and, if so, to bring them back up with their much-needed stores.

'On the way down, I had the surprise of my life. Coming towards me were nine vehicles of my "B" Platoon. They were not scheduled to arrive until D+5 (11 June) and I just couldn't believe it. They had found room on an LCT and came on anyway.'

Having sorted out his men, Major Cuthbertson rode back to the bridges yet again, still not meeting anyone on the way. He got back there at 1700 hrs, where he took matters into his own hands and set out to find General Gale's Headquarters. His problem was to get across the bridges which the enemy had under heavy fire.

'The paratroopers laid down a protective smoke screen over the bridges, so I crossed in a fog and followed one of the lanes leading off on the other side. ... I eventually arrived at the Airborne HQ in a farm near Ranville, which was itself under sporadic mortar-fire.'

It transpired that both the Airborne officer guides he had been due to meet had been wounded, but General Gale ordered him to bring up his convoy after dark and off-load the stores in a nearby quarry.

'While I was with the Headquarters, at 1800 hrs we all listened to the King's speech, a most moving moment. Just as it finished, there was a mighty roar as hundreds of gliders and aircraft flew over, bringing the 6th Air Landing Brigade to reinforce the heavily pressed Airborne Division. There was an enormous cheer from everyone, immediately followed by a German mortar attack.'

Setting off yet again on his motorcycle, Major Cuthbertson raced back to his rendezvous at Colleville. That night he made his fifth trip along winding French lanes to the Caen Canal bringing up the much needed stores. For his efforts on D-Day, Major James Cuthbertson was awarded the Military Cross.

Not only fighting troops were involved on D-Day. The troops at the front had to be supplied with ammunition and fuel, and their wounded had to be evacuated, and these tasks depended on the men of the Royal Army Service Corps, like Major Cuthbertson's company. One of the men engaged in supply was Douglas Grey of the 27th Armoured Brigade. 'My job was to supply the tanks of the 27th Armoured Brigade with petrol, oil and lubricants. My personal transport was a motor-cycle which was attached to the side of a Sherman tank of the East Riding Yeomanry, commanded by Sergeant East. There was little room on the landing craft and the only place I could find to try and sleep was between the two diesel engines. As we came to land at H+6 (approximately 1 p.m.) on "Sword" beach at Lion-sur-Mer, I was able to have a brief look out at the beaches from the top of the tank before Sergeant East asked me to return to the inside. Shells were passing overhead from the battleships and I was particularly astounded to watch the mul-tiple rocket flak ships firing inland. I was more than glad we were not on the receiving end.

'My motorcycle was lowered from the tank and I said farewell to Sergeant East and his crew, who I never saw again. I then found, to my consternation, that it was impossible to steer the motorcycle as I had attached so much equipment to it. I set off in what I thought was the right direction for Brigade HQ, but was stopped by some of our infantry who told me not to proceed

as the enemy was just round the corner. I thereupon retraced
my steps and managed to negotiate all the traffic moving from
the beaches and located Brigade HQ in Hermanville.

'My task until my trucks landed was to locate the "porpoises"
which were loaded with ammunition and towed in by the tanks,
and have their loads picked up. I might add that I was not very
successful in finding them. Eventually my trucks arrived and we
harboured up south of Hermanville. Conditions near the
beaches and around the Sector Stores Dumps, whence all
replenishment had to be made, were very difficult. There were
only about two up and down routes and they were in use by all
new units landing and all beach and DUKW transport. Congestion was very severe throughout the day. Bombings by day and
night were frequent and even until D+2 isolated snipers
remained in some houses behind the beaches.

'At about 2000 hrs some of the POL (Petrol, Oil and Lubri-
cant) vehicles were sent forward with ammunition vehicles to
replenish tanks in their forward positions. Throughout the
night, which was one of considerable air activity, the work of
replenishing the tanks went on, all vehicles then returning to
the Sector Stores Dumps at "Queen" beach to refill. They
arrived back at location as dawn was breaking.'

As more and more men came ashore, the assaulting battalions
pushed inland, against increasing German resistance. Behind
the assault battalions Lord Lovat's Commandos came ashore.
The following accounts come from men of 45 (Royal Marine)
Commando.

Emlyn Jones was in the Signal Troop. 'Only seconds to go
now before we hit the beach, though naval ratings, both port
and starboard were firing guns at the enemy targets oblivious of
the fire that was coming back. This is it ... ramp down ... let's
move. The Bren gunner has frozen at the top of the ramp and
won't move. Then we found out that only one ramp could be
used. While waiting those few minutes for my turn, I found
myself quietly singing "Abide with me". Why? I don't know
but it seemed appropriate at the time. If ever we needed God by
our side, this was the time.

'At the foot of the ramp was a sailor lying prostrate with his face blown off. Poor devil, wish I had held my tongue about the Navy. Must push on. Mortars and shells raining down while struggling through the sand and dunes with the wounded and dead all around, but no time to stop. Medics following will attend to the wounded. Above all this bedlam we heard the skirl of the bagpipes. Bill Millin, Lord Lovat's piper, playing "Blue Bonnets". It was heart-stirring music, even to a Welshman.'

Despite all the briefings and planning, the anxiety of battle caused mistakes. John Day of 45 Commando recalls what happened later that day when his commanding officer took a wrong turn while moving up to the Merville Battery. 'The Commando set off at about 3 p.m., moving eastwards towards Sallenelles. I led "E" Troop immediately behind the CO's party. All was quiet and the countryside seemed peaceful, with no sign of Germans or civilians. Having passed through Sallenelles the two leading troops, quite correctly, turned right, up a narrow track leading to Merville. This move was not noticed by the CO's group which continued straight along the road, towards Franceville-Plage. When we were about 400 yards from Sallenelles I heard heavy small-arms fire ahead and saw the CO's group scatter off the road. The left-hand, seaward side of the road was completely open and as a few shots had come close to us, I moved "E" Troop back about 50 yards to a clump of trees by a track junction which provided some cover. As we took up position I saw about ten Germans, some 300 yards away to our left, running along a skyline towards a pill-box. An "E" Troop Bren gunner hurried them on their way.

'By now the firing ahead of us had ceased but I could see no sign of the CO's group, so I thought I should go forward to find out what was happening. Leaving the TSM in charge of the troop, I walked alone down the road. Suddenly, when I was about 150 yards from the troop position, I became the object of a great deal of unwanted attention, rifle-fire probably coming from the pill-box we had just spotted on the seaward side. The only nearby cover was a line of trees behind a wire fence on the other side of the road, so I dashed towards this haven and hurled myself at the fence.

'Unfortunately my rucksack caught in the fence but the

whip-cracks of bullets were too close to permit a second attempt. I dropped to the ground and crawled along a shallow
ditch until it seemed safe to get to my feet and run to rejoin "E"
Troop. I had heard so often of men being killed before they had
a chance to engage the enemy, and this had nearly happened to
me. My Tommy gun being useless at the range required, I got
behind a Bren gun and fired a couple of bursts at the pill-box. I
could not claim to have hit anyone, but it made me feel better.'

Colin Fletcher was the machine-gun officer in the MG
section of 'F' Troop, 45 Commando. 'On the run-in, only one
man in my troop was wounded: Corporal Gooch, hit by shrapnel in the jaw. I do not think I was aware that he had been hit
until after we were ashore, but I seem to remember being told
that it was while we were still aboard. He stayed with us for
quite some time – maybe two or three days, though I can't be
sure just how long. I remember his being brought to me –
probably by my medical orderly, L/Corporal Glidden – with a
first-aid dressing still on his cheek, and the cheek swelling so
badly that he clearly had to be sent back. We never saw him
again.

'We had our first machine-gun action at Pegasus Bridge soon
after noon in support of an attack on a pill-box by an airborne
unit. We crossed the two bridges and moved on northward to a
small quarry overlooking the river. There we came under
command of Major Tony Lewis, commander of 6 Commando
Heavy Weapons Troop, to form a little sub-unit composed of
our MG section and that from 6 Commando. As far as I
remember, the day ended for us when we dug in near the
quarry.'

While the initial objectives on the beach were falling to the 8th
Infantry Brigade, both the follow-up brigade, No. 185, and the
support brigade, No. 9, were doing their best to get off the
beaches and move inland towards Caen. The follow-up brigade
consisted of the 2nd Battalion, the Royal Warwickshire Regiment, the Second Battalion, the King's Shropshire Light Infantry and the First Battalion, Royal Norfolk Regiment. Their
armoured support was provided by the Staffordshire Yeomanry, equipped with Sherman tanks.

This brigade was to move south towards the 3rd Division objective for D-Day – Caen. 2nd Warwicks moved up behind Lord Lovat's Commando Brigade, and captured Blainville-sur-Orne, some kilometres south-east of the Orne bridges. The King's Shropshire Light Infantry and 1st Royal Norfolks in turn were to move right and left of 1st Suffolk from the 8th Brigade once the Suffolks had secured their objective, the strongpoint codenamed 'Hillman'. 1st Norfolks were to move to St Aubin d'Arquenay and then on to a second objective called 'Rover', south of 'Hillman'.

Corporal Edwin Byatt with 'B' Company, 1st Suffolks, recalls the attack on another strongpoint, codenamed 'Morris'. 'We went at the double from the beach, leaving snipers and other pockets of resistance to be mopped up by others following. "Morris" was still firing on the beach and with shells going overhead the noise was terrific. We managed to find some cover on the approach and got in position to attack. The Navy were to stop shelling when we were ready to go in and if we didn't send up the "Success" signal by a certain time, 30 minutes I think, they would start firing again, which would mean firing on us as well as on the Germans.

'The air photos we had studied had shown the trenches round the gun emplacements, so each section knew where to make for. I remember laying flat by the Bangalore torpedo team, ready to blow the wire, wondering what it was going to be like. The shelling stopped and we were just going to blow and attack when white flags were waved. We hoped it wasn't a trick, but they surrendered, 60 or 70 officers and men, which was just as well for us. Their positions were well covered and formidable, but the shelling and bombing had softened them up, although the emplacement looked intact. I think the speed with which we had got there also helped a lot. So the "Success" signal went up and our morale then was sky-high.'

'Morris' fell relatively easily; 'Hillman' was to prove much more difficult. This large dug-in complex was heavily defended and totally surrounded by two barbed-wire fences and mines. The 'Hillman' position was a mass of concrete emplacements and armoured gun cupolas removed from old French tanks, which were virtually impervious even to anti-tank gunfire. The defending German force comprised the Headquarters Company and infantry of the 736th Grenadier Regiment.

The task of taking 'Hillman' was given to 'A' Company of the 1st Suffolks, with a detachment of 246 Field Company, Royal Engineers to clear the mines and barbed wire, allowing the company to rush the first trenches and then fight their way through the position.

Eric Rowland of 'A' Company, 1st Suffolks takes up the story: 'A breaching party crawled through standing corn and managed to blow the first belt of wire with Bangalore torpedoes. A mine-clearing section of Royal Engineers then cleared a path through the mines and the second belt of wire was blown, but an attempt to rush the gap resulted in several casualties.'

Sapper Richard Ellis was one of those clearing the mines. 'We were told to tape a path through the minefield, where we came under machine-gun fire. I led the way into the minefield at the crouch and dived behind a small mound; the machine-gun rounds were bouncing off it and the third man of our team was hit in the chest. After lying there for a while I began to ease myself forward. Pinning marker tape around the mines, I picked up on the detector and crawled on until I reached a triple barbed-wire fence. I then crawled back down the tape, very aware of an extremely dry mouth and perspiration running down my face.'

With the mines pinpointed, another Bangalore team blew the final barbed-wire concertinas. Eric Rowland went forward again. 'I crawled forward so that I was lying on the path through the mines. Heavy machine-gun fire greeted every attempt at movement. Every now and again a bullet would ricochet off an angle-iron stake beside me. Eventually, word was passed back that we were to dash, one at a time, through the gap and into a small crater just inside the wire, and from there get into a trench. I relayed this message to the chap lying behind me and told him to pass it on – the rest of "A" Company being in among the corn. I then carried out the order and managed to get into the trench unharmed and joined the small party gathered there.'

Corporal Rayson of 9 Platoon remembers the move up to the outer defences of 'Hillman'. 'We crawled through a field of barley and waited till the Engineers lifted some mines and taped a track through. Another party got rid of the wire with Banga-lore torpedoes. Then we went in. The first two, a corporal and a private, were killed as soon as they got through the gap. A machine gun in a tank turret was mounted right in front of the gap. The turret was made of what looked like glass. We all got down and he kept us down. Bullets whizzed above our heads. One hit the pick-axe on my back, one went through my gas cape rolled up on my belt ... this proves my behind was higher than my head. The Bren gunner, lying behind me, had one hit his shovel, the bits going in his backside. After a while, things went quiet. We hit the turret twice, but didn't smash it, although we got rid of the gunner.'

Eric Rowland, now in a shell-hole on the German side of the wire, was ordered to move again. 'My platoon officer ordered me to crawl out of the trench as he needed someone to give covering fire for a Bren gunner he intended to send out. I did as I was ordered, feeling very vulnerable, but luckily I was not seen, probably due to the fact that vision was limited and the Germans concentrated on the gap in the wire. The officer then asked me if I could see anything that warranted a Bren. I said "No," so he told me to return to the trench. He then asked me what had happened to the rest of the company and why they hadn't joined us. He realized that our position was pretty hopeless and told us to get off the position as best we could – i.e., one at a time.'

Corporal Rayson was one of those who had entered the 'Hillman' position. 'Suddenly, along came the Company Com-mander. "Come on, Rayson," he said. I got up only to be knocked down by someone running behind him. I followed him only to be fired at as I got through the gap. I got down and then up again, and ran through a hole in the bank where the others had gone. I found myself in a deep trench. I couldn't see over the top, but following the trench to the left, then to the right, and so on, I eventually caught up with the others – although there weren't many of us left. As we were wondering what to do next, a runner came round the corner and told us to get out as quickly as we could. We didn't need encouraging. A flail tank then appeared from somewhere and made a large track through the minefield, then up came three Sherman tanks, and in we went again.'

Eric Rowland takes up the story: 'This time we got in to the position with little trouble and proceeded to mop up. We took several prisoners, but we could not clear the objective properly because so much of it was underground. However, we neutralized it and withdrew to dig in for the night. I decided to make a cup of cocoa using a Tommy cooker and my enamel mug, and proceeded to burn my fingers. Considering what we had been through that day, I got off lightly! The next day the remainder of the German garrison surrendered, and that was the end of "Hillman".'

Corporal Rayson also found that he needed a brew after consolidating on the position. 'We couldn't get down into the position owing to some steel doors which we couldn't open, but to wake them up we put several grenades down the ventilation shafts, plus a few smoke ones. After this we dug in around the place. Things got quieter, so we opened the 48-hr ration packs and brewed up some tea in our tin mugs. The tea – tea, sugar and milk, looked like an Oxo cube, but at least it tasted like tea, although even the Naafi tea was better.'

With 'Hillman' neutralized the 1st Suffolks started to consolidate their position, holding the ground for 185 Brigade to push through towards Caen. Corporal Edwin Byatt was there with 'B' Company of the 1st Suffolks. 'By now, 185 Brigade, with the 2nd Warwicks and so on, were going for Caen. They had been held up waiting for their tank support. The tanks had been held up getting off the beaches, so 185 had to go on their own, and they soon ran into trouble with 21st Panzer Division. I had placed my section for all-round defence. We dug two-man slit trenches. I shared mine with a very good young chap, George Jarvis, aged only 19 (I was an old man of 24). Unfortunately George Jarvis was killed three weeks later.

'Some self-propelled guns came to our position and started firing. I remember saying to George that they would draw fire down on us in return, so we dug deeper. To our left we could see 6th Airborne holding the bridges and firing going on there. They were doing a wonderful job and were reinforced by now. It was as well that we had moved away from the "Morris" position as the German artillery was ranged on to it and gave it a good shelling.'

While the 1st Suffolk were fighting their battle for 'Hillman' the 185th Infantry Brigade and the reserve brigade, the 9th Infantry Brigade, were making their way inland.

Geoff Peters was a twenty-four-year-old corporal in the Signals Platoon of the 2nd Warwicks. 'We were landing between Ouistreham and Lion-sur-Mer in LCAs. We had about 80lbs of kit on our backs, and I had a wireless set added to all that. I didn't realize till later that the big aerial sticking up was attracting snipers. I was looking out from the boat and it was as if I were watching a war film. Our craft got hit about a hundred yards out, and hit again, and hit again, so we suddenly realized that all our careful plans were going to pot. The Signals Sergeant was killed as was one of the signallers. When we came to go ashore the ramp wouldn't go down so we finished up scrambling over the side. I was running behind a tank when it was hit as well. There was a lot of firing and shelling.

'We reached the forming-up position for the Warwicks. The Norfolks and the KSLI were in our brigade, and the job of the 185th Brigade was to push through and ignore some things and get to Caen on the first morning. Things started to go wrong because we had got our plans, but the Germans had got their plans.

'The KSLI were supposed to push up the road to Caen, riding on tanks. We were going on the right to knock out some strongpoints, with the Norfolks on the left. When it came to the push the Norfolks were so heavily engaged at some strongpoint, we hadn't got them. Then the tanks didn't turn up for the KSLI – they were bogged down on the beach. So within half an hour of landing all our plans were changed, and the Warwicks and the KSLI had to push on up the road to Caen on our own. When we got to Bénouville at Pegasus Bridge, the Airborne were expecting a counter-attack, and we sent a company of our lads to help them, so we were down to three-quarters of our strength, less what we had lost already. Then we started coming under quite a bit of fire, small-arms and shell-fire, and it was a plodding game then. There were villages ... Beuville, Biéville, just villages that sounded nothing and looked just a dot on the map, but it was a big thing to us to take them. In fact, we never got into Caen that day.'

Major Eric Lummis of the 1st Suffolks was a witness to the problems that the soldiers suffered as they came ashore, mainly from German artillery. 'We managed to find a way through and at last arrived at what had been marked as the D-Day transit area. My Suffolk company was followed by the first reinforcement companies of the two other battalions in 8 Brigade and that of the 2nd Battalion of the King's Shropshire Light Infantry, who were the lead Battalion of the follow-up brigade – 185 Brigade. As I was nominally in charge of all these companies, I allocated areas and we settled down to dig slit trenches. To our surprise civilians started appearing. One offered me a glass of cider, another man and his wife invited me into their home and gave me a cup of tea.

'We had just about completed our trenches when further troops arrived. First some of the Beach Group, followed by vehicles of 9 Brigade headquarters with their commander in a Bren carrier. A few minutes later there were three or four bangs close by. The shells caught the HQ, wounding the Brigadier and his Intelligence Officer and killing three others, including the Canadian liaison officer from the Canadian Brigade on our right. We saw the Brigadier and his Intelligence Officer being taken off in a Jeep. In the brigade's place came a mortar detachment from a Royal Marine Commando who were still engaged in trying to clear a strongpoint on the beach in Lion.'

Corporal Albert Smith, a member of the Anti-Tank Platoon of the 1st Norfolks, continues the tale: 'It is strange how you remember the silly things, like seeing a barrage balloon brought ashore. The German guns quickly ranged in on it and began pin-pointing their fire on to the landing area. The last I saw of this balloon it was floating gently away down the coast.'

As the fighting moved inland, more and more of the local inhabitants ventured out of their shelters. Major Eric Cooper Key, commanding 'B' Company of 1st Norfolks that day, recalls a typically British incident. 'There was one piece of light relief shortly after we landed. Major Humphrey Wilson, the Battalion 2nd I/C, had a group of Frenchmen surrounding him, and most of them were jabbering at him. He turned to me and said, "Eric, these bloody fools don't understand their own language." He was replying in his best known foreign tongue – Urdu!'

Many a British soldier was to admire the stoicism of the French that day. Alfred Rampling, a private serving with 'A' Company, 1st Norfolks, recalls a Frenchman he met, while all around the battle raged. 'We carried on and reached a small village. The residents were going about their daily tasks, and there was one old chap pushing a barrow full of cabbages, carrots and so on. He had just come back from his allotment. "*Bonjour, Monsieur*," he kept saying, and went on his way. All this time the Germans were getting within range of us and mortar bombs were cutting into our ranks.'

The brigade signals officer, Captain Philip, was also under pressure as 185 Brigade moved forward. With an impatient brigadier desperately wanting to move forward to his battalions he had to try and find the necessary transport. 'We set off again, inland along the dusty road. Most of the roads in our area were only partially surfaced and all were dusty. After about a mile we arrived at the village rendezvous which was to be our first HQ. I felt at a complete loss. There was nothing I could do. Our small party had the wireless sets going and the IO had a map – and that was it. A horrible feeling of uselessness came over me and I wandered around somewhat aimlessly, wondering however on earth we were going to fight a battle on these slender resources. Then suddenly the miracle began to happen. Quite out of the blue one of my vehicles drove up. I can't even remember which one it was, but I fell on the necks of the crew as though they were long-lost brothers.

'And then another came, and another, and yet another. All the vehicles which I had seen distributed to various ports scattered along the south coast of England and which I thought I might never see again, were now all homing in on this tiny village in Normandy, picked off a map during the planning stage. I could hardly believe my eyes. It was a masterpiece of planning and organization, and we were back in business.

'There was only one fly in the ointment. The Brigadier was desperate to get up and see the battalions, but his command carrier had not arrived. There was no other transport available, and then I came across a French boy wheeling a bicycle. I spoke

to the boy, borrowed the bicycle and wheeled it over to the
Brigadier. It was much too small for him but that didn't matter.
I can see him now, happily disappearing down the village street,
compelled to pedal with his knees coming up outside the
handlebars. I suppose he must have been the only senior British
commander ever to have cycled into battle! I subsequently
found the carrier a few days later in a drowned vehicle park just
behind the beaches, but by that time the crew had rejoined the
section and were running the replacement carrier that quickly
appeared.'

By midday the 3rd Infantry Division was ashore on 'Sword'
beach and staking out claims inland. Lord Lovat's No. 4 Commando had taken Ouistreham and the other Commando units
were linking up and reinforcing the paratroops on the Ranville
heights above Bénouville. The 9th Infantry Brigade had landed
and pushed out from Hermanville, 185th Brigade were in front
of Biéville, 8th Brigade were at Bénouville supporting 6th
Airborne Division across the bridges at Ranville. The only
trouble spot was the stretch of coast between St Aubin and
Lion-sur-Mer and stretching back inland through Douvres and
Périers to Caen, which was still in German hands. The two
Royal Marine Commandos, 41 and 48, were now fighting to
close this gap and link up the Canadian 'Juno' beach with
'Sword'.

The last brigade of 3rd Division to come ashore on 'Sword' was
the 9th Infantry Brigade. This comprised the 2nd Battalion, the
Lincolnshire Regiment, the 1st Battalion, the King's Own
Scottish Borderers and the 2nd Battalion, the Royal Ulster
Rifles. Armoured support was provided by Sherman tanks of
the East Riding Yeomanry attached from 27th Armoured Brigade. 'Sword' beach was under artillery fire as this brigade came
ashore.

Trooper King was with 'B' Squadron of the East Riding
Yeomanry. 'The morning of the 6th began with a clear dawn. As
soon as it became light, the "Rhino" raft was brought round and
the task of transferring began. The big lorry which was the last
on was the first off, and finally we headed for the French shore.
A great ball of black smoke began to rise and fill the sky, and at

its base huge flashes from the naval shelling and rockets from the special boats. Between us and land there were great water spouts, as the German guns returned fire. We approached "wading depth", when streams of machine-gun tracer riddled the lorry and the crew jumped out and ran behind the tanks.

'With bullets all over us we got up the beach and into a small excavation with infantry huddled around and under the tanks. We could not see or hear or know who was shelling who. Eventually the shelling eased and in the lull a group of prisoners with an escort ran down the beach to a boat. Just before they made it came two bright flashes and mines exploded among them, leaving a tangled heap of grey and khaki.'

Corporal Jack Hodgson was with 'A' Company, 9th Field Ambulance, and landed with 9th Infantry Brigade. 'Our Medic Section consisted of eighteen men. We were trained in first aid and our job was looking after the wounded in the forward areas and evacuating them to the rear. The rest of the troops on our craft were from the 2nd Battalion, the Lincolnshire Regiment.

'Our landing area was "Sword" beach at Hermanville–La Brèche. I was soon stepping around dead soldiers and at our assembly point we were relieved to find we had all arrived safely. In single file we moved off with the infantry towards Hermanville-sur-Mer, then took a left turn to Lion-sur-Mer. Near the outskirts of this village we medics stopped at a small stone building, which was to be our Regimental Aid Post, and the infantry carried on into the village. After only ten minutes or less we received our first casualty, a young infantryman with a severe flesh wound on his right forearm. He was quickly dealt with. Our next wounded soldier, a German, was carried in on a stretcher. The third was British. He was dead and we buried him under an apple tree. The tree was still there in 1990.'

Captain Philip, the Signals Officer with 185 Brigade Headquarters recalls the airborne reinforcements coming in by glider on the evening of 6 June. 'There were several incidents, but undoubtedly the most important was the landing of the Air Landing Brigade on our left. To refer to it as impressive is almost an understatement. The first indication we had was the sound of aircraft engines. Then suddenly we saw the beginning of a vast armada of some 250 four-engined bombers each towing a glider. In next to no time the sky was full and the stream seemed never-ending, though I guess the whole operation could not have lasted more than an hour at the most. The aircraft flew in at around 2,000 to 3,000 feet. The gliders cast off over the beaches, though this was too far away for us to see in detail and we only knew it had happened when the distance between glider and tug began to increase.

'I had always assumed that a glider's descent was by a gentle downward path. I soon learned that I was wrong. The pilot brought the aircraft over the landing zone without losing much height, presumably to stay above small-arms fire and to pick out a suitable landing spot. Then suddenly they would go into a horrifying steep dive, flatten out just above the ground and skid to a halt, though I must admit that from where we were we couldn't see the actual touchdown. The tugs had turned slightly to starboard and were flying directly over us, their tow ropes still dangling below. As they approached we could see the bomb doors open and the supply containers neatly grouped in the bomb racks.

'Suddenly they were all released simultaneously and descended amid a flutter of brightly coloured parachutes, each identifying the contents of its container. In a few instances the parachute failed to open and the container plunged earthwards at an alarming speed. Finally, the aircraft dropped the dangling tow rope and headed for home. To add to the spectacle the heavy German AA guns around Caen were banging away merrily, filling their part of the sky with black blobs. The Halifax bombers turned away too soon to come within effective range and, as far as I could see, none was hit.'

Geoff Peters of the 2nd Warwicks has another memory of this glider landing. 'Later on D-Day, 185 Brigade had reached the Bénouville–Beuville area and I was with "D" Company, the forward company. When the gliders came in one of them slid across a field and hit two of our signallers who were operating a set in the ditch. They had their earphones on and didn't hear it coming ... one of them was decapitated.

'We dug in that night in a small village and I was lucky in that place. We just had a 24-hour pack ... bits of cheese and stuff. The first big trench I sat down in for the night was in somebody's back garden, with onions all round me, and I was able to eat my little bit of cheese with some spring onions.

'Although it seemed a long way from home, it was homely from the fact of being in a battalion like the Warwicks ... they were all local Birmingham lads, and in between the shells falling and the general noise of war, you could hear a heated argument going on about the merits of Villa and Birmingham City football clubs in a couple of slit trenches just behind you, and it seemed then as if you weren't so far from home.'

For the 3rd British Infantry Division, D-Day was one of mixed success. All the brigades managed to get ashore and inland with less casualties than was initially anticipated, but they did not secure their objective, Caen. In the face of growing resistance from the enemy, particularly 21st Panzer Division, their advance slowed in the early afternoon. Nevertheless, the men who got ashore were happy to be alive and content with their achievement. Four years after Dunkirk, the British Army was back again in France.

Memorial to North Shore Regt and 48 Commando RM, St-Aubin-sur-Mer

—— CHAPTER TWELVE——

After D-Day

'It had always been difficult to imagine
D+1.'
Norman Scarfe
3rd (British) Infantry Division

The men involved in planning and fighting Operation 'Overlord', had always found it hard to think beyond D-Day. Plans were drawn up with future operations in mind, but D-Day was so important, the issue so vital and the battle so finely balanced that just to get ashore and stay ashore would seem victory enough.

Total Allied casualties on D-Day amounted to some 10,000 men killed, wounded and missing. According to the US Official History, published by the US Department of the Army in 1951, the 101st Airborne lost 1,240 men, including 182 definitely killed and 501 missing, presumed captured or killed. The 82nd Airborne lost 1,259, including 156 definitely killed and 756 missing, presumed captured or killed. Casualties on D-Day along 'Utah' beach were mercifully low, but the heaviest of all fell on 'Omaha', where some 2,000 men were killed, wounded or missing at the end of the day. The initial figures came to 1,190 for the 1st Infantry, 743 for the 29th Infantry, and 441 for Corps troops. These figures were later revised downwards slightly as men rejoined their units, but the accurate figures are still not known. Casualties along the British and Canadian front amounted to about 1,000 men per beach.

German casualties were very high, especially among the 352nd and 91st Infantry Divisions, where the men fought stubbornly. Total German casualties on D-Day have never been accurately established but certainly ran into thousands, with many thousands more wounded or taken prisoner.

The accounts in this book have concentrated on the events of D-Day and end at midnight, 2359 hrs in military parlance, on 6 June. This chapter takes the story on a little and describes what happened to some of the people met in these preceding pages.

Two days after the landings, General Montgomery wrote his appreciation of the post D-Day situation in a private letter to his friend and colleague, General Dempsy.

8-6-44

My dear Simbo

    You may like the following news of our battle.

1. There is no doubt that the Germans were surprised, and we got on shore before they had recovered. The speed, power, and violence of the assault carried all before it.
2. Generally, the beach obstacles presented no difficulty; where they were troublesome it was because of the rough weather – and on some beaches it was pretty rough.
3. DD Tanks
   (a) Used successfully on UTAH beaches.
   (b) Failed to reach the shore on OMAHA beaches and all sank – too rough.
   (c) Were not launched on 50 Div front as it was too rough; were landed 'dry' behind the leading flights; casualties to AVRE sappers high as a result, and to leading infantry.
   (d) Landed 'dry' on Canadian front.
   (e) Used successfully on 3 Div front.
   Generally it can be said that the DD tanks proved their value, and casualties were high where they could not be used.
4. As a guess, prisoners about 6,000 so far. They consist of Germans, Russians, Poles, Japanese, and two Turks.

5. British casualties about 1,000 per assault Division.
   American casualties not known.
   High proportion of officer casualties, due to sniping behind our front.
   Two Bde Cmds wounded:
       Cunningham   9 Bde
       Senior   151 Bde
   Good many COs killed, including Herdon, OC 2 Warwicks.
   No general officers are casualties.

6. The Germans are fighting well; Russians, Poles, Japanese, and Turks, run away, and if unable to do so, surrender.

7. Our initial attack was on a wide front, and there were gaps between landings. The impetus of the assault carried us some way inland and many defended localities were by-passed; these proved very troublesome later. In one case a complete German Bn, with artillery, was found inside 50 Div area; it gave some trouble but was eventually collected in (about 500 men). There is still one holding out – the radar station west of Douvres; it is very strong and is held by stout-hearted Germans.

8. Snipers in beach areas have been very troublesome, as a result of para 7. The roads have been far from safe and we have lost several good officers. I have been all right myself, though I have toured the area all day. There have been women snipers, presumably wives of German soldiers; the Canadians shot 4 women snipers.

9. The Germans are doing everything they can to hold on to CAEN. I have decided not to have a lot of casualties by butting up against the place, so I have ordered Second Army to keep up a good pressure at CAEN, and to make its main effort towards VILLERS-BOCAGE and EVRECY and thence SE towards FALAISE.

10. First US Army had a very sticky party at OMAHA, and its progress at UTAH has not been rapid.
    I have therefore ordered it to join up its two lodgement areas and to secure CARENTAN and ISIGNY. It will then thrust towards LA HAYE DU PUITS and cut off the Cherbourg peninsula.

11. The two armies have now joined hands east of BAYEUX.

No time for more.

Yrs ever

B. L. Montgomery

P.S.
The country here is very nice; green fields; very good crops; plenty of vegetables; cows and cattle; chickens, ducks, etc.

The few civilians there are appear well fed, the children look healthy, the people have good boots and clothing.

The locals did not believe the British would ever invade France or come over the Channel; they say that the German officers and men thought this also – which may account for the tactical surprise we got.

B.L.M.
0900 hrs
9 June

That was the view of the Commanding General, written fifty years ago. Other people have their own memories.

André Heintz, the young French Resistance worker, kept an account of what happened in Caen after the landings. 'I kept a short diary of the period – in fact 36 pages for the first day only – which I wrote afterwards from a few notes – but afterwards I gave up! That "longest day" – so long awaited for – was in fact a grand day and a most wonderful experience; not much hope of living through it and yet we did, but we were happy at the idea it would bring freedom to others at last.

'A man who was found dead in the ruins of the city after the battle when they started clearing the cellars had kept a diary until the end. That diary was found beside him in the cellar where he had been trapped. His strength was failing as he wrote the last line and he must have given up hope by then, and yet he said: "I feel that I am dying and it's terrible to think that I shall never see that day of the liberation I have been so long waiting for but I know that because of my death others will be liberated; so long live France, long live the Allies."

'This is a poor translation from French into English of what that man was writing, but it is a fair statement of what we were feeling at the time.

'I could also tell you how my sister and I made the first red cross in the city with the blood of the wounded that day. My sister was a nurse in the improvised hospital, a former lunatic asylum where Beau Brummell had been confined. My sister helped the surgeons who were operating on British soldiers as well as civilians. She had seen several bombs falling on one of the wards near her, killing some people, and she was conscious that something had to be done to warn the Allies that so many wounded were being gathered and tended in that spot. By then, two other hospitals had been hit; all the firemen in the city had been killed, with all their equipment lost. The only place where coffins could be made had been destroyed, so we wanted to do something quickly.

'Painting red crosses on the buildings would have taken too long and finding paint itself was a problem. We decided to look for the red carpets that were usually laid in the church for weddings but we could not find the key nor anyone who could help us. So my sister decided to take four of the big sheets that had been used in the operating theatre, already smeared with blood. We dipped them into the pails of blood that stood there and went to spread them on the forcing frames of the hospital garden. We thought that the reflection of the glass would help in spotting this international sign, but as we were spreading the fourth sheet, making the fourth side of the cross, a small plane came down and we thought it was going to strafe us.

'Although tempted to abandon the job and run into hiding, we still decided to risk it and finish our red cross. We did not know much about British planes then, as the battle was just beginning, but we noticed that it was moving its wings, rocking slightly, and soon we realized it was a spotter plane. It was obvious that it had spotted the red cross and was trying to let us know. The next day, however, when we went back to the huge vegetable garden to check if the red cross still lay as it should on the forcing frames, we realized that it was not red any more but had turned a dark brown, so we added some mercurochrome – though this was scarce – to the blood before we dipped the sheets again in order to stain them more efficiently.

'When I was told later by the surgeons to clear the mess and empty those pails, as I was throwing the blood from one of the pails, a severed hand fell out. I must confess that it took me years before I could admire again any of Dürer's or Rodin's studies of hands or even look at a painting representing hands. We were still sensitive then; I was twenty-four in 1944.'

Jack Capell was still with the wire section of the 8th Infantry Regiment, 4th Infantry Division. 'On 7 June the regimental command post was near Ste-Mère-Eglise and that was where Cisk and I rejoined the company. On 9 June the command post moved to Fréville. On the 10th we encountered heavy fighting south of Montebourg. We remained in or near that location for the next nine days. One night the German counter-attack was so intense that I felt our position would be overrun by morning. I wondered about the rest of the wounded men I had been unable to take back to the aid station, as I had previously taken wounded men back in my Jeep. I was so tired that I fell asleep in my fox-hole. In the morning I found the Germans had not continued their advance either because they were in no condition to do so or because they didn't realize how weak we were. We remained at something of a stand-off with the Germans from 10 June through 19th.

'One morning I was taking a nap beside my fox-hole when one of my men told me the General was coming. I thought this must be Teddy Roosevelt because he was the only General who regularly inspected the front line. I shall never forget Teddy Roosevelt – he was truly the soldier's friend. Teddy Roosevelt died in Normandy of exhaustion on the night of 12 July.

'We were cheered one day by the arrival of nine American tanks in our sector; by nightfall six of them had been knocked out. The situation appeared grim again. We hoped that if the D-Day landings were successful and a good beachhead established, the German defences would collapse. By the time we got to Cherbourg we realized there was going to be a long war ahead.

'Thus we began to value the "Million-dollar wound". This meant a wound serious enough to get a man to hospital but not serious enough to kill or permanently maim him. Atterbury, of our wire section, was hit by shrapnel in the buttocks area. It did not appear to be serious but was enough to get him evacuated. We congratulated him as he lay on the ground smiling, awaiting evacuation to a hospital in England. Next day we asked the medic who attended to him if he was indeed on his way to England. The medic informed us that Atterbury had died at the aid station.

'Self-inflicted wounds began to occur more frequently after mid-June. One day I was sitting in my fox-hole, when I noticed a man put his foot on the edge of his hole, aim his rifle at it and blow the end off. This was the most common self-inflicted wound at the time.

'Some men took to drinking heavily since there was abundant liquor available in evacuated farmhouses and towns. There was as much brandy as anyone could drink. Nearly every farm in Normandy had an apple orchard and at least one vat of hard cider. Whenever a GI drank too much in combat he was usually killed or wounded after a short time. In some cases this led to acts of foolish bravery. A fellow in our company who drank too much strapped grenades around his waist, grabbed his rifle and raced for the enemy lines, announcing he was going to kill every German he could find. We found him dead the next day.'

By 7 June the German Army were hurling themselves in force against the bridgehead. Colonel Helmut Ritgen of Panzer Lehr Division takes up the story. 'From 6 June onwards, 21st Panzer had been thrown piecemeal into battle to counter the British airborne landings. This armoured attack towards the shore was halted prematurely when British paratroopers landed in our rear. On D–Day night the British I Corps had captured a coastal strip six miles long though not yet very deep. In vain the exhausted German defenders looked for reinforcements but all local reserves had been used up.

'C-in-C West had ordered increased readiness to move for Panzer Group West, which included 12th SS Panzer, Panzer Lehr, and the 17th SS Panzer Grenadier Division. 12th SS Panzer was put under command of Army Group "B" and Kurt Meyer led them towards a sector of the 711th Infantry Division east of the Orne. Movement was difficult because of air strikes and too many failures of the radio sets. Marching at night turned out to be reasonably safe and Panzer Lehr made their way to the Flers–Vire area on previously reconnoitred routes.

'My battalion was attacked by aircraft during a supply halt near Alençon. Bomb and gun bursts set tanks and POL trucks on fire, soldiers were killed and wounded. Similar incidents happened to all columns. Some mushroom clouds of smoke were guiding the fighter bombers to their targets. In spite of increased vehicle distances and dispersion to small groups, marching in daylight under repeated air attack was a risky venture, costing time and losses.

'While the columns of Panzer Lehr Division headed for their objectives under rolling air interdiction, General Bayerlein was severely cut up when his car was attacked from the air. His aide and his driver were killed. He himself got away, slightly wounded but violently shaken.'

Back on the British and Canadian beaches, men and equipment were still pouring ashore. Harold Addie, Royal Navy seaman came into 'Juno' beach on an LCT and gives an account of the scene. 'On landing we hit a mine which damaged the stern, screws and rudder, but we were not holed, but when the tide receded we were not able to get off the beach. The beach was being tidied up now and the dead were being dragged along and placed in stacks for collection. As we were high and dry, a Geordie friend and myself asked permission to go ashore. We found a hole in the Atlantic Wall and went through it. There were still dead Germans in the bunkers, and we collected some souvenirs lying about, namely belts and tin hats. We went into the town of Bernières and were amazed to find a shop open selling newspapers and German magazines, but our progress was stopped by the troops in one street, because a sniper was still holed out in a church steeple. The railway station was deserted and we returned across the field to the craft.

'That night the fighting was still going on in the town and along the coast to St Aubin. During the next day LCT 530 came alongside. It had been hit and was sinking. We tried to use our generators to pump out the water but it was a losing battle and we had to let it go. It was not until 10 June that we were finally towed back across the Channel.'

Over in the Cotentin, the 4th Infantry Division was butting its way towards Cherbourg. On D+5 Colonel 'Red' Reeder of the 12th Infantry Regiment was hit by shell-fire near Montebourg. 'I stopped to talk a moment to some replacements sitting behind a hedgerow, who had just arrived from England. I felt sorry for them because they looked frightened. I said, "Great to have you fellows with us. You're joining a winning outfit. The 12th Infantry has been beating the Germans for six days."

'When we walked across an open field, a single shell cracked over my head and I went down. My left leg was on fire. I sat up and looked at it and saw that it was horribly mangled above the ankle. My left elbow was torn open. I screamed and could not help it. Bill Mills, who was wounded and stunned in the same explosion, recovered quickly and placed a tourniquet on my leg. His blood splashed on me as he gave me a shot of morphine from his paratrooper's first-aid kit. I was thankful for Bill Mills. I lay there in the dirt for maybe fifteen minutes, then a Jeep rolled up carrying six wounded on a stretcher, and I saw the top man being removed for me. "Oh, no, you don't," I called. "Take those men to the Aid Station, then come back for me."

'When I woke up I was in a huge black tent, the wounded on stretchers lay in neat rows. Two shadows appeared. One I recognized in the dim light as the head of the beach hospital. The other, who wore a steel helmet, knelt on one knee.

'"Red," he said, "this is General Collins." He fumbled with my shirt. "I am pinning on you the Distinguished Service Cross. Brad – General Bradley – said to tell you he was sorry that he could not come himself, and he wants you to know he sent an aviator to London to get this. This is the first DSC to be awarded in Normandy."

'General Collins stood up. "Red, is there anything I can do for you?"

'"Make Van Fleet a General," I said.

'"The recommendation is already in," he replied, "but what can I do for you?"

'"Tell the regiment it won the first DSC," I said, "and that I will be back."'

Another man wounded was George Nicolson with 'D' Company, the 7th Green Howards. 'I survived until 13 August, when I was wounded in the head by shrapnel. By then I was the last surviving member of the platoon that came ashore on D-Day. The officer and two men were killed on D-Day, and the rest were wounded ... so they got the lot of us in the end.

'At the time of the 40th Anniversary of D-Day I was interviewed by a teacher from a local secondary school, whose class was studying the Second World War. She asked me if the Army put us up in hotels during the fighting, and if hot food came up every day in lorries; the more you write about how war really was, the better.'

Inland from 'Juno', the Canadians were getting locked into their bitter fight with 12th SS Panzer Division. The 25th SS Panzer Grenadier Regiment of 12th SS Panzer was commanded by Standartenführer Kurt Meyer and on 7 June 1944 this regiment shot twenty-three Canadian prisoners at Buron, a village north-west of Caen. 12th SS continued to shoot its prisoners throughout the Normandy campaign, and there was certainly retaliation for these atrocities. In December 1945 a Canadian Military Court Martial found Kurt Meyer guilty of murder and sentenced him to be shot. The sentence was later commuted to life imprisonment and he was released in 1954.

S. J. Dann was a soldier in No. 6 Commando, holding the Ranville heights. 'We had been briefed to expect a German counter-attack four days after the landing. Facing us at the time was the 744th Infantry Regiment, and we expected an attack from the 857th and 858th Infantry Regiments backed up by 21st Panzer. During the night of 9/10 June we could hear a lot of movement from the enemy as there was only a cornfield between us. The night passed quietly though we could hear tracked vehicles which we assumed were mobile 88s. Just after "Stand-to", I was shaving when the Brigadier, Derek Mills-Roberts, came along (Lord Lovat had by then been wounded by shell-fire and evacuated), and gave us his "Not a step back, fight to the last man, the last drop of blood" routine. It looked like being a lousy day.

'At 0800 hrs all was still and quiet, and then all hell broke loose. Mortar shells and machine guns, but all the fire fell on the edge of the orchards. We held our fire and waited until we saw the helmets of the German infantry as they advanced through the corn. They came at a steady pace and penetrated several yards into the orchard, where they stopped and looked about. By all the rules we should have occupied the leading edge and looking down the forward slope to their positions. Instead the CO had us dig in at the back of the orchard. Very crafty. On a given word we opened up with everything. These included a Bren, a Vickers K gun, an American Browning, and a German MG-34. The Germans were lifted off the ground by the weight of fire.

'The next attack came in from our right flank but this was a weak affair which soon died out. Then, at about 1100 hrs, it was our turn again with a barrage of mortars and shells, and this time their shelling was accurate. Their infantry crawled through the corn and fired on us from the hedgerow, and when they thought we had been softened up enough, they charged. They made half the distance before faltering and falling back. Then they hit the right flank again and there was the danger of a break-through. Our TSM took one man from each trench and got them across to 4 Troop. A stick of mortar bombs landed near me and a man behind was killed and three others wounded. I dived into the first slit trench I found but got out a lot quicker. The two occupants had been hit. One was very dead and the other had a serious back wound. I met him again thirty-five years later, still paralysed from the waist down.

'The attack died down. The German troops had infiltrated into the small wood on our right and brought up a self-propelled 88mm gun. We had a stalemate situation. We could not move out and were down to our last magazine for the Bren. Then came one of my lasting memories of the war, one I remember when I go back to Normandy each year for the D-Day pilgrimage and walk down that road. The Germans were behind a low wall and one of them suddenly jumped over the wall and ran towards us, firing from the hip with a Schmeisser. He had 50 yards to go and stood no chance. A short burst stitched his chest and he fell. Later on we moved down and I turned him over. He was a tall blond, pure German, wearing an Iron Cross 2nd Class, the Afrika ribbon and several other campaign ribbons. I thought what a terrible waste, what a way to finish his career and life. We picked up the two German wounded and flushed out a couple of poor specimens hiding in the bushes and returned to the farm.

'About 1800 hrs the Germans had had enough and withdrew. Peace reigned over our little piece of Normandy. We had been engaged by three battalions, we were now about 350 in number, but I think we did a good job. We had about one-third of the unit as casualties.'

No. 6 Commando were still in action eleven months later in May 1945, when the war came to an end. They were then deep in Germany, had fought many battles, and overrun the concentration camp at Belsen. When the German Field Marshal Milch surrendered his baton to the Commando Brigadier, Derek Mills-Roberts, the Brigadier, disgusted with the sights uncovered at Belsen, broke the baton over the Field Marshal's head.

Over on the western flank, the American airborne troops were still in action and continued to fight in Normandy until mid-July, when they were withdrawn to the UK. The 508th PIR returned to a tumultuous welcome from the people of Nottingham, and David Pike, a local historian, has left an account of this time. 'The troopers were very, very weary, some were even in a state of shock. They had been in action continuously for 31 days and of the 2,056 young men who had landed on D-Day only 995 were returning back to England. The rest were missing or casualties, and 307 had been killed.

'The 508th landed at Southampton to a hero's welcome. People were waving and cheering as the troopers left the LSTs and boarded trains for Nottingham. The welcome at Southampton was greatly appreciated by the troopers, but it was nothing compared with the welcome they got when the train pulled in at Nottingham. There were two ATS bands and hundreds of people waiting to welcome the 508th back "home".

'As the bands played "Over There", there were shouts of "God bless you, Yank". The troopers walked slowly through the crowd, the tiredness plainly visible on their faces. People were crying and it was at this moment that the 508th came to realize that Nottingham was indeed their second home. In fact the 508th's History stated that one trooper had suggested that the regiment should not have received foreign service pay at all during their stay in Nottingham, such was the bond of friendship that was felt between the 508th and the citizens of Nottingham.

'After reaching Wollaton Park 50 per cent of the regiment was immediately given a seven-day furlough, the other 50 per cent would have the same the following week. Just how fierce the fighting had really been suddenly hit the troopers the minute they returned to their tents. They could tell by looking at the empty cots how high the casualties were. In fact, on more than one occasion, a trooper would find that he was the lone survivor from his eight-man tent, and it has been brought to my notice that on discovering this, many a trooper simply sat on a bed and cried his eyes out for his missing buddies.'

Howard Hughes from California says: 'The only sad time I had in Wollaton Park was when we came back from Normandy. We left with about 130 of the finest men I have ever met and when we returned five weeks later only 30 of us came back. I remember someone singing "Danny Boy", the tears came down my cheek when I looked around and saw all the men who were no longer with us. It was a sad day, I lost so many good buddies. We had been like one big family.'

Two months later, in September 1944, the American Airborne were in action again, parachuting into Holland as part of the 'Market Garden' operation, taking bridges on the road to Arnhem, where the British 1st Airborne Division made a memorable stand.

The D-Day landings of 1944 were a glorious victory, but war is not glorious. If the accounts in this book have not already made that clear, this final account will do so.

Sergeant Rainer Hartmetz was fighting the American paratroopers when he was wounded. 'I was on the left flank of my squad with Gottlieb's squad 150 metres away on the right. Machine-gun fire was coming from that flank and my boys could not move, for they were pinned down by the machine-gun fire. Then soldiers began to pass me by shouting that Gottlieb was hit, and by the loss of him my machine gun wasn't any more protected. If now the American infantry would assault along our hedgerow they could roll up our line and fight down our riflemen one after the other. My squad would be lost and the big dying begin.

'I had only one thought – to replace Gottlieb. I had 150 metres to run towards the American hedgerow, and the apple tree half way had the leaves and the branches flying away, hit by bullets. It was a run like the 100 metres in High School, with only my magazines and the machine pistol in my hand. I crashed into Gottlieb's fox-hole. He was pale in the face, eyes wide open. I fired a magazine into the hedgerow to keep the Americans down, then I turned back to Gottlieb. He was hit in the hip and I said, "Now let's see ..." when I got a push in the right shoulder.

'It was like a hit from a mighty hammer. All seemed to be

smashed and torn apart. I let the weapon fall and tried to grip my arm with my left hand, but I couldn't find it. Blood ran out of the sleeve, over my hand and soaked my pants. Gottlieb got up and started firing to give me cover. I crawled out of the fox-hole into the next fox-hole, where a man cut my blouse away and dressed my shoulder. I hardly dared to look at the wound but I did. It seemed to be as large as the palm of the hand, a deep, bloody crater, surrounded by a lot of small holes. Two bandages were soaked, so he took a third one. I became tired and leaned my head on the wall of the fox-hole.

'I wanted to close my eyes and repose a little. All energy was gone. Lutz got me awake and my energy came back again. "You can't stay here. If they start cleaning the position they'll kill you," he said, and he helped me out of the hole. I ran, the rest of the field jacket hanging on the left shoulder, the upper part of my body naked. They were firing and I had the feeling they were using me for target practice. I passed my machine-gun position, and saw the gun crew fall down like they were swept away by a hand. One of them cried in pain. It was a cry like an animal. They died. All of the boys died.

'I walked and walked, each step became harder. The bandages wouldn't stop the blood. I saw suddenly big drops of blood on my dusty boots. My neck became stiff and I became tired. I wanted to sit down in the ditch and sleep a little, but I knew I would never wake up again. Then it all became black before my eyes and I couldn't stay on my legs. I let myself fall into the ditch and as I fell I thought, "That's it! They will never know how it happened."

'I felt that someone kept me in a sitting position, and I could see again. First I couldn't figure out what was going on. It was two men in khaki, one of them lit a cigarette and gave it to me. It was a Camel. The two khakies were Americans. At first I thought they had caught me, but then I could see they were wounded themselves and had no weapons. After a while we got up and they supported me. We reached a crossroad with a German first aid station.

'It was a dreadful night, tired, pain, and not able to sleep. In the morning hours they put us on trucks and brought us to the south in the region of St Lô. Another castle, another ambulance place. We lay lined up in a long tent. Paratroopers, infantrymen, tank crews, and between us some Americans. The end of the tent was parted by a curtain of a tent sheet. Behind that the surgery room. From time to time a doctor appeared. Around his waist was a blood-spotted apron. He had shadows under the eyes. Passing our line he chose the men for operations. They carried me on a stretcher behind the curtain. There were two tables. On the other one worked an American surgeon who had been taken prisoner.

'The German doctor cut off my bandages. "We have to cut clean the lip of the wound, boy. It doesn't hurt much." The doctor cut and the pain was terrible. Then it was over. I couldn't have stood it a minute longer. I was exhausted. They brought me back and gave me something to drink. Then I was placed by the exit of the tent. Beside me was a small table. Two Paymasters were sitting there and talked while having a meal. I heard that since the morning hours England was bombed by "V" weapons, the new German rocket bombs. They talked of that with satisfaction. I thought of the boys in the hedgerows.

'They prepared us for the transport, to clear the place for newcomers. A dozen of us were lying on stretchers in the middle of the courtyard, waiting for the trucks. The sky was grey and it started raining. First some drops, then very strong. The ambulance personnel took cover in the entrance of the castle. Nobody took any notice of us. The rain splashed on our faces and soaked the rest of our uniforms and the bandages were full of water. We felt like forgotten dogs.'

BIBLIOGRAPHY

Stephen Ambrose, *The Supreme Commander*, New York, 1970.

Stephen Ambrose, *Pegasus Bridge*, Allen & Unwin, 1984.

General Omar Bradley, *A Soldier's Story*, Eyre & Spottiswoode, 1951.

Canada's Battle in Normandy, 1944, Dept of Defense, Ottawa, 1946.

Paul Carell, *Invasion – They're Coming*, London, 1962.

D-Day, accounts by The Eisenhower Foundation, University Press of Kansas, 1971.

W. F. Dawson, *The All-American (*82nd Airborne), privately printed, 1950.

Kenneth Edwards, *Operation Neptune*, Collins, 1947.

General Dwight D. Eisenhower, *Crusade in Europe*, Heinemann, 1949.

Major L. F. Ellis, *Victory in the West* (Vol. 1), HMSO, 1962.

Bernard Fergusson, *The Watery Maze*, Collins, 1956.

General Sir Richard Gale, *With the 6th Airborne Division in Normandy*, London, 1948.

Frederick de Guingand, *Operation Victory*, Collins, 1960.

George Harrison, *Cross Channel Attack*, US Dept of the Army, 1951.

Max Hastings, *Overlord*, Michael Joseph, 1984.

Gordon Holman, *Stand by to Beach*, Hodder & Stoughton, 1944.

David Howarth, *Dawn of D-Day*, Collins, 1959.

John Keegan, *Six Armies in Normandy*, Pan Books, 1982.

B. H. Liddell Hart (ed.), *The Rommel Papers*, London, 1953.

Brigadier the Lord Lovat, *March Past*, Weidenfeld & Nicolson, 1978.

Oberst Hans von Luck, *Panzer Commander*, Prager, 1992.

Captain J. R. Madden, 'Ex Coelis', *Canadian Army Journal*

Field Marshal Sir Bernard L. Montgomery, *Normandy to the Baltic*, World Publishing, 1958.

Jacques Mordel, *Dieppe – The Dawn of Decision*, Souvenir Press, 1962.

General Sir Fredrick Morgan, *Overture to Overlord*, Hodder & Stoughton, 1950.

Maj.-General James Moulton, *Haste to the Battle (48 Commando)*, Cassell, 1963.

Ross Munro, *Gauntlet to Overlord*, Macmillan, 1945.

Robin Neillands, *By Sea and Land (The Royal Marine Commandos)*, Weidenfeld & Nicolson, 1987.

Robin Neillands, *The Raiders (The Army Commandos)*, Weidenfeld & Nicolson, 1989.

General Matthew B. Ridgeway, *Soldier*, Harper & Row, 1956.

Cornelius Ryan, *The Longest Day*, Simon & Schuster, 1959.

Hilary St George Saunders, *The Green Beret*, Michael Joseph, 1949.

Hilary St George Saunders, *The Red Beret*, Michael Joseph, 1951.

Norman Scarfe, *Assault Division*, Collins, 1952.

The 79th Armoured Division, privately published, London, 1950.

Hans Speidal, *We defended Normandy*, London, 1951.

Jack Thomson and others, *First Infantry Division*, privately published, New York, 1947.

Warren Tute, *D Day*, Pan Books, 1974.

George Weller, *The Story of the Paratroops*, Random House, 1958.

Chester Wilmot, *The Struggle for Europe*, Collins, 1952.

David Young, *Four-five (45 Commando, Royal Marines)*, Leo Cooper, 1972.

Brigadier Peter Young, *Storm from the Sea*, William Kimber, 1959.

INDEX